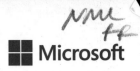

D0121135

Exam Ref 70-347
Enabling Office 365
Services
2nd Edition

Orin Thomas

Exam Ref 70-347 Enabling Office 365 Services, Second Edition

Published with the authorization of Microsoft Corporation by:
Pearson Education, Inc.

ISBN-13: 978-1-5093-0478-3
ISBN-10: 1-5093-0478-9

Library of Congress Control Number: 2017963302
1 18

Trademarks

Microsoft and the trademarks listed at *https://www.microsoft.com* on the "Trademarks" webpage are trademarks of the Microsoft group of companies. All other marks are property of their respective owners.

Warning and Disclaimer

Every effort has been made to make this book as complete and as accurate as possible, but no warranty or fitness is implied. The information provided is on an "as is" basis. The authors, the publisher, and Microsoft Corporation shall have neither liability nor responsibility to any person or entity with respect to any loss or damages arising from the information contained in this book or programs accompanying it.

Special Sales

For information about buying this title in bulk quantities, or for special sales opportunities (which may include electronic versions; custom cover designs; and content particular to your business, training goals, marketing focus, or branding interests), please contact our corporate sales department at corpsales@pearsoned.com or (800) 382-3419.

For government sales inquiries, please contact governmentsales@pearsoned.com.

For questions about sales outside the U.S., please contact intlcs@pearson.com.

Editor-in-Chief	Greg Wiegand
Acquisitions Editor	Laura Norman
Development Editor	Troy Mott
Managing Editor	Sandra Schroeder
Senior Project Editor	Tracey Croom
Editorial Production	Backstop Media
Copy Editor	Christina Rudloff
Indexer	Julie Grady
Proofreader	Christina Rudloff
Technical Editor	Tim Warner
Cover Designer	Twist Creative, Seattle

Contents at a glance

Contents

What do you think of this book? We want to hear from you!

Microsoft is interested in hearing your feedback so we can continually improve our
books and learning resources for you. To participate in a brief online survey, please visit:

https://aka.ms/tellpress

Chapter 2   Provision SharePoint Online site collections   73

What do you think of this book? We want to hear from you!

Microsoft is interested in hearing your feedback so we can continually improve our
books and learning resources for you. To participate in a brief online survey, please visit:

https://aka.ms/tellpress

Introduction

The 70-347 exam deals with advanced topics that require candidates to have an excellent working knowledge of Office 365, Exchange Online, SharePoint Online, OneDrive for Business, Skype for Business Online, and Office 365 Security and Compliance. Some of the exam comprises topics that even experienced Office 365, Exchange Online, SharePoint Online, and Skype for Business Online administrators may rarely encounter unless they are consultants who deploy new Office 365 tenancies on a regular basis.

Candidates for this exam are Information Technology (IT) Professionals who want to validate their advanced Office 365, Exchange Online, SharePoint Online, Skype for Business Online, OneDrive for Business management skills, configuration skills, and knowledge. To pass this exam, candidates require a strong understanding of how manage and configure Office 365 clients and end user devices, provision SharePoint Online site collections, configure Exchange Online, OneDrive for Business, and Skype for Business Online for end users and manage, migrate to, and administer Exchange Online, OneDrive for Business Online and Skype for Business Online. To pass, candidates require a thorough theoretical understanding as well as meaningful practical experience implementing the technologies involved.

This book covers every major topic area found on the exam, but it does not cover every exam question. Only the Microsoft exam team has access to the exam questions, and Microsoft regularly adds new questions to the exam, making it impossible to cover specific questions. You should consider this book a supplement to your relevant real-world experience and other study materials. If you encounter a topic in this book that you do not feel completely comfortable with, use the "Need more review?" links you'll find in the text to find more information and take the time to research and study the topic. Great information is available on MSDN, TechNet, and in blogs and forums.

Organization of this book

This book is organized by the "Skills measured" list published for the exam. The "Skills measured" list is available for each exam on the Microsoft Learning website: *https://aka.ms/examlist.* Each chapter in this book corresponds to a major topic area in the list, and the technical tasks in each topic area determine a chapter's organization. If an exam covers six major topic areas, for example, the book will contain six chapters.

Microsoft certifications

Microsoft certifications distinguish you by proving your command of a broad set of skills and experience with current Microsoft products and technologies. The exams and corresponding certifications are developed to validate your mastery of critical competencies as you design and develop, or implement and support, solutions with Microsoft products and technologies both on-premises and in the cloud. Certification brings a variety of benefits to the individual and to employers and organizations.

> **MORE INFO   ALL MICROSOFT CERTIFICATIONS**
>
> For information about Microsoft certifications, including a full list of available certifications, go to *https://www.microsoft.com/learning*.

Microsoft Virtual Academy

Build your knowledge of Microsoft technologies with free expert-led online training from Microsoft Virtual Academy (MVA). MVA offers a comprehensive library of videos, live events, and more to help you learn the latest technologies and prepare for certification exams. You'll find what you need here:

https://www.microsoftvirtualacademy.com

Quick access to online references

Throughout this book are addresses to webpages that the author has recommended you visit for more information. Some of these addresses (also known as URLs) can be painstaking to type into a web browser, so we've compiled all of them into a single list that readers of the print edition can refer to while they read.

Download the list at *https://aka.ms/examref3472E/downloads*.

The URLs are organized by chapter and heading. Every time you come across a URL in the book, find the hyperlink in the list to go directly to the webpage.

Errata, updates, & book support

We've made every effort to ensure the accuracy of this book and its companion content. You can access updates to this book—in the form of a list of submitted errata and their related corrections—at:

https://aka.ms/examref3472E/errata

If you discover an error that is not already listed, please submit it to us at the same page.

If you need additional support, email Microsoft Press Book Support at *mspinput@microsoft.com*.

Please note that product support for Microsoft software and hardware is not offered through the previous addresses. For help with Microsoft software or hardware, go to https://support.microsoft.com.

We want to hear from you

At Microsoft Press, your satisfaction is our top priority, and your feedback our most valuable asset. Please tell us what you think of this book at:

https://aka.ms/tellpress

We know you're busy, so we've kept it short with just a few questions. Your answers go directly to the editors at Microsoft Press. (No personal information will be requested.) Thanks in advance for your input!

Stay in touch

Let's keep the conversation going! We're on Twitter: *http://twitter.com/MicrosoftPress*.

Preparing for the exam

Microsoft certification exams are a great way to build your resume and let the world know about your level of expertise. Certification exams validate your on-the-job experience and product knowledge. Although there is no substitute for on-the-job experience, preparation through study and hands-on practice can help you prepare for the exam. We recommend that you augment your exam preparation plan by using a combination of available study materials and courses. For example, you might use the Exam ref and another study guide for your "at home" preparation, and take a Microsoft Official Curriculum course for the classroom experience. Choose the combination that you think works best for you.

Note that this Exam Ref is based on publicly available information about the exam and the author's experience. To safeguard the integrity of the exam, authors do not have access to the live exam.

CHAPTER 1

Manage clients and end-user devices

One of the challenges in deploying and managing Office 365 for traditional IT departments is that Office 365 is designed around the idea that users are able to install and configure their own applications, rather than having the deployment and management of applications occur centrally by an IT department. In this chapter, you'll be reminded of not only how you can enable or restrict users from performing their own deployments, but how you can manage the deployment of Office 365 applications centrally, monitor the functionality of those applications, as well as allow for the configuration of Office applications. You'll also be reminded of some of the differences between the volume license versions of Office 2013 traditionally deployed and managed by IT departments, and Office 365 ProPlus, the version available through Office 365.

> **IMPORTANT**
> **Have you read page xv?**
> It contains valuable information regarding the skills you need to pass the exam.

Skills in this chapter:

- Skill 1.1: Manage user-driven client deployments
- Skill 1.2: Manage IT deployments of Office 365 ProPlus
- Skill 1.3: Set up telemetry and reporting
- Skill 1.4: Plan for Office clients

Skill 1.1: Manage user-driven client deployments

One of the great advantages of Office 365 is that it provides end users with the opportunity to perform self-service deployment of software to their own devices. While this has definite advantages, empowering users to this degree can also lead to problems, such as users exceeding their allocation of Office 365 ProPlus licenses. This skill deals with how you can restrict self-provisioning of Office 365 ProPlus, Windows Store apps and mobile apps, how to manage and revoke activation, as well as Office 2016 for Mac.

> **This skill covers the following topics:**
> - Restrict self-provisioning of Office 365 ProPlus
> - Windows Store apps and mobile apps
> - Manage activation
> - Office 2016 for Mac

Restrict self-provisioning of Office 365 ProPlus

Depending on the policies of your organization, you might want to allow users to install software directly from the Office 365 portal, to restrict this ability entirely, or to allow users to install some applications but restrict them from installing others. Office 365 ProPlus is the version of Microsoft Office that is available to appropriately licensed users in an Office 365 tenancy. Office 365 ProPlus includes the following software products:

- Access
- Excel
- InfoPath
- OneNote
- Outlook
- PowerPoint
- Publisher
- Word

Depending on the Office 365 subscription associated with a tenancy, the Skype for Business, Project, and Visio applications might also be available.

To configure which Office software users are able to install from the portal, perform the following steps:

1. When signed in to Office 365 with a user account that has Administrator permissions, open the Office Admin Center, and click Software Download Settings under Office Software as shown in Figure 1-1.

FIGURE 1-1 Manage User Software

2. To restrict users from deploying software from the Office 365 portal, clear the check box next to the listed software.

For example, in Figure 1-2 the slider next to SharePoint designer has been cleared.

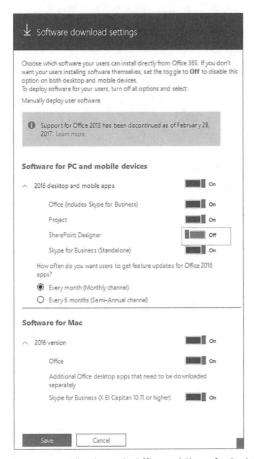

FIGURE 1-2 Allowing only Office and Skype for Business

The software that users will be able to install depends upon the type of Office 365 subscription. Different Office 365 subscriptions have different software options. It is also likely that software options will change. Table 1-1 lists the software that is available for each Office 365 software option.

TABLE 1-1 Software available with each Office 365 software option

Software option	Software made available to users
Office	■ Office 365 ProPlus ■ Office 2016 for Mac 2016
Office and Skype for Business	■ Office 365 ProPlus ■ Office 2016 for Mac 2016 ■ Skype for Business
Skype for Business	Skype for Business
Project	Project Pro for Office 365
Visio	Visio Pro for Office 365
SharePoint Designer	SharePoint Designer 2016

While you can make Office 365 software available to users through the Office 365 portal, this doesn't mean that users will automatically be able to successfully install this software. When allowing users to self-provision software from the Office 365 portal, keep the following in mind:

- To successfully run Office 365, users will need an Office 365 license.
- For users to be able to install the software they downloaded from the Office 365 portal, they will need to have local administrator privileges on their computer. This means that self-provisioning of software through the Office 365 portal is a suitable strategy in Bring Your Own Device (BYOD) scenarios where the user is the owner of the computer and is responsible for its configuration. Self-provisioning of software is less of a concern for most environments where each user is assigned a computer with a Standard Operating Environment (SOE), as users in these environments rarely have local administrator credentials.
- If you do not make Office software available to users, they will see a message that informs them that Office installations have been disabled when they navigate to the Software page in the Office 365 portal.
- Office 365 ProPlus is only run on the following operating systems:
  - Windows 7
  - Windows 8
  - Windows 8.1
  - Windows 10
  - Windows Server 2008 R2
  - Windows Server 2012
  - Windows Server 2012 R2
  - Windows Server 2016

By default, if a user installs Office 365 ProPlus from the Office 365 portal, all programs included with Office 365 ProPlus (Access, Excel, InfoPath, OneNote, Outlook, PowerPoint, Publisher, and Word) will also install. Administrators can configure deployments so that only some, not all, of these programs will install. You can configure which programs are excluded from Office 365 ProPlus using the Office Deployment Tool. You will learn more about configuring the Office Deployment Tool later in this chapter.

Office 365 and mobile devices

Microsoft has made Word, Excel, PowerPoint, and OneNote apps available for the Windows 10 Mobile, iOS, and Android mobile platforms. There are several ways that you can install these apps on these devices.

The first is to navigate to the Office 365 portal using the mobile device on which you want to install each application. From here you can click Get Office Apps as shown in Figure 1-3.

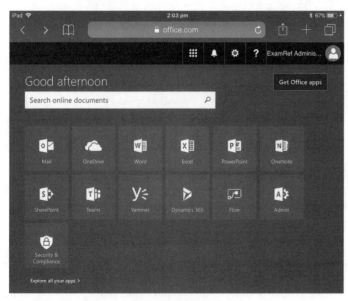

FIGURE 1-3 List of apps available for the iPad platform

Clicking Get Office Apps will open a page on Microsoft's website that will provide a link to the app's page in the appropriate vendor's app store. Figure 1-4 shows the Apple App Store page that opens when the Excel link on the Office 365 portal is opened. The application can then be downloaded from the App Store and installed on the device.

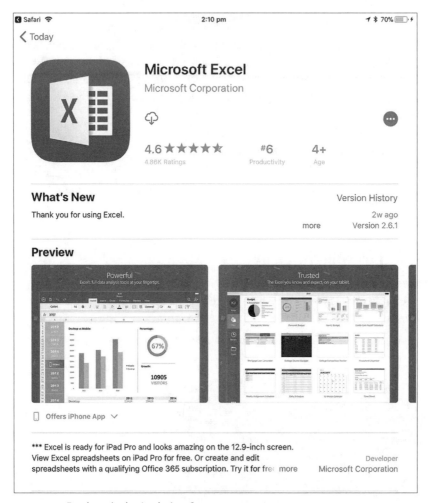

FIGURE 1-4 Excel app in the Apple App Store

These applications can also be installed directly from each mobile device operating system vendor's app store. To use all of the available features of each app, such as accessing documents in OneDrive for Business that are associated with your organization's Office 365 subscription, it will be necessary to sign in to the app using your Office 365 user account credentials. Premium features include:

- The ability to track changes, change page orientation, insert chart elements, and add WordArt and picture effects in the Word app.

- Use Pivot Tables, add, and modify chart elements in the Excel app.
- Use Presenter View with speaker notes, perform audio and video edits, and use picture styles in the PowerPoint app.
- Technical support options from Microsoft.

Select the Sign In option of an app, shown in Figure 1-5, to connect the app to an Office 365 subscription.

FIGURE 1-5 Sign In to Office 365

MORE INFO **OFFICE 365 AND MOBILE DEVICES**

You can learn more about deploying Office 365 at: *https://support.office.com/ en-us/article/Office-365-mobile-setup---Help-7dabb6cb-0046-40b6-81fe-767e0b1f014f?CorrelationId=93e770bc-f158-40da-8052-f27b45564eee.*

Manage activation

Office 365 ProPlus must be activated for users to be able to create and edit documents. While this can vary depending on the subscription level, each Office 365 user account generally allows for the activation of five concurrent instances of Office 365 ProPlus. Activation usually occurs automatically when a user downloads and installs Office 365 ProPlus from the Office 365 portal.

Reduced functionality mode

If Office 365 ProPlus is not in an activated state, it enters a reduced functionality mode. Reduced functionality mode allows users to open and view documents, but restricts them from creating new documents or making modifications to existing documents. When Office 365 ProPlus is in reduced functionality mode, users are prompted to reactivate the product on a regular basis.

Regular reactivation

Once Office 365 ProPlus has been activated on a computer, additional activation checks must be performed every 30 days. These automatic activation checks occur automatically when the computer connects to the internet. If the computer does not connect to the internet for more than 30 days, Office 365 ProPlus will enter reduced functionality mode. This 30-day period is an important consideration for certain types of scenarios and will determine whether it's okay to deploy Office 365 ProPlus or if it is necessary to deploy an appropriate edition of Office 2013.

For example, imagine that you are responsible for selecting a version of Office for the laptop computers of a scientific team that is going to work in Antarctica. As part of this scenario, you learn that the scientific team will be away from the main base for a period of 45 days, and during this 45-day period, those laptops will be unable to make an internet connection. In this scenario, you should not choose to deploy Office 365 ProPlus because you don't want members of the scientific team to have Office 365 ProPlus go into reduced functionality mode while away from the base.

You can check which licenses have been assigned to a user from the User properties page in the Office 365 portal as shown in Figure 1-6.

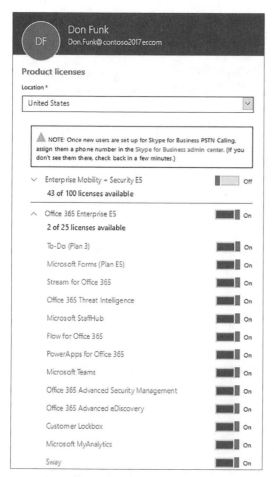

FIGURE 1-6 Software Licenses

Deactivating Office 365 ProPlus

A user can have a maximum of five installations tied to their Office 365 account. Should a user who has reached their five-installation limit need to install Office 365 ProPlus on a new computer, they can deactivate one of their existing installations as a way of reclaiming the license. Deactivating an installation does not remove the software from the computer on which it is installed. While it is possible to run the software after it has been deactivated, the software will be in reduced functionality mode.

To deactivate an existing Office 365 ProPlus activation, a user must perform the following steps:

1. Sign in to the Office 365 portal with their Office 365 user account.

2. Navigate to the software page at *https://portal.office.com/Account#installs*. You can also reach this page by navigating to My Account and then clicking Install Status.

3. On the software page, shown in Figure 1-7, locate the computer for which you want to deactivate an existing activation and then click Deactivate.

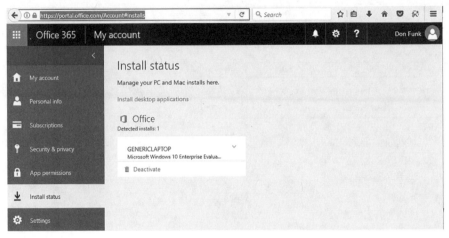

FIGURE 1-7 Deactivate installation

4. You will be prompted to confirm that you want to deactivate the installation, as shown in Figure 1-8.

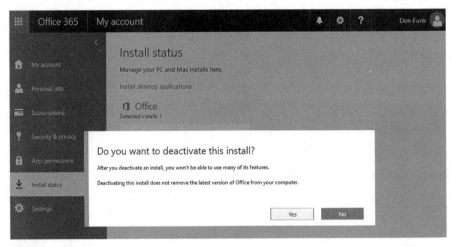

FIGURE 1-8 Deactivate install

5. If you attempt to start an Office 365 ProPlus application after the product activation has been deactivated, you will be presented with the Product Deactivated dialog box, shown in Figure 1-9.

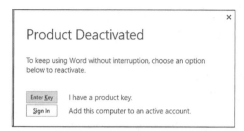

FIGURE 1-9 Product Deactivated

6. You can either manually enter an Office product key to reactivate the installation, or sign in with your Office 365 subscription and attempt to perform activation, as shown in Figure 1-10.

FIGURE 1-10 Activate Office

7. If you have not reached your activation limit, you will be able to successfully activate the deactivated copy of Office 365 ProPlus, as shown in Figure 1-11.

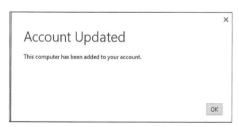

FIGURE 1-11 Account Updated

Office 2016 for Mac

Office 365 ProPlus is currently only available for computers running Windows operating systems. Until Office 365 ProPlus is also available for OS X, users with computers running the macOS operating system can obtain Office 2016 for Mac 2016 from the Office 365 portal and activate the program using their Office 365 credentials. Office 2016 for Mac 2016 includes Word, PowerPoint, Excel, and Outlook. Activating Office 2016 for Mac with the Office 365 user credentials consumes one of the five available licenses, as shown in Figure 1-12.

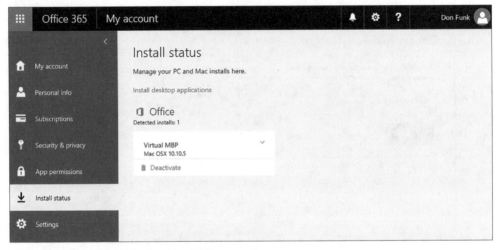

FIGURE 1-12 List of installs showing Mac OS X

To install Office 2016 for Mac, sign on to a computer running macOS with a user account that has administrator credentials and perform the following steps:

1. Using a web browser, navigate to *https://portal.office.com* and sign in with your Office 365 user credentials shown in Figure 1-13.

FIGURE 1-13 Signing in to Office 365 on a Mac

2. On the Office 365 Welcome page, shown in Figure 1-14, click Install Office 2016.

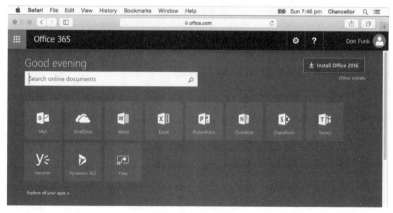

FIGURE 1-14 Office 365 console

3. If you click Install Office 2016, the operating system will be detected and the appropriate installer will automatically be downloaded to your computer. If you click Other Installs, the computer operating system is also automatically detected and Office 2016 for Mac 2016 will be offered as shown in Figure 1-15. Click Install to trigger a download of the disk image containing the Office 2016 for Mac 2016 installation files.

FIGURE 1-15 Install Office For Mac 2016

4. When the installer for Office 2016 for has downloaded, locate it in the Downloads folder as shown in Figure 1-16 and then double click on the installer. This launches the Microsoft Office 2016 for Mac installer.

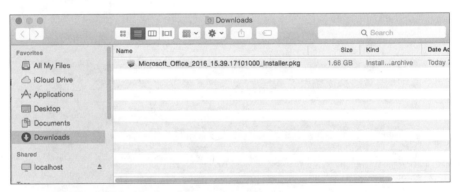

FIGURE 1-16 Office 2016 for Mac installer

5. On the Welcome page of the Microsoft Office For Mac Installer, shown in Figure 1-17, click Continue.

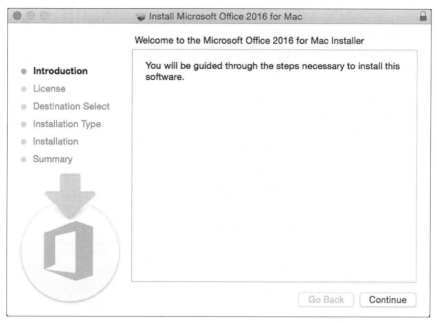

FIGURE 1-17 Introduction for Office installer

6. Review the Software License Agreement, as shown in Figure 1-18, and click Continue.

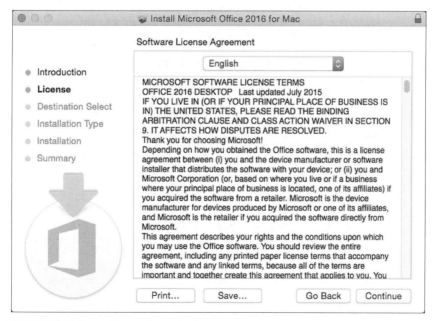

FIGURE 1-18 Software License Agreement

7. When prompted to agree with the license agreement, you will need to click Agree, as shown in Figure 1-19, to continue with the installation.

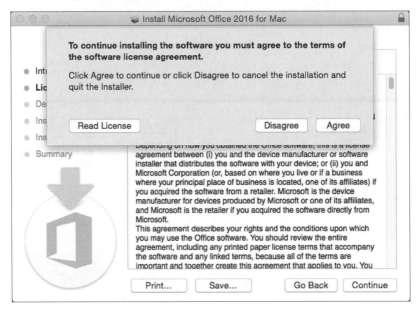

FIGURE 1-19 Agree to the license agreement

8. On the Installation Type page, click Install. Click Customize to change the installation options, such as placing the files on a separate disk.

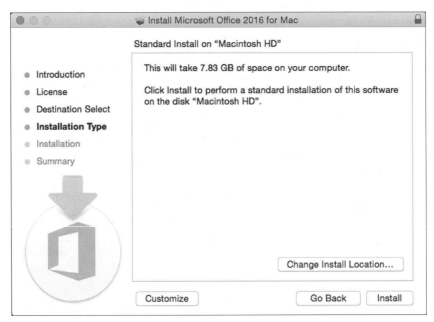

FIGURE 1-20 Standard installation

9. The installer prompts you for the credentials. (Remember, you must have the credentials of a user who has permission to install software on the macOS computer.) Provide your credentials, as shown in Figure 1-21, and then click Install Software.

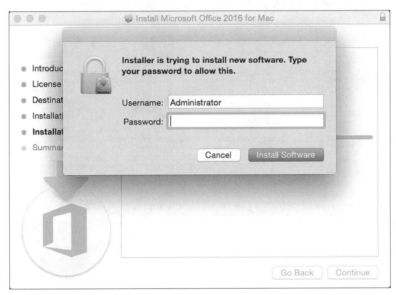

FIGURE 1-21 Provide administrative permission

10. After a period of time, the installer will report the installation has completed successfully. Click Close to exit the wizard, as shown in Figure 1-22.

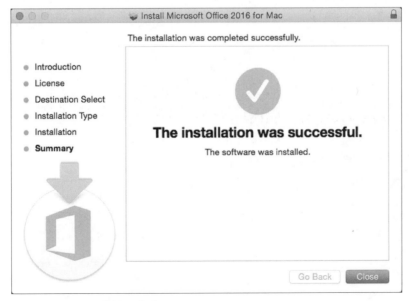

FIGURE 1-22 Successful installation

11. Once the installation has finished, you can start an office program from the Applications folder as shown in Figure 1-23.

FIGURE 1-23 Office programs in the Applications folder

12. When you start one of the Office programs for the first time, you'll be prompted to sign in to your Office 365 account as shown in Figure 1-24. Click Sign In.

FIGURE 1-24 Sign In To Office

13. When prompted, enter the email address associated with the Office 365 account, as shown in Figure 1-25.

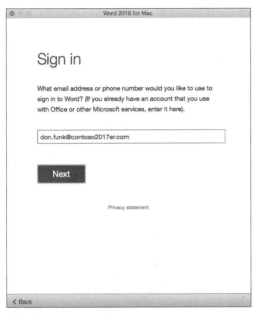

FIGURE 1-25 Provide Office 365 credentials

14. On the next screen, shown in Figure 1-26, provide the password associated with the Office 365 account.

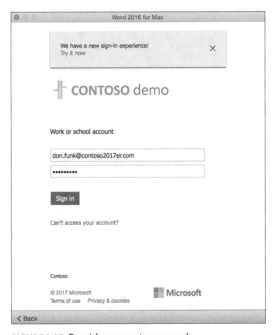

FIGURE 1-26 Provide account password

15. On the How would you like Office to look? page, shown in Figure 1-27, select a theme and click Continue.

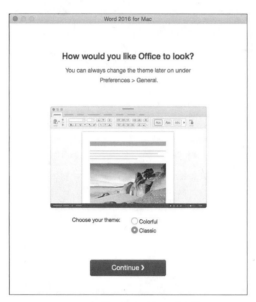

FIGURE 1-27 Personalize Your Copy Of Office For Mac

16. On the Your All Set page, shown in Figure 1-28, click Start Using Word, or whichever Office program you chose to run first.

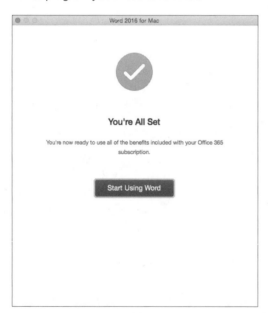

FIGURE 1-28 Configure updates

17. Word will then be installed and is activated on your Mac computer as shown in Figure 1-29.

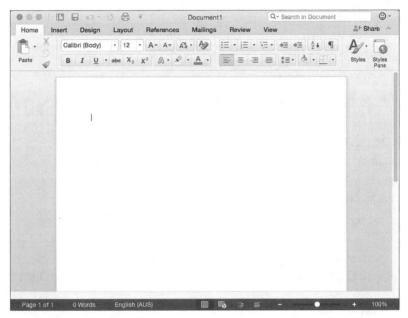

FIGURE 1-29 Word from Office 2016 on Mac

EXAM TIP

Remember that users can deactivate an Office 365 ProPlus activation through the Office 365 portal.

Skill 1.2: Manage IT deployments of Office 365 ProPlus

In most organizations, the IT department is still responsible for installing and maintaining software on the computers used by that organization. Just because Office 365 ProPlus is traditionally installed manually by a user doesn't mean that it can't be installed and managed centrally by an IT department. This Skill deals with managing the deployment of Office 365, including managing streaming updates, managing the Office deployment tool, and customizing deployment.

Manual deployment

The typical method of deploying Office 365 ProPlus on a computer is for a user to access the installation files from the Office 365 portal. You can install Office 365 ProPlus on a computer by performing the following steps:

1. Sign in to the computer with a user account that is a member of the local administrators group.

2. Open a web browser and sign in to the Office 365 portal at *https://portal.office.com*. You can click Install Office 2016 if you want to install using the default, or click Other Installs if you want to choose between the 32 bit and the 64 bit option.

3. If you want to install the 64-bit version of Office ProPlus, select the language and click Advanced as shown in Figure 1-31.

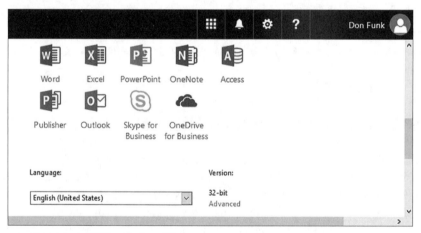

FIGURE 1-30 Install Office On Your PC

4. Once you click Advanced, you can select between the 32-bit and the 64-bit option as shown in Figure 1-31. Once you've selected the appropriate option, click Install. This will begin the download of the Office 365 ProPlus installer Click-to-Run setup file.

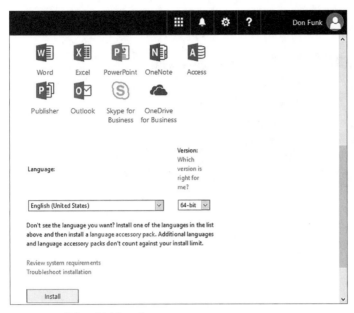

FIGURE 1-31 Select 64-bit option

5. Choose to Save or Run the installation file. It's often sensible to save the file and then run it as this simplifies the process of running the installer again should something interrupt the installation process.

6. Once the Click-to-Run installer has downloaded, double click on it to initiate installation. On the User Account Control dialog box, verify that the Program name is set to Microsoft Office, as shown in Figure 1-32, and then click Yes. The installation process will commence.

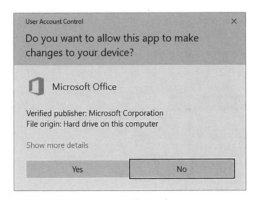

FIGURE 1-32 User Account Control

7. On the "You're all set!" page, shown in Figure 1-33, click Close.

FIGURE 1-33 Office is installed

8. Open one of the Office ProPlus applications. The first time you run one you'll be presented with the "Office is almost ready" screen shown in Figure 1-34. Click Accept and start Word, or whichever Office ProPlus application you selected to run first.

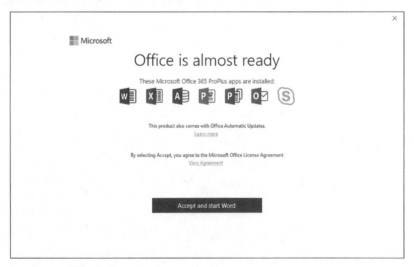

FIGURE 1-34 Office is almost ready

9. On the Word Recent page shown in Figure 1-35, click Sign In To Get The Most Out of Office.

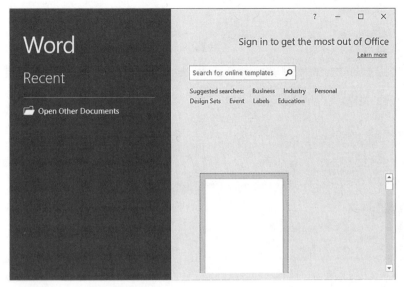

FIGURE 1-35 Word Recent page

10. On the Sign In page, shown in Figure 1-36, enter the email address of your Office 365 account and click Next.

FIGURE 1-36 Sign In

11. On the Work or school account page shown in Figure 1-37, enter the password and click Sign In.

FIGURE 1-37 Enter work or school account credentials

12. Once you have signed in, your account will be listed on the Recent page as shown in Figure 1-38 and documents stored in Office 365 will be available.

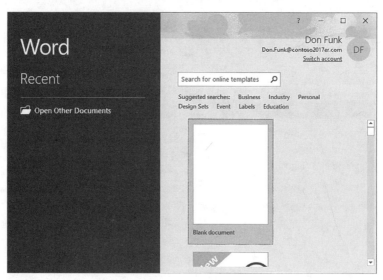

FIGURE 1-38 Signed in to Office 365

Central deployment

With special preparation, Office 365 ProPlus can be downloaded to a local shared folder and then deployed centrally. To use this central deployment method, the IT department must use the Office Deployment Tool to download the Office 365 ProPlus software from Microsoft servers on the internet. While it is possible to deploy Office 365 ProPlus centrally, successful installation of Office 365 ProPlus requires the ability for the software to activate against Microsoft Office 365 servers on the internet. You can't use a volume licensing solution, such as a Key Management Services (KMS) server, to activate Office 365 ProPlus, even when you are deploying it centrally.

Update channels

Office 365 provides new features and updates to Office programs on a regular basis. Depending on your organization, you can choose between an update channel that provides new features as they become available, or you can choose an update channel that provides new features less frequently. The following Office 365 update channels are available:

- **Monthly channel**   This channel provides users with the most recent features. Updates occur on a monthly basis.
- **Semi-annual channel**   This channel provides users with new features on a less frequent basis. Updates occur in January and July.
- **Semi-annual channel targeted**   Use this channel for pilot users and compatibility testers when you are using semi-annual channel. This allows these users to test updates and changes before they are released in the semi-annual channel. Updates to this channel occur in March and September.

You configure which update channel is used by editing the configuration.xml file for the Office Deployment Tool or by configuring the Update Channel group policy setting under Computer Configuration\Administrative Templates\Microsoft Office 2016 (Machine)\Updates when the Office 2016 group policy template files are installed.

Office Deployment Tool

The Office Deployment Tool allows IT departments to perform the following tasks:

- **Generate a Click-to-Run for Office 365 installation source**   This allows administrators to create a local installation source for Office 365 rather than requiring that the files be downloaded for each client from the internet.

- **Generate Click-to-Run for Office 365 clients**   This allows administrators to configure how Office 365 ProPlus is installed. For example, it can block the installation of PowerPoint.

- **Creating an App-V package**   Allows administrators to configure Office 365 ProPlus to work with application virtualization.

- **Configure update channel**   Allows administrators to configure some users is a pilot group to get more frequent updates to Office 365 than other users.

To install the Office Deployment Tool, perform the following steps:

1. On the computer on which you want to deploy the Office Deployment Tool, open a web browser and navigate to the following address: *https://www.microsoft.com/en-us/download/details.aspx?id=36778*.

2. On the Office Deployment Tool For Click-To-Run webpage, shown in Figure 1-39, click Download.

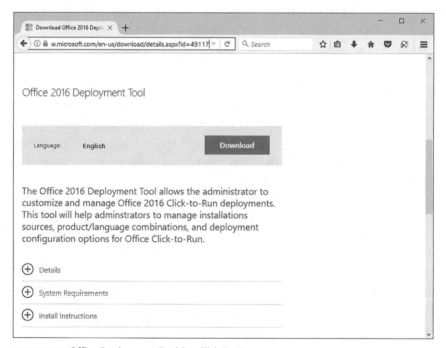

FIGURE 1-39 Office Deployment Tool For Click-To-Run

3. Save the installer file to a location on the computer. Figure 1-40 shows the file down-loaded to the Downloads folder.

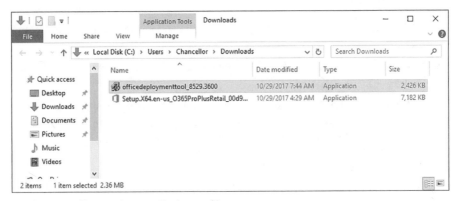

FIGURE 1-40 Office Deployment Tool setup file.

4. After the deployment tool has downloaded, double-click it to start the deployment tool setup.

5. On the User Account Control dialog box, click Yes.

6. On the Microsoft Software License Terms page, select the Click Here To Accept The Microsoft Software License Terms option, and click Continue.

7. On the Browse For Folder page, select the folder in which to store the files associated with the tool. While these files can be extracted anywhere, you will need to interact with the tool frequently so you should create a folder in the root folder of a volume.

8. Two files will be extracted: Configuration.xml and Setup.exe, as shown in Figure 1-41.

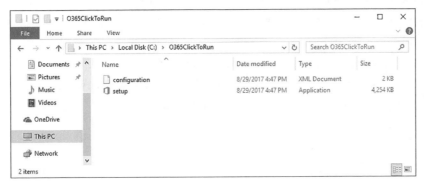

FIGURE 1-41 Deployment Tool folder

The Office Deployment Tool is a command line utility that provides administrators with three general options:

- The download mode allows administrators to download the Click-to-Run installation source for Office 365 ProPlus as well as language pack files to a central on-premises location.

- The configure mode allows for the configuration and installation of Click-to-Run Office products and language packs.

- The packager mode allows for the creation of an App-V package from downloaded Click-to-Run installation files.

The Office Deployment Tool must be run from an elevated command prompt in the /configure and /packager modes. To run the Office Deployment tool in download mode against a configuration file stored in the *c:\ClickToRun* folder, use the syntax:

```
Setup.exe /download c:\ClickToRun\configuration.xml.
```

To run the Office Deployment Tool in configure mode, when the tool is hosted on the share \\SYD-Deploy\O365 and the configuration file is stored on the share \\SYD-Deploy\Configs, run the command:

```
\\SYD-Deploy\O365\Setup.exe /configure \\SYD-Deploy\Configs\Configuration.xml
```

> *MORE INFO* **OFFICE DEPLOYMENT TOOL**
>
> You can learn more about the Office Deployment Tool at: *https://technet.microsoft.com/en-us/library/jj219422.aspx.*

Configuration.xml

You use the Configuration.xml file to perform the following tasks:

- Add or remove Office products from an installation.
- Add or remove languages from the installation.
- Specify display options, such as whether the installation occurs silently.
- Configure logging options, such as how much information will be recorded in the log.
- Specify how software updates will work with Click-to-Run.
- Specify update channel.

Figure 1-42 shows the example Configuration.xml file that is available with the Office Deployment Tool.

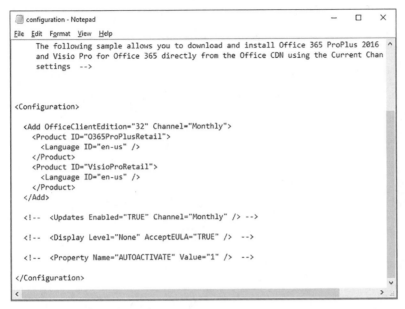

```
configuration - Notepad                                    —   □   ×
File  Edit  Format  View  Help
     The following sample allows you to download and install Office 365 ProPlus 2016  ^
     and Visio Pro for Office 365 directly from the Office CDN using the Current Chan
     settings  -->


<Configuration>

  <Add OfficeClientEdition="32" Channel="Monthly">
    <Product ID="O365ProPlusRetail">
      <Language ID="en-us" />
    </Product>
    <Product ID="VisioProRetail">
      <Language ID="en-us" />
    </Product>
  </Add>

  <!--  <Updates Enabled="TRUE" Channel="Monthly" /> -->

  <!--  <Display Level="None" AcceptEULA="TRUE" />  -->

  <!--  <Property Name="AUTOACTIVATE" Value="1" />  -->

</Configuration>
```

FIGURE 1-42 Configuration.xml

Important attributes include:

- **SourcePath** When you run the tool in download mode, the SourcePath attribute determines the location where the Click-to-Run files will be stored. When you run the tool in configure mode, the SourcePath attribute determines the installation source.

- **OfficeClientEdition** This value is required and either must be set to 32 or 64. This determines whether the x86 or x64 version of Office applications are retrieved or installed.

- **Version** If this element is not set, the most recent version of files will be either downloaded or installed. If a version is set, then that version of the files will either be downloaded or installed.

- **Display** The display element allows you to specify what information the user sees during deployment. The options are:

  - **Level=None** The user sees no UI, completion screen, error dialog boxes, or first run UI.

  - **Level=FULL** The user sees the normal Click-to-Run user interface, application splash screen, and error dialog boxes.

  - **AcceptEULA=True** The user does not see the Microsoft Software License Terms dialog box.

  - **AcceptEULA=False** The user will see the Microsoft Software License Terms dialog box.

- **ExcludeApp**   You use this element to exclude applications from being installed. Valid values of this attribute are as follows:
  - Access
  - Excel
  - Groove (used for OneDrive for Business)
  - InfoPath
  - Lync (used for Skype for Business)
  - OneNote
  - Outlook
  - PowerPoint
  - Project
  - Publisher
  - SharePointDesigner
  - Visio
  - Word
- **Language ID**   This element allows you to specify which language packs are installed. For example, en-us for US English. You can have multiple Language ID elements, one for each language that you wish to install.
- **Logging**   This element allows you to disable logging, enable logging, and specify the path where the log file is to be written.
- **Product ID**   This element allows you to specify which products to install. The available options are:
  - **O365ProPlusRetail**   Office 365 ProPlus
  - **VisioProRetail**   Visio Pro
  - **ProjectProRetail**   Project Professional
  - **SPDRetail**   SharePoint Designer
- **Remove**   If this element is set ALL=TRUE then all Click-to-Run products are removed.
- **Updates**   The Updates element allows you to configure how updates are managed and includes the following options:
  - **Enabled**   When set to true, Click-to-Run update system will check for updates.
  - **UpdatePath**   If this element is not set, updates will be retrieved from Microsoft servers on the internet. If the element is set to a network, local, or HTTP path, then updates will be sourced from the specified path.
  - **TargetVersion**   Allows you to have updates applied to a specific Office build version. If not specified, the most recent version is updated.

- **Deadline**   Specifies the deadline by which updates must be applied. You can use Deadline with Target Version to force Office applications to be updated to a specific version by a specific date. The Deadline will only apply to a single set of updates. To ensure that Office applications are always up-to-date, it is necessary to revise the deadline when new updates are available.

- **Channel**   Specified which update channel will be used. Options include Monthly, Broad, and Targeted for the monthly, semi-annual, and semi-annual targeted channels.

MORE INFO   **CONFIGURATION.XML**

You can learn more about the format of Configuration.xml at: *https://technet.microsoft.com/en-us/library/jj219426.aspx.*

EXAM TIP

Remember the different elements used in the Configuration.xml file.

Skill 1.3: Set up telemetry and reporting

Office 365 ProPlus and Office 2016 both support the gathering of telemetry data about how Office applications are being used in an environment. This skill deals with how you configure the collection of telemetry through Group Policy, how you configure a central repository for telemetry issues, how you can view local telemetry data, and what steps you can take to deploy the telemetry agent to computers that have versions of Office that do not automatically include telemetry functionality.

This skill covers the following topics:

- Enable telemetry through Group Policy
- Set up telemetry service
- Report user issues
- Deploy agents

Set up telemetry service

Office Telemetry is a compatibility-monitoring framework. You can use it to assess Office compatibility issues. Office Telemetry provides similar functionality to the following Office 2010 compatibility tools:

- Office Migration Planning Manager
- Office Code Compatibility Inspector

- Office Environment Assessment Tool

Office Telemetry works with both Office 2016, Office 2013, and Office ProPlus, and is included with the applications. Some Office Telemetry features are available for earlier versions of Office if the Office Telemetry agent is installed on each computer running the previous version of Office.

> **MORE INFO**   **OFFICE TELEMETRY**
>
> You can learn more about Office Telemetry at: *https://support.office.com/en-us/article/Best-practices-for-Office-Telemetry-570c7fb3-d7a5-49cd-8cbf-7300ea656328*.

Deploy Telemetry Dashboard

The Telemetry Dashboard allows you to view information collected by the Telemetry Processor, a special server that you deploy on the network to collect telemetry information. The Telemetry Dashboard is installed automatically when you install Office 365 ProPlus, Office Professional Plus 2016, Office Standard 2016, Office Professional Plus 2013, and Office Standard 2013. The Telemetry Dashboard is a specially configured Excel worksheet that connects to a database hosted on a supported SQL instance. You can start the Telemetry Dashboard in the following manner:

- On computers running Windows 7, Windows Server 2008, or Windows Server 2008 R2, click Telemetry Dashboard for Office 2013 in the Office 2013 Tools folder under Microsoft Office 2013.

- On computers running Windows 8 or Windows 8.1, type Telemetry Dashboard on the Start Screen.

- On computers running Windows Server 2012 or Windows Server 2012 R2, open the Search charm from the Start menu and type **Telemetry Dashboard**.

- On computers running Windows 10 or Windows 2016, click the Start menu and type **Telemetry Dashboard** as shown in Figure 1-43.

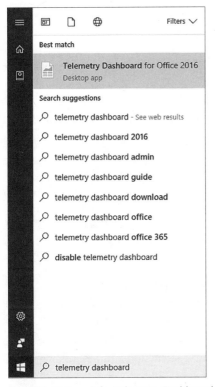

FIGURE 1-43 Search for Telemetry Dashboard

You must have Excel installed to open the Telemetry Dashboard For Office 2016. To use the Telemetry Dashboard, you need to configure a computer to function as the Telemetry Processor and a computer to host the SQL Server database used by the Telemetry Dashboard. The computer that functions as the Telemetry Processor and the computer that hosts the SQL Server database used by the Telemetry Dashboard can be the same computer.

You can use the following versions of SQL server to host the back-end database for the Telemetry Dashboard:

- SQL Server 2005
- SQL Server 2005 Express Edition
- SQL Server 2008
- SQL Server 2008 Express Edition
- SQL Server 2008 R2
- SQL Server 2008 R2 Express Edition
- SQL Server 2012

- SQL Server 2012 Express
- SQL Server 2014
- SQL Server 2014 Express
- SQL Server 2016
- SQL Server 2016 Express

The Telemetry Dashboard contains links from which you can download SQL Server Express. Microsoft recommends that you host the Telemetry Processor role on a computer running one of the following operating systems:

- Windows Server 2008
- Windows Server 2008 R2
- Windows Server 2012
- Windows Server 2012 R2
- Windows Server 2016

Before deploying the Telemetry Processor, ensure that you have the following information:

- Name of the SQL Server Instance on which the Telemetry Dashboard will be created or where the database is already present.
- Permission to create and configure the database on the SQL Server. This needs to be a domain account that has been assigned the systems administrator role on the SQL Server instance.
- Permission to create a shared folder or the UNC path of an existing folder.
- 11 GB or more of free hard drive space on the computer that hosts the Telemetry Processor role.

To deploy the Telemetry Processor, perform the following steps:

1. Open the Telemetry Dashboard spreadsheet and then click the Getting Started worksheet in the workbook.

2. Click the arrow next to Install Telemetry Processor, as shown in Figure 1-44.

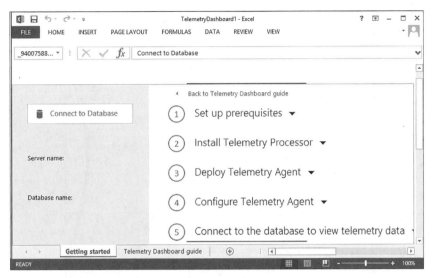

FIGURE 1-44 Getting Started

3. Under Install Telemetry Processor, click either the x86 or x64 link, as shown in Figure 1-45. For deployment of the Telemetry Processor on Windows Server 206, select the x64 option. While the x86 version will run, Windows Server 2016 requires an x64 processor and the x64 version of the Telemetry Processor will be able to utilize more resources than the x86 version.

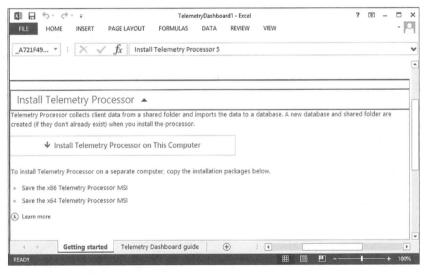

FIGURE 1-45 Install Telemetry Processor

4. Safe the file to a location where you will be able to retrieve it. Figure 1-46 shows the file osmdp64.msi being saved to the desktop.

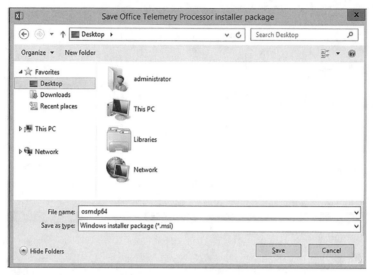

FIGURE 1-46 Office Telemetry Processor Installer Package

5. Once the file has saved, double-click it to run the Telemetry Processor Installer.

6. On the Welcome To The Microsoft Office Telemetry Processor page of the Setup Wizard, shown in Figure 1-47, click Next.

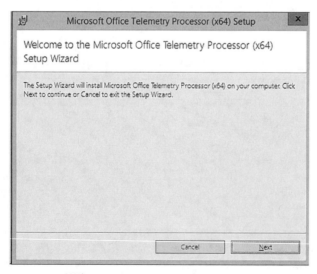

FIGURE 1-47 Welcome page

7. On the Completed the Microsoft Office Telemetry Processor page, ensure that Run The Office Telemetry Processor Settings Wizard Now option is selected, as shown in Figure 1-48, and click Finish.

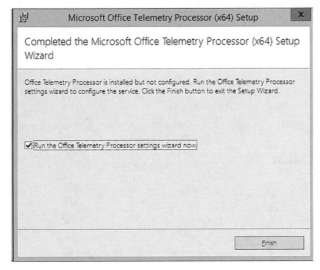

FIGURE 1-48 Installation complete, now run setup

8. On the Getting Started page of the Office Telemetry Processor Settings Wizard, review the information, as shown in Figure 1-49, and then click Next.

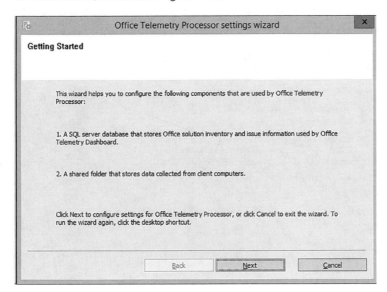

FIGURE 1-49 Setup requirements

9. On the Database Settings page, enter the name of the database server and click Connect. The connection will be made using the credentials of the currently signed-on user. Enter a name for the database and then click Create. Figure 1-50 shows a database named OfficeTelemetry. When the database is created, click Next.

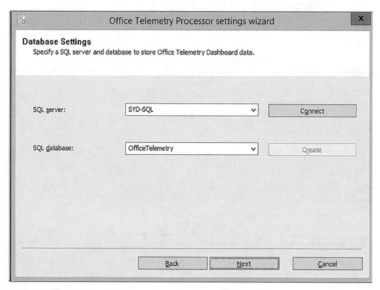

FIGURE 1-50 Database Settings

10. On the Office Telemetry Processor Settings Wizard dialog box, shown in Figure 1-51, click Yes to configure database permissions and database role settings.

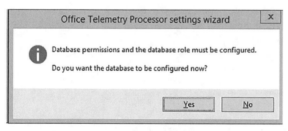

FIGURE 1-51 Database Permissions configuration

11. On the Shared Folder page, shown in Figure 1-52, click Browse.

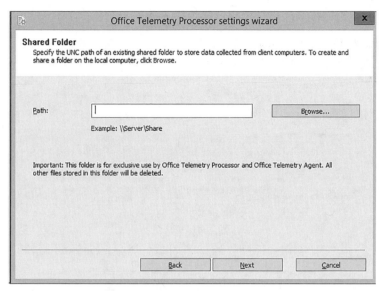

FIGURE 1-52 Shared Folder configuration

12. Create and select a shared folder, as shown in Figure 1-53. If you are going to use an existing folder, ensure that it is empty.

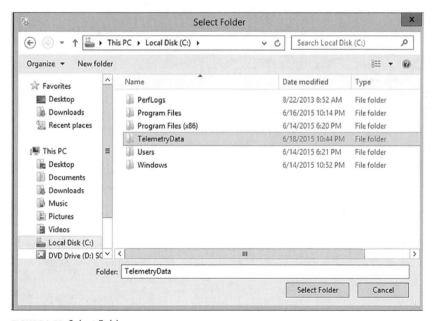

FIGURE 1-53 Select Folder

13. On the Shared Folder page, shown in Figure 1-54, click Next.

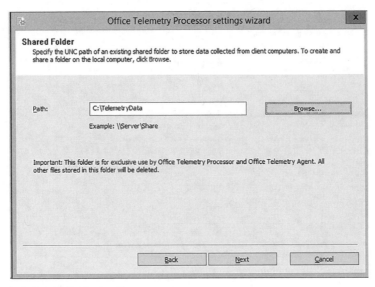

FIGURE 1-54 Folder location

14. Review the information on the information dialog, shown in Figure 1-55, which informs you that authenticated users will be granted the ability to create files and write data in the folder without being able to browse the contents of that folder, and then click Yes.

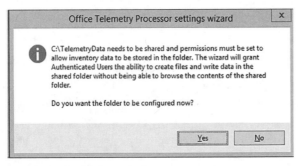

FIGURE 1-55 Permissions warning

15. On the Microsoft Customer Experience Improvement Program page, shown in Figure 1-56, decide if you want to participate in the Customer Experience Program.

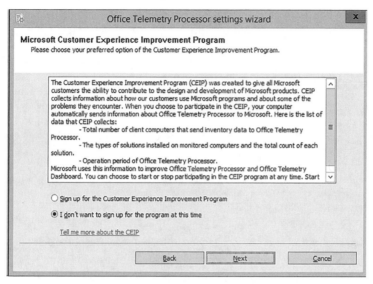

FIGURE 1-56 Customer Experience Improvement Program

16. On the Configuration Successful page, click Finish.

17. Once the Telemetry Processor is deployed, return to the Telemetry Dashboard spreadsheet and on the Getting Started tab, under section 5: Connect To The Database To View Telemetry Data, as shown in Figure 1-57, click Connect To Database.

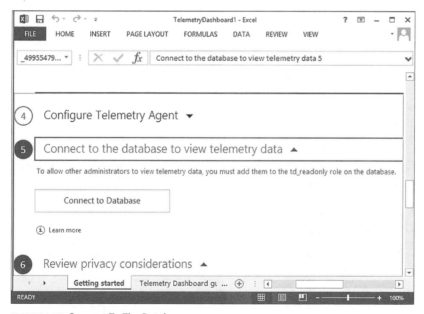

FIGURE 1-57 Connect To The Database

18. The Data Connection Settings dialog box, shown in Figure 1-58 should be automatically populated with the name of the SQL instance and the name of the database. Click Connect.

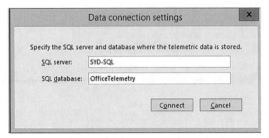

FIGURE 1-58 Data Connection Settings

19. Until you have configured telemetry collection, the Telemetry Dashboard will display a message informing you that there is no telemetry data, as shown in Figure 1-59.

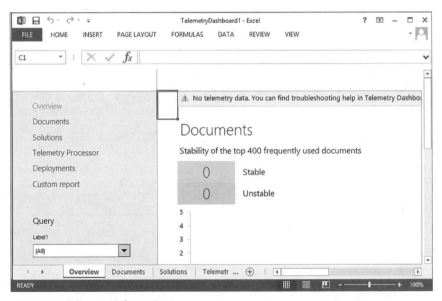

FIGURE 1-59 Telemetry information

MORE INFO **DEPLOY TELEMETRY DASHBOARD**

You can learn more about deploying the Telemetry Dashboard at: *https://technet.microsoft. com/library/f69cde72-689d-421f-99b8-c51676c77717.*

Enable telemetry through Group Policy

Before you can enable telemetry through Group Policy, you need to install the Office 2016 Group Policy administrative template. This functions for both Office 2016 and Office ProPlus.

You can download the administrative template from the Microsoft website at: *https://www.microsoft.com/en-us/download/details.aspx?id=49030*.

You'll need to download the file to a domain controller and then run it. When running the file downloaded from the internet, you will be asked to agree to the license terms, as shown in Figure 1-60. When you have agreed to the license terms, click Continue.

FIGURE 1-60 Software License Terms

You will be asked to choose a temporary directory in which to extract the template files. Once you have extracted the files, you will need to do the following:

- Copy the file Office16.admx to the C:\Windows\PolicyDefinitions folder.
- Copy the language appropriate Office16.adml file to the C:\Windows\PolicyDefinitions\ Language folder. For example, if using EN-US for US English, copy the Office16.adml file from the EN-US folder where you extracted the templates to the C:\Windows\PolicyDefinitions\en-US folder, as shown in Figure 1-61.

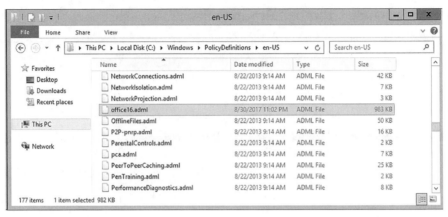

FIGURE 1-61 Office16.adml

When the ADMX and ADML files are copied across to the appropriate folders, you'll be able to edit the following policies, which are located in the User Configuration\Policies\Administrative Templates\Microsoft Office 2016\Telemetry Dashboard node shown in Figure 1-62.

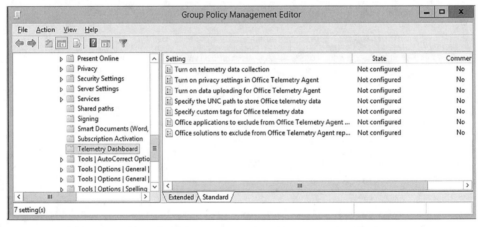

FIGURE 1-62 Telemetry Dashboard policies

TURN ON TELEMETRY DATA COLLECTION

The Turn On Telemetry Data Collection policy must be enabled, as shown in Figure 1-63, for telemetry data collection to be enabled. If this policy is not enabled, Office telemetry data collection will not occur.

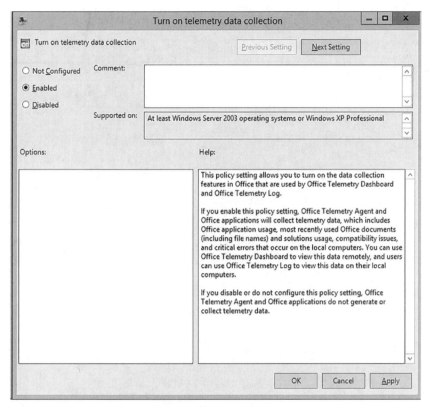

FIGURE 1-63 Turn On Telemetry Data Collection

TURN ON DATA UPLOADING FOR THE TELEMETRY AGENT

When you enable this policy, shown in Figure 1-64 Office telemetry data is uploaded to a shared folder specified in another policy. If you don't enable this policy, Office telemetry data is stored on the client and cannot be accessed at a central location through the Telemetry Dashboard.

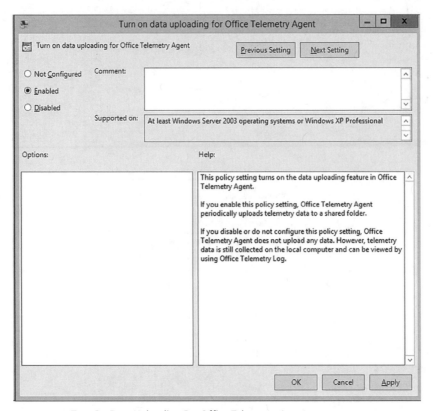

FIGURE 1-64 Turn On Data Uploading For Office Telemetry Agent

SPECIFY THE UNC PATH TO STORE OFFICE TELEMETRY DATA

If you have configured telemetry data to be uploaded to a shared folder using the Turn On Data Uploading For The Telemetry Agent policy, you'll need to configure this policy, shown in Figure 1-65, to specify the address to which the data will be uploaded.

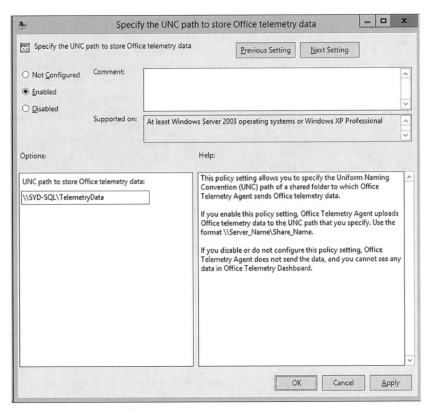

FIGURE 1-65 Specify The UNC Path To Store Office Telemetry Data

SPECIFY CUSTOM TAGS FOR OFFICE TELEMETRY DATA

The Specify Custom Tags For Office Telemetry Data allows you to apply tags to telemetry data forwarded to the shared folder used by the Telemetry Processor. You can specify up to four separate tags, as shown in Figure 1-66.

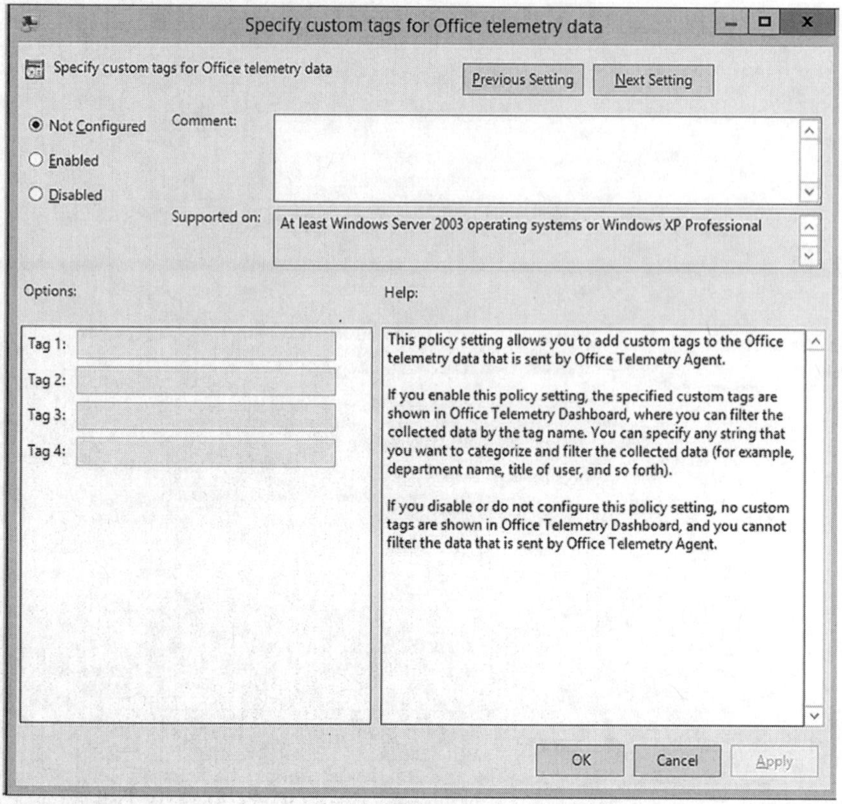

FIGURE 1-66 Specify Custom Tags For Office Telemetry Data

TURN ON PRIVACY SETTINGS IN TELEMETRY AGENT

Enabling this policy, shown in Figure 1-67, obfuscates the file name, file path, and title of Office documents before telemetry data uploads into the shared folder. If this policy is not enabled, the file name, path, and title of documents remain visible.

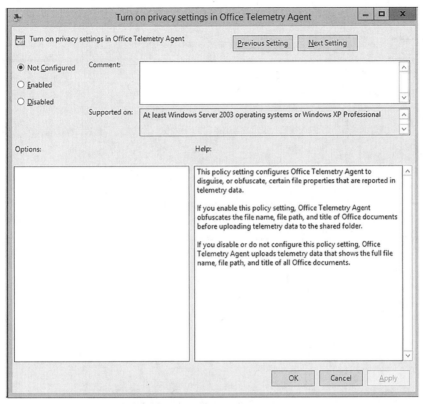

FIGURE 1-67 Turn On Privacy Settings In Office Telemetry Agent

OFFICE APPLICATIONS TO EXCLUDE FROM TELEMETRY AGENT REPORTING

You can use the Office Applications To Exclude From Office Telemetry Agent Reporting policy to exclude telemetry data from specific applications from being forwarded to the shared folder used by the Telemetry Processor. Figure 1-68 shows a configuration where telemetry from the Publisher and Visio applications will be excluded from being sent to the Telemetry Processor.

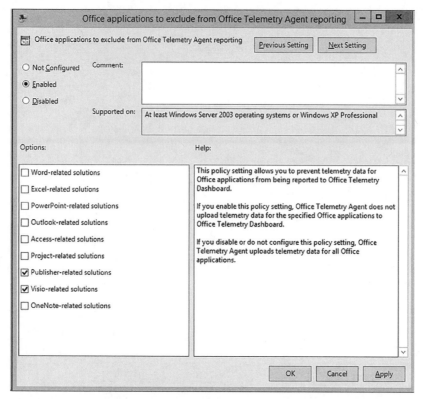

FIGURE 1-68 Office Applications To Exclude From Office Telemetry Agent Reporting

OFFICE SOLUTIONS TO EXCLUDE FROM TELEMETRY AGENT REPORTING

Configuring the Office Solutions To Exclude From Telemetry Agent Reporting policy allows you to stop telemetry data from the following Office solution categories from being forwarded to the Telemetry Processor:

- Office document files
- Office template files
- COM add-ins
- Application-specific add-ins
- Apps for Office

Figure 1-69 shows this policy configured so that telemetry from Office template files and COM add-ins won't be forwarded to the Telemetry Processor.

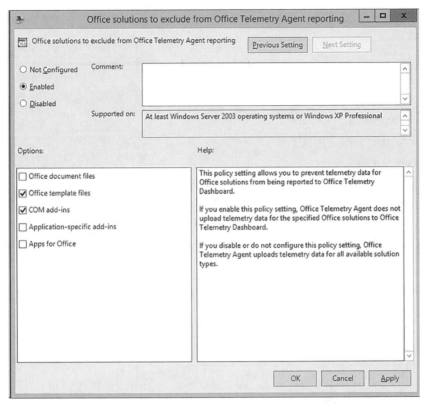

FIGURE 1-69 Office Solutions To Exclude From Office Telemetry Agent Reporting

> **_MORE INFO_ TELEMETRY AGENT POLICY**
>
> You can learn more about configuring group policies related to the Telemetry Agent at _https://technet.microsoft.com/library/f69cde72-689d-421f-99b8-c51676c77717#agentpolicy._

Deploy agent

Office Telemetry works natively with Office 2016 and Office ProPlus. Office Telemetry also works natively with Office 2013. This is because the Office Telemetry Agent is built into the Office 2016, Office 2013, and Office 365 ProPlus software. To use Office Telemetry with Office 2003, Office 2007, and Office 2010 it is necessary to deploy special agent software. This agent will collect data about any installed Office add-ins as well as any documents that have been recently accessed. The Office Telemetry agent for previous versions of Office collects inventory and usage data only. The Office Telemetry agent for previous versions of Office does not collect application event data.

The Telemetry Agent is supported on the following 32-bit and 64-bit versions of Windows:

- Windows 10
- Windows 8.1
- Windows 8
- Windows 7
- Windows Vista with Service Pack 2
- Windows XP with Service Pack 3
- Windows Server 2016
- Windows Server 2012 R2
- Windows Server 2012
- Windows Server 208 R2
- Windows Server 2008
- Windows Server 2003

It is important to remember that the separate Telemetry Agent software is only required if versions of Office prior to Office 2013 and Office ProPlus are in use. You can get the MSI files that allow for the installation of the Telemetry Agent through the Deploy Telemetry Agent section of the Getting Started worksheet of the Telemetry Dashboard, as shown in Figure 1-70.

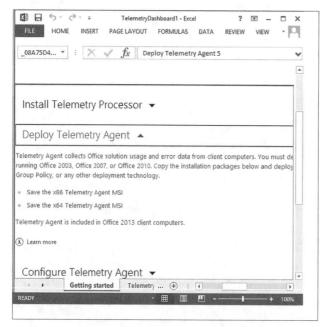

FIGURE 1-70 Deploy Telemetry Agent

Clicking on either the x86 or x64 Telemetry Agent MSI links will prompt you to save the Telemetry Agent Installer Package, as shown in Figure 1-71. These MSI files can then be deployed to computers using Group Policy, Microsoft Intune, System Center Configuration Manager, or any other software deployment solution.

FIGURE 1-71 Save Telemetry Agent Installer Package

Telemetry Dashboard details

When connected to the telemetry database, the Telemetry Dashboard includes the following worksheets:

- **Overview worksheet** This worksheet provides information about how documents and solutions are functioning on monitored computers. This worksheet provides a high-level view of solution and document stability.

- **Documents worksheet** This worksheet provides a list of documents collected by Telemetry Agent scans and telemetry documents. This worksheet will provide you with information about the most frequently used documents in your organization.

  - **Document details worksheet** Available through the documents worksheet, allows you to see which users are accessing a document.

  - **Document issues worksheet** Available through the documents worksheet, allows you to learn about unique events related to a specific document, such as if the document was open during an application crash.

  - **Document sessions worksheet** Available through the documents worksheet, shows session information during which issues occurred including data, user name, computer name, and domain information.

- **Solutions worksheet** Provides information about solutions collected by the Telemetry Log and Telemetry Agent scans. Solutions include COM add-ins, application specific add-ins, and apps for Office.

- **Solution details worksheet** Available through the solutions worksheet, allows you to see which users are using a solution.

- **Solution issues worksheet** Available through the solutions worksheet, allows you to discover the details of unique events related to a solution.

- **Solution sessions worksheet** Available through the solutions worksheet, allows you to determine session information about events related to a solution, such as when it occurred, the user, and computer on which the event occurred.

- **Telemetry Processor worksheet** Provides information about the health of the Office Telemetry infrastructure. This worksheet is shown in Figure 1-73.

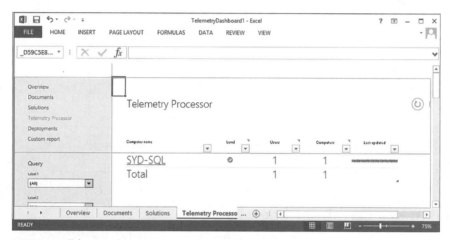

FIGURE 1-72 Telemetry Processor

- **Agents worksheet** Provides information about the users who have computers forwarding data to the Telemetry Processor.

- **Deployments worksheet** Provides information about the number of Office clients deployed in the organization.

- **Custom report worksheet** Creates relationships based on data in the database in a pivot table.

> *MORE INFO* **TELEMETRY DASHBOARD DETAILS**
>
> You can learn more about the Telemetry Dashboard at: *https://support.office.com/en-us/article/Best-practices-for-Office-Telemetry-570c7fb3-d7a5-49cd-8cbf-7300ea656328.*

Configure Telemetry Agent through registry

In some scenarios, you will want to enable the collection of telemetry data from computers that are not members of an Active Directory domain and hence are not subject to Group Policy. In this scenario, you can create and import registry settings that will configure the telemetry agent. You can do this by using a text file with the .reg extension and then importing it into the registry. The example below shows the settings required to configure a computer to upload its data to the shared folder \\SYD-SQL\TelemetryData.

```
[HKEY_CURRENT_USER\Software\Policies\Microsoft\Office\15.0\osm]
"CommonFileShare"="\\\\SYD-SQL\\TelemetryData"
"Tag1"="<TAG1>"
"Tag2"="<TAG2>"
"Tag3"="<TAG3>"
"Tag4"="<TAG4>"
"AgentInitWait"=dword:00000258
"Enablelogging"=dword:00000001
"EnableUpload"=dword:00000001
"EnableFileObfuscation"=dword:00000000
"AgentRandomDelay"=dword:000000F0
```

Report user issues

The Office Telemetry Log is a local log file that is automatically installed when you install Office 2016 or Office 365 Pro Plus. The Office Telemetry Log tracks the solution types listed in Table 1-2 for Office 2016 and Office 365 ProPlus applications.

TABLE 1-2 Office Telemetry Log properties

Solution type	Applications	Description
Task pane apps	Excel, Word, Project	Apps located in the task pane of the client application
Content apps	Excel	Apps integrated into an Office document
Mail apps	Outlook	Apps that appear in Outlook, often when a message contains specific words or phrases
Active documents	Word, PowerPoint, Excel	<ul><li>Office binary files (.doc, .ppt, .pps, .xls)</li><li>Office OpenXML files (.docx, .pptx, .ppsx, .xlsx)</li><li>Macro-enabled files with Visual Basic for Applications (VBA) code (.docm, .dotm, .pptm, .potm, .xlsm, .xltm)</li><li>Files with ActiveX controls</li><li>Files with external data connections</li></ul>
COM add-ins	Word, PowerPoint, Excel, Outlook	COM add-ins, including Office development tools in Visual Studio application-level add-ins
Excel Automation add-ins	Excel	Excel-supported automation add-ins built on COM add-ins
Excel XLS RTD add-ins	Excel	Excels worksheets that use the RealTimeData worksheet function
Word WLL add-ins	Word	WLL are work-specific add-ins built with compilers that support the creation of DLLs
Application add-ins	Word, PowerPoint, Excel	Application-specific files that contain VBA code (.dotm, .xla, .xlam, .ppa, .ppam)
Templates	Word, PowerPoint, Excel	Application-specific templates (.dot, .dotx, .xlt, .xltx, .pot, .potx)

A file or solution must be either loaded or opened within the local Office application before information about it will be present in the Telemetry Log.

To open the Telemetry Log, on the start menu type **Telemetry Log For Office 2016** as shown in Figure 1-73. You use Telemetry Log For Office 2016 even if Office ProPlus is installed.

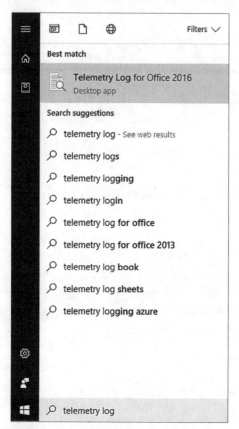

FIGURE 1-73 Telemetry Log Search

The events worksheet of the Telemetry Log shows event information. This is the primary view of the log that you would use if attempting to diagnose user issues using the Telemetry Log.

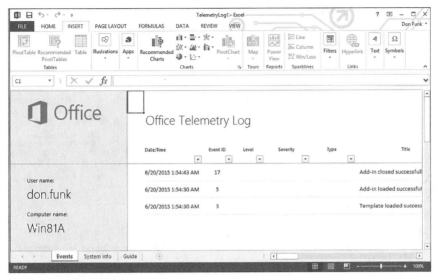

FIGURE 1-74 Telemetry Log

The System Info worksheet provides you with information about the computer on which the Telemetry Log is being run, including user name, computer name, system type, Windows edition, time zone, Telemetry Log version, and Office edition.

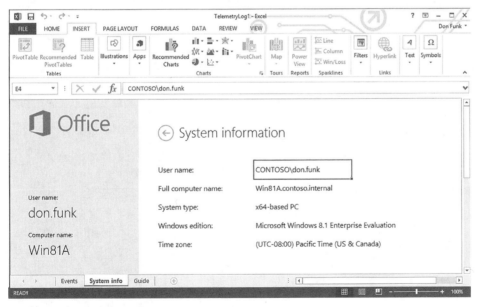

FIGURE 1-75 System Information

EXAM TIP

Remember which policies must be enabled to allow telemetry data to be forwarded to the Telemetry Processor.

Skill 1.4: Plan for Office clients

Just installing Outlook from the Office 365 portal doesn't configure it with a person's Office 365 user name and password. This skill deals with configuring Outlook and Skype for Business clients to use Office 365 accounts. It also deals with the Office Web Apps, known as Office Online, and the differences between Click-to-Run and MSI deployment formats.

This skill covers the following topics:

- Outlook client
- Skype for Business client
- Office on Demand
- Office Web Apps
- Click-to-Run versus MSI
- Modern authentication

Outlook client

The main task that is necessary to complete once Outlook is installed on a client computer is configuring access to the Exchange Online mailbox. You can add an Office 365 email account to the Outlook client by performing the following steps:

1. Open Outlook from the Start menu.
2. On the Welcome to Outlook, shown in Figure 1-77, verify that the Office 365 email account is listed and click Connect.

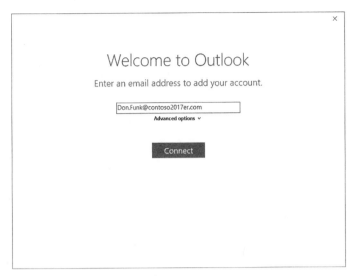

FIGURE 1-76 Welcome To Outlook

3. On the Windows Security dialog box, shown in Figure 1-77, enter the password for the Office 365 account and click OK.

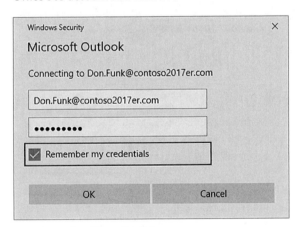

FIGURE 1-77 Provide credentials

4. On the Account setup is complete page, shown in Figure 1-78, click OK. Outlook will open.

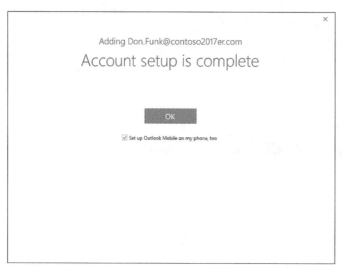

FIGURE 1-78 Account setup complete

MORE INFO **USING OUTLOOK WITH OFFICE 365**

You can learn more about Configuring Outlook for Office 365 at: *https://support.office. com/en-us/article/Add-an-email-account-to-Outlook-for-PC-6e27792a-9267-4aa4-8bb6- c84ef146101b.*

Skype for Business client

The Skype for Business client allows users to connect to Skype for Business to host or join meetings and instant message other Skype for Business users. To connect to Skype for Business, the user must enter their Office 365 email address, as shown in Figure 1-79 and then click Sign In.

FIGURE 1-79 Skype For Business

Users may be prompted for their Office 365 password. Once they have successfully authenticated with the Skype for Business servers, they will be able to add contacts and join meetings from the client.

> **MORE INFO** **SKYPE FOR BUSINESS**
>
> You can learn more about the Skype for Business client at: *https://support.office.com/en-us/article/Install-Skype-for-Business-8a0d4da8-9d58-44f9-9759-5c8f340cb3fb.*

Office Online

Office Online, also known as Office Web Apps, allows you to access the basic functionality of a variety of Microsoft Office applications through a supported web browser. You can open Word Online, Excel Online, PowerPoint Online, and OneNote Online directly from the Office 365 portal, as shown in Figure 1-80.

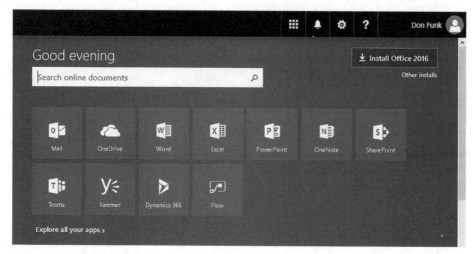

FIGURE 1-80 Office Online

People with Office 365 User Accounts will be able to access documents stored in organizational locations such as OneDrive for Business and SharePoint Online. Documents will also be able to be opened directly from the Outlook Web App. Figure 1-81 shows the interface of the Word Online Office Web App.

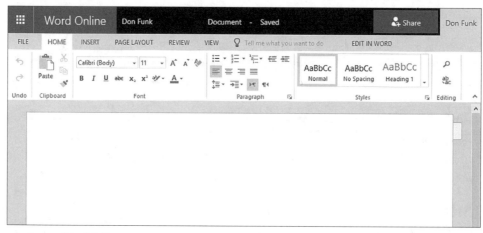

FIGURE 1-81 Word Online

MORE INFO **OFFICE ONLINE**

You can learn more about Office Online at: *https://support.office.com/en-us/article/Get-started-with-Office-Online-in-Office-365-5622c7c9-721d-4b3d-8cb9-a7276c2470e5*.

Click-to-Run vs. MSI

Click-to-Run and MSI are two different formats through which Office applications can be distributed to users. Click-to-Run offers the following features:

- **Streaming installation**   Streaming installation allows an application to be run before installation has completed. When the installation of an application is streamed, the first part of the application installed provides the minimum functionality necessary to get the application running. This allows the user to begin working with the application while installation completes.

- **Slipstreamed Servicing**   The Click-to-Run functionality of Office 365 ProPlus means that updates are included in the installation. Rather than installing Office in a traditional manner and then running a Windows Update check to locate and install any relevant updates, relevant updates are already included within the Click-to-Run installation files. Slipstreamed Servicing means that end users have the most secure and up-to-date version of the application immediately, rather than having to wait for the post-deployment update cycle to complete.

- **User-based licensing**   User-based licensing means that the Office 365 ProPlus license is associated with the Office 365 user account, not the computer that the user is signed on to. Depending on the type of license associated with the user and the tenancy, the user is able to install Office 365 ProPlus on up to five different computers. It is possible to remove licenses from computers that have had Office 365 ProPlus installed on them at an earlier point in time.

- **Retail activation**   Office 365 ProPlus is activated using retail rather than volume license methods. Activation occurs over the internet. As you learned earlier, this means that the computer must connect to the Internet every 30 days, otherwise Office ProPlus will enter reduced functionality mode.

- **SKU-level application suites**   Unless an administrator configures an appropriate configuration file, Office 365 ProPlus installs all products in the suite. The products that are installed will depend on the specifics of the Office 365 subscription, but this usually means Access, Excel, InfoPath, OneNote, Outlook, PowerPoint, Publisher, and Word. The products that are installed will be installed to all users in the tenancy. It is not possible to choose to install the PowerPoint program to some users but not to others when all users are using the same Click-to-Run installation file and configuration file. It is possible to have separate sets of applications deployed to users, but this requires separate configuration files for each set of applications.

- **Scenario limitations**   You cannot use Office 365 ProPlus with Remote Desktop Services, Windows To Go, or on networks that do not have a connection to the Internet.

MSI files are a method through which applications are packaged. MSI files allow organizational IT departments to automate the deployment applications, such as Office, using tools such as Microsoft Intune and System Center Configuration Manager. MSI files are appropriate for organizations that have a managed desktop environment and are less suitable for the types of "Bring Your Own Device" scenarios in which Click-to-Run products, such as Office 365 ProPlus, are suitable. MSI files offer the following features:

- **Classic installation**   MSI files can be installed by double-clicking on the installer file, and can be deployed using Group Policy, Microsoft Intune, System Center Configuration Manager, or third-party application deployment products. The application is not available to the user until the installation of the application is complete. This differs from the Click-to-Run method's streaming technology, which allows a user to begin using an application with a reduced set of features before the installation of the application completes.

- **Layered servicing**   MSI files represent the application at the time that it was packaged as an MSI file. This means that after deployment it will be necessary for the IT department to apply any necessary software updates to the application. Depending on the age of the MSI file and the number of software updates that have been released since the application was first packaged, it can take quite some time for the application to be updated to the current patch level after the application is deployed. This substantially increases the amount of time between an application being deployed and the user being able to use the application to perform their job role. IT departments can update MSI files with the latest updates and patches, but this is a complex, usually manual, process which requires deploying the application to a reference computer, updating the application, and then performing a technique known as a capture that creates the new updated MSI file. With Click-to-Run technology, the application updates are slipstreamed into the application by Microsoft, meaning that the application is current with updates as soon as it is deployed.

- **Volume licensing**   The versions of Office that you can deploy from an MSI file, including Office 2013 and Office 2016, have editions that support volume licensing. Volume licensing gives you the option of using a volume license key. Volume licensing is not something that is automatically supported by the MSI format and depends on the properties of the deployed software. Office 365 ProPlus does not support volume licensing. Volume licensing is only available to organizations that have volume licensing agreements with Microsoft.

- **Volume activation**   Like volume licensing, volume activation is not a property of an MSI file, but a feature that is supported by some versions of Office that use this packaging format. Volume activation allows large numbers of products to be activated, either through use of a special activation key used each time the installation is performed, or through technologies such as a Key Management Services (KMS) server on the organization's internal network. Volume activation is only available to organizations that have volume-licensing agreements.

- **Selective application installation**   Rather than deploying all products in the Office suite, the MSI-based deployment method makes it simple for organizations to deploy individual products in the suite. For example, it is possible to choose to deploy Word and Excel to some users, and PowerPoint to others.

- **Scenario limitations** Unlike Click-to-Run Office 365 ProPlus, which uses retail activation, the volume-licensed versions of Office 2016 can be used on Remote Desktop Services servers, can be deployed on Windows To Go USB devices, and can be deployed on networks that do not have internet connectivity.

While there are differences between the Click-to-Run Office 365 ProPlus and MSI-based Office 2016, there are also certain similarities:

- Both can be configured through Group Policy.
- Both provide telemetry visible through the Telemetry Dashboard.
- Extensions designed for the Office 2016 version of a product will work with the Office 365 version of that product.

> *MORE INFO* **CLICK-TO-RUN VERSUS MSI**
>
> You can learn more about Click-to-Run versus MSI at: *http://blogs.technet.com/b/office_resource_kit/archive/2013/03/05/the-new-office-garage-series-who-moved-my-msi.aspx.*

Office Configuration Analyzer Tool

The Office Configuration Analyzer Tool (OffCAT) provides you with diagnostic information about Office programs installed on a computer. This includes most parameters of each Office program's configuration. OffCAT is useful in diagnosing known problems with Office programs. When you perform an OffCAT scan and a known problem is found, you'll be provided with a link to the relevant Knowledge Base article. Figure 1-82 shows the output of an OffCAT scan.

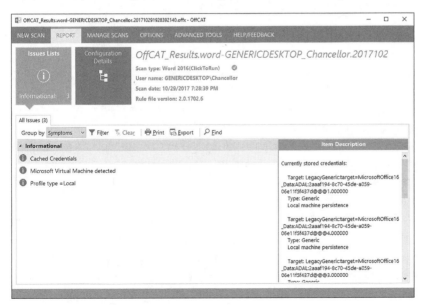

FIGURE 1-82 Office Configuration Analyzer

Modern Authentication for Office 365 Clients

Modern authentication leverages Active Directory Authentication Library based sign-in for Office client applications. Modern authentication uses OAuth 2.0 standards and is supported on the Windows, mac OSX, iOS, and Android operating systems. The Office 2013 versions of applications that interacted with Office 365 used legacy authentication rather than modern authentication unless registry keys were specially configured on each client. Legacy authentication used either the Microsoft Online Sign-In Assistant or basic authentication. Office 2016 client applications use modern authentication by default and no extra configuration if required.

EXAM TIP

Remember that volume-licensing scenarios require MSI rather than Click-to-Run.

Thought experiment

In this thought experiment, demonstrate your skills and knowledge of the topics covered in this chapter. You can find answers to this thought experiment in the next section.

There are an increasing number of iPad and Android tablet users at Contoso who want to use these mobile devices to perform work tasks. Several of the users of Android tablets have already installed apps from the Google Play Store, but are unable to access documents stored in SharePoint online. Some of the iPad users have heard that Office apps are available, but don't know where to start when it comes to obtaining them.

For your desktop computers, you are interested in centrally deploying Office 365 ProPlus using Click-to-Run files. To monitor this deployment, you are in the process of preparing to use the Telemetry Dashboard.

Don Funk is a user at Contoso. Don has just purchased a new consumer laptop for use at home and wants to set up Outlook and Skype for Business. Don signs in to his domain joined work computer using the contoso\don.funk user name. Don signs in to Office 365 using the don.funk@contoso.com user name. Single sign-on is configured with Office 365.

With this information in mind, answer the following questions:

1. What instruction should you give to iPad users about locating Office apps?

2. What instruction should you give to Android tablet users who have already installed apps from the Google Play Store?

3. Which tool should you use to obtain the Office 365 ProPlus Click-to-Run files from the Microsoft servers on the Internet?

4. Which file should you edit to retrieve a specific version of the Office 365 ProPlus Click-to-Run files?

5. What is the role of the Telemetry Processor?

6. How do you configure a non-domain joined computer with Office 365 ProPlus to forward telemetry data to a specific specially configured shared folder used with the Telemetry Dashboard?

7. Which user name should Don use when configuring Outlook email on the new computer?

8. Which user name should Don use when configuring Skype for Business on the new computer?

Thought experiment answers

This section contains the solutions to the thought experiment.

1. You should tell the iPad users to sign in to the Office 365 portal. This will allow them to view the available Office 365-related apps for iPad. It will also provide them with direct links to those apps in the app store.

2. You should instruct them to sign in to their Office 365 accounts in each app so that they can gain access to documents stored in enterprise locations.

3. You should use the Office Deployment Tool, also known as the Office Deployment Tool for Click-to-Run, to obtain the Office 365 ProPlus Click-to-Run files from the Internet.

4. You must edit the configuration.xml files to specify a specific version of the Office 365 ProPlus files.

5. The Telemetry Processor takes data forwarded to the shared folder and processes it, forwarding it to the SQL Server database.

6. You need to edit the registry of the non-domain joined computer to configure it to forward telemetry data to a specific specially configured shared folder used with the Telemetry Dashboard.

7. Don Funk should use the user name don.funk@contoso.com when configuring Outlook email on the new computer.

8. Don Funk should use the user name don.funk@contoso.com when configuring Skype for Business on the new computer.

Chapter summary

- You can use the Office 365 Admin Console to restrict the applications that users can self-deploy. However, you can only allow or block them from Office 365 ProPlus. You cannot allow or block individual programs within Office 365 ProPlus such as Word and Excel.

- Users can self-provision apps for mobile devices from the Office 365 portal. Selecting an application in the portal will open the device vendor's app store to the chosen application.

- Each Office 365 user can run five activated copies of Office 365 ProPlus and/or Office 2016 for Mac.

- Unactivated copies of Office 365 ProPlus run in reduced functionality mode.

- Reduced functionality mode allows documents to be viewed, but does not allow new documents to be created or existing documents to be modified.

- Users can deactivate existing activations. When a user does this, the application enters reduced functionality mode.

- An activated copy of Office 365 ProPlus must be able to communicate with Microsoft servers on the Internet every 30 days. If this communication does not occur, Office 365 ProPlus will enter reduced functionality mode.

- The Office Deployment Tool is a command line utility used if you want to centralize the deployment of Office 365 Click-to-Run files from a location on your local area network.

- You can use the Office Deployment Tool to download the Office 365 Click-to-Run files and language pack files from Microsoft servers on the Internet.

- You use the Office Deployment Tool in download mode to retrieve files from the Microsoft servers on the internet.

- You use the Office Deployment Tool in configure mode to install Office 365 using an installation source on the local area network.

- The configuration.xml file is used with the Office Deployment Tool in both download and configure mode. In download mode it allows you to specify which files are downloaded. In configure mode it allows you to specify how Office Click-to-Run applications and language packs are installed and how updates are applied.

- The Telemetry Dashboard is a specially configured Excel workbook that connects to a SQL Server database and displays telemetry information from Office 2016, Office 2013 and Office 365 ProPlus.

- The Telemetry Processor is a computer that collects telemetry data and writes information to a SQL Server database.

- Telemetry collection settings are configured through Group Policy or by configuring the registry.

- Office 2016, Office 2013 and Office 365 ProPlus have telemetry collection built into the applications.

- Previous versions of Office require the deployment of a telemetry collection agent.

- A local version of the Telemetry Log can be accessed to help in the diagnosis of problems related to Office.

- Outlook can be configured by providing a user's Office 365 user name, which also functions as their email address and password.

- Skype for Business can be configured by providing a user's Office 365 user name, which also functions as their email address and password.

- Office Online provides browser-based versions of Word, Excel, PowerPoint, and OneNote. These versions provide only basic functionality.

- The Click-to-Run format has limitations that make it unsuitable for organizations that need to use volume licensing or do not allow client computers to connect to the internet.

- The Office Configuration Analyzer Tool (OffCAT) allows you to diagnose common problems with Office applications.

- Office 2016 client applications use modern authentication by default and no extra configuration if required.

CHAPTER 2

Provision SharePoint Online site collections

SharePoint Online allows collaboration for people within an organization, and also allows collaboration with people who are external to the organization. For many organizations, SharePoint Online has taken the place of the traditional shared file server when it comes to sharing documents. Understanding how to configure and manage SharePoint Online site collections is critical for an Office 365 administrator. Administrators must ensure that resources are externally shared when appropriate, and that access to resources is restricted when required.

Skills in this chapter:

- Skill 2.1: Configure external user sharing
- Skill 2.2: Create SharePoint site collection
- Skill 2.3: Plan a collaboration solution

Skill 2.1: Configure external user sharing

This skill deals with the settings related to allowing people external to your organization's Office 365 tenancy access to content stored within SharePoint Online. There are a variety of sharing options, from allowing read and edit access to people with Microsoft accounts, to allowing read and edit access to anyone who has the correct URL for a document.

> **This skill covers the following topics:**
> - Enable external user sharing globally
> - Enable external user sharing per site collection
> - Share with external users
> - Remove external user access

Understanding external users

External users are people who need to collaborate with people in your organization using content hosted on SharePoint Online, but who haven't been provisioned with an organizational Office 365 or SharePoint Online license.

The use rights available to external users depend on the features available to the SharePoint Online tenancy with which they are collaborating. For example, if your organization has an E3 Enterprise Plan, and a SharePoint site uses enterprise features, the external user is able to use and view those enterprise features.

External users can perform the following tasks:

- Can use Office Online to view and edit documents in the browser. Can use their own version of Office to interact with content hosted in SharePoint Online, but are not eligible for licenses to the tenancy's Office 365 Office ProPlus software.

- Perform tasks on the site commensurate with their permission level. For example, adding an external user to the Members group grants that user Edit permissions. They are able to add, edit, and delete lists, list items, and documents.

- View other site content, including navigating to subsites to which they have been invited, and view site feeds.

External users are restricted from being able to perform the following tasks:

- Create personal sites.

- Edit their profiles.

- View the company-wide newsfeed.

- Add storage to the tenant storage pool.

- Enact searches against "everything" or access the Search Center.

- Access the site mailbox.

- Access PowerBI features, including Power View, Power Pivot, Quick Explore, and Timeline Slicer.

- Use eDiscovery.

- Open downloaded documents protected by Azure Rights Management (it is still possible to open these documents using Office Online).

- Access SharePoint Online data connection libraries.

- Use Excel Services features, such as Calculated Measures and Calculated Members, decoupled Pivot Tables and PivotCharts, Field List, and Field support, filter enhancements, and Search Filters.

- Use Visio Services.

Enabling external user sharing globally

The external sharing options configured at the SharePoint Online tenancy level override those configured at the site collection level. You can configure the following global external sharing options shown in Figure 2-1.

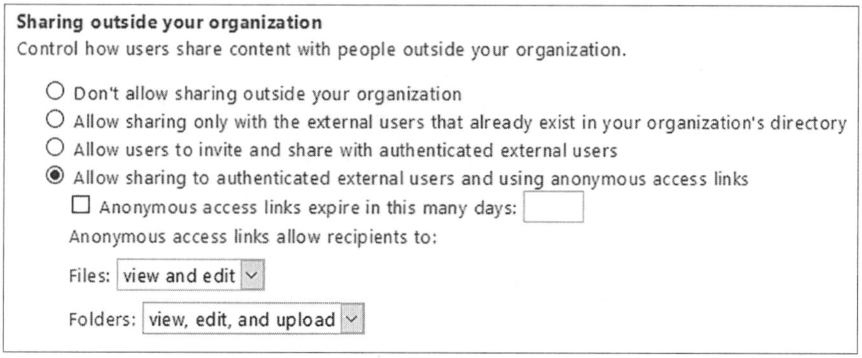

FIGURE 2-1 External Sharing settings

- **Don't Allow Sharing Outside Your Organization**   Choosing this option prevents all users on all sites within the SharePoint Online tenancy from sharing sites or content with external users.

- **Allow Sharing Only With The External Users That Already Exist In Your Organization's Directory**   Selecting this setting allows sites, folders, and documents to be sharable with external users that exist within the Office 365 user directory. A user is added to the directory if they have previously accepted a sharing invitation or have been imported from a separate Office 365 or Azure Active Directory instance.

- **Allow Users To Invite And Share With Authenticated External Users**   Choosing this option allows sites, folders, and documents to be shared with users who have a Microsoft account. This includes accounts such as outlook.com accounts or users from other Office 365 or Azure Active Directory instances.

- **Allow Sharing With Authenticated External Users And Using Anonymous Access Links**   This option allows documents and folders to be shared via anonymous links. Anyone with the link can view or edit the document or upload data to the folder. This applies only at the document and folder level and does not apply at the site level.

To configure external user sharing for the SharePoint Online tenancy, perform the following steps:

1. Sign in to the Office 365 Admin Center with a user account that has SharePoint Online administrator privileges.

2. Under Admin, click SharePoint. This opens the SharePoint Admin Center.

3. In the SharePoint Admin Center, click Sharing, as shown in Figure 2-2.

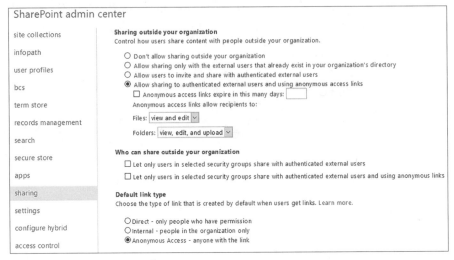

FIGURE 2-2 SharePoint Admin Center

4. In the Sharing section, choose between one of the following options:

- Don't Allow Sharing Outside Your Organization

- Allow Sharing Only With External Users That Already Exist In Your Organization's Directory

- Allow Users To Invite And Share With Authenticated External Users

- Allow Sharing To Authenticated External Users And Using Anonymous Access Links

Turning off external sharing has the following consequences:

- If you disable and then re-enable external sharing, external users who have been granted access to content regain access.

- If you disable and then re-enable external sharing, site collections that had sharing enabled have sharing re-enabled.

- If you want to block specific site collections from having sharing re-enabled, disable external sharing on a per site collection basis prior to re-enabling external sharing.

- When you disable external sharing on a specific site collection, any configured External User permissions for that site collection are permanently deleted.

- Turning off external sharing at the site collection level disables guest links, but does not remove them. To remove access to specific documents, you need to disable anonymous guest links.

- Changes made to external access do not occur immediately, and might take up to 60 minutes.

You can use the Set-SPOSite with the `SharingCapability` parameter to configure sharing options. You can use the following options with this parameter:

- ExternalUserSharingOnly
- ExternalUserAndGuestSharing
- ExistingExternalUserSharingOnly
- Disabled

> **MORE INFO   EXTERNAL SHARING**
>
> You can learn more about external sharing at *https://support.office.com/en-us/article/Manage-external-sharing-for-your-SharePoint-Online-environment-c8a462eb-0723-4b0b-8d0a-70feafe4be85*.

Enabling external user sharing per site collection

Only SharePoint Online administrators are able to make changes to the SharePoint Online tenancy's external user sharing settings. Site collection administrators are allowed to configure sharing settings on a per site collection basis as long as external user sharing is set to one of the following options:

- Allow External Users Who Accept Sharing Invitations And Sign In As Authenticated Users.
- Allow Both External Users Who Accept Sharing Invitations And Anonymous Guest Links

The sharing options at a site collection level are similar to those that are available at the SharePoint Online tenancy level, and are shown in Figure 2-3.

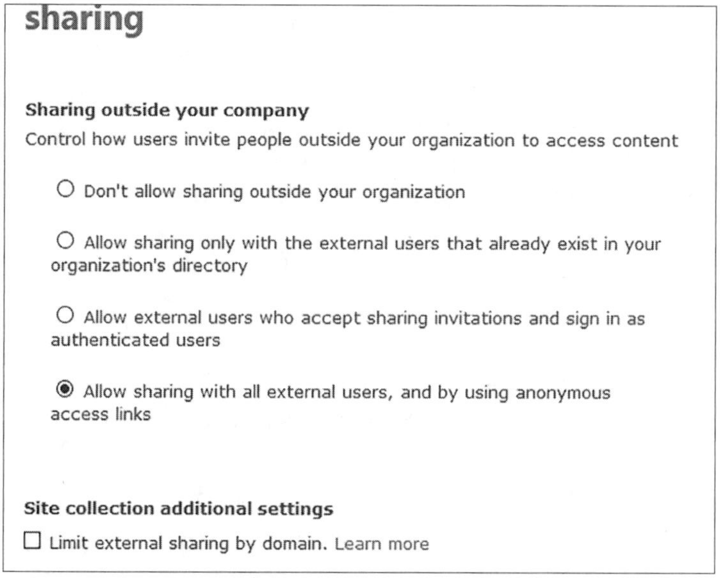

sharing

Sharing outside your company
Control how users invite people outside your organization to access content

- ○ Don't allow sharing outside your organization

- ○ Allow sharing only with the external users that already exist in your organization's directory

- ○ Allow external users who accept sharing invitations and sign in as authenticated users

- ● Allow sharing with all external users, and by using anonymous access links

Site collection additional settings
- ☐ Limit external sharing by domain. Learn more

FIGURE 2-3 Site collection sharing

These options have the following properties:

- **Don't Allow Sharing Outside Your Organization** Prevents all users on all sites in the collection from sharing sites or content with external users. Users are unable to share content or sites with users who are not members of their organization's Office 365 tenancy. If sharing had been enabled previously, any permissions assigned to external users are deleted.

- **Allow Sharing Only With The External Users That Already Exist In Your Organization's Directory** Allows access to users that are already present in the Office 365 directory, either because they have accepted an invitation before or because their account has been imported from another Office 365 or Azure Active Directory instance.

- **Allow External Users Who Accept Sharing Invitations And Sign In As Authenticated Users** Allows users with Microsoft accounts who have been sent invitations to access sites and content in a site collection. Site owners and users with Full permission can share sites and documents with external users who sign in with a Microsoft account. Invitations that are redeemed by external users are tied to the redeeming Microsoft account, and access cannot be shared with other Microsoft accounts.

- **Allow Sharing With All External Users, And By Using Anonymous Access Links** Allows sites within a site collection that have been authenticated with Microsoft accounts to be shared with users. Site owners and users with Full Control permissions are able to share sites and documents with external users. Invitations that are redeemed by external users are tied to the redeeming Microsoft account. Access cannot be shared with other Microsoft accounts. Site owners and users with Full Control permissions are able to share documents through an anonymous link. When sharing documents with external users or through anonymous links, View or Edit permission can be assigned. Anonymous links can be shared with the original sharer, having no control over which external parties access anonymously shared content after the guest link has been forwarded.

Settings configured at the SharePoint Online tenancy level determine those available at the individual site collection level. If sharing is only allowed for external users at the SharePoint Online tenancy level, the option to allow anonymous guest links to be sent at the site collection level will not be available. If sharing is blocked at the SharePoint Online tenancy level, then sharing will not be possible at the site collection level. Modifications to the external sharing settings for the My Site site collection apply to any existing personal sites as well as any personal sites created in the future.

To configure sharing at the site collection level, perform the following steps:

1. Sign in to the Office 365 Admin Center with a user account that has SharePoint Online administrator privileges.

2. Under Admin, click SharePoint. This opens the SharePoint Admin Center.

3. In the Site Collections area, select the site collection for which you want to configure sharing, and click Sharing in the Site Collections toolbar, as shown in Figure 2-4.

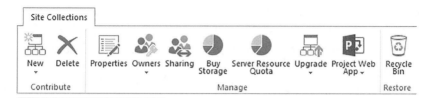

FIGURE 2-4 Site Collections

4. On the Sharing dialog box, shown in Figure 2-5, specify the type of sharing you wish to enable, and click Save.

FIGURE 2-5 Sharing options

Sharing settings configured at the site collection level determine the sharing options available at the document level. If sending anonymous links is not allowed at the site collection level, it will not be allowed from a document hosted within a site in that collection.

> **MORE INFO**   **SITE COLLECTION SHARING**
>
> You can learn more about sharing at the site collection level at *https://support.office. com/en-us/article/Manage-external-sharing-for-your-SharePoint-Online-environment-c8a462eb-0723-4b0b-8d0a-70feafe4be85*.

Sharing with external users

After sharing is appropriately configured at the SharePoint Online tenancy level and at the site collection level, there are three basic methods that allow you to share content with external users:

- Share an entire site and invite users to sign in using a Microsoft account (including Office 365 accounts from separate organizations, such as workplaces or schools).

- Share individual documents by inviting external users to sign in using a Microsoft account.

- Send users a guest link that allows users external to the organization access to each individual document that you want to share anonymously.

Sharing a site

To share a site with an external user, perform the following steps:

1. Sign in to Office 365 with an account that has permission to share the site. Select SharePoint from the list of Apps, as shown in Figure 2-6.

FIGURE 2-6 Office 365 Apps

2. In the list of sites, select the site that you want to share.

3. In the upper right-hand corner of the Site page, click Share Site, as shown in Figure 2-7.

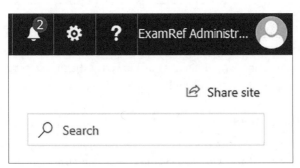

FIGURE 2-7 Share

4. On the Share Site dialog box, shown in Figure 2-8, provide the name of the person with whom you want to share the site, specify the permission level, and click Share. You can choose between the following levels:

- Read

- Edit

- Full Control

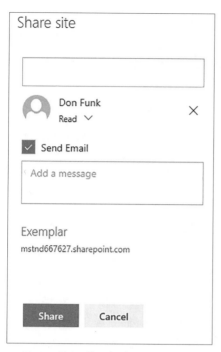

FIGURE 2-8 Team Site sharing

An invitation is automatically sent to the person or people who you invited. If the invitation isn't accepted within seven days, it expires. Users accepting an invitation must sign in with a Microsoft account, such as an Outlook.com or Hotmail.com account, or an Office 365 account.

You can determine which external users a SharePoint Online site collection has been shared with by performing the following steps:

1. Sign in to Office 365 with an account that has permission to share the site and select SharePoint from the list of Apps.

2. In the list of sites, select the site that you want to share.

3. Click the Gear icon in the upper right-hand corner, and then click Site Permissions.

4. On the Share Site dialog box, click Shared With, as shown in Figure 2-9. The dialog box lists all users with whom the site collection has been shared.

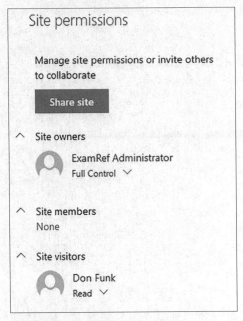

FIGURE 2-9 Site permissions

Sharing a document

There are two ways to share a document: sharing with an external user who must authenticate and sharing through an anonymous guest link.

To share with an external user who must authenticate using a Microsoft account, which includes the option of using an Office 365 account, perform the following steps:

1. Sign in to Office 365 with an account that has permission to share the site, and select SharePoint from the list of Apps.

2. In the list of sites, select the site that hosts the document that you want to share.

3. Select the document that you want to share, and then click Share, as shown in Figure 2-10.

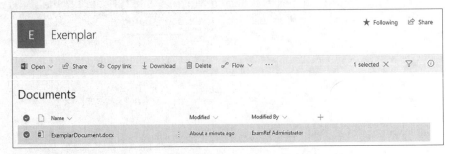

FIGURE 2-10 Share Document

4. On the Send Link page, specify what level of sharing and permission you would like to provide. You can choose between the permissions Can Edit and Can View. Figure 2-11 shows the document ExemplarDocument shared to Kim Akers' account with the permission that allows the user of that account to edit the document.

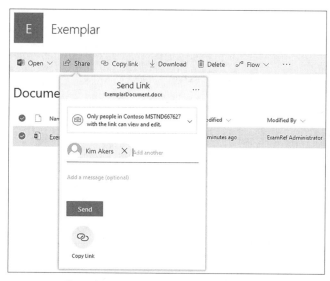

FIGURE 2-11 Share document

5. Click Send to share the document.

You can view which users and groups have access to a document by clicking Advanced from the Share Manage Access dialog box and viewing the Permissions assigned. Figure 2-12 shows the permissions assigned to the ExemplarDocument.docx document.

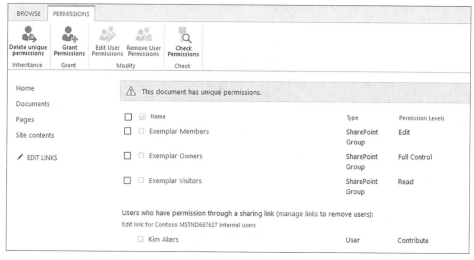

FIGURE 2-12 Permissions

The process of creating a shared link is similar. Sign in to Office 365, locate the document that you want to share, and then open the Sharing dialog box. Click Copy Link, as shown in Figure 2-13.

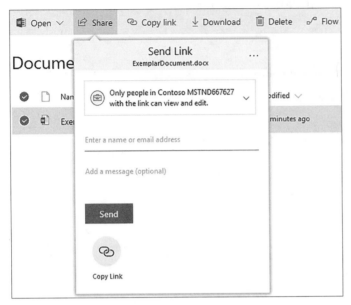

FIGURE 2-13 Copy Link

MORE INFO **SHARE SITES OR DOCUMENTS WITH EXTERNAL USERS**

You can learn more about sharing sites or documents with external users at *https://support. office.com/en-us/article/Share-sites-or-documents-with-people-outside-your-organiza- tion-80e49744-e30f-44db-8d51-16661b1d4232.*

Removing external user access

You can revoke external user access to a site only after a user has accepted their invitation. You can revoke access by removing the external user's permission to the site. To revoke access, perform the following steps:

1. Sign in to Office 365 with an account that has permission to share the site and select SharePoint from the list of Apps.

2. In the list of sites, select the site that you want to share.

3. Click Site Contents, and then click Site Settings, as shown in Figure 2-14.

FIGURE 2-14 Site Settings

4. Under Users And Permissions, click People And Groups, as shown in Figure 2-15.

FIGURE 2-15 Site Settings

5. Select the external user from whom you want to revoke access.

6. From the Actions menu, click Remove Users From Group.

7. When prompted about removing users from the group click OK.

You can use the Remove-SPOExternalUser PowerShell cmdlet to remove external users from accessing SharePoint online. There is no way, at the SharePoint Online tenancy level, to determine all of the sites to which an external user has been granted access. It is necessary to view the settings for individual sites to determine if a specific external user has been granted access to the site. There is also no method, at the SharePoint Online tenancy level, to determine which documents have been shared externally.

> **MORE INFO** **REVOKE USER ACCESS**
>
> You can learn more about revoking user access at *https://support.office.com/en-us/article/Share-sites-or-documents-with-people-outside-your-organization-80e49744-e30f-44db-8d51-16661b1d4232*.

EXAM TIP

Remember that the sharing settings configured at the SharePoint Online level overrides the settings that can be configured at the site collection level.

Skill 2.2: Create SharePoint site collection

This skill deals with creating and managing SharePoint site collections. To master this skill, you'll need to understand how to configure a user as a site collection administrator, how to configure resource quotas, how to apply storage quotas, and other aspects of managing site collections within SharePoint Online.

> **This skill covers the following topics:**
> - Site collection administrators
> - Resource quotas
> - Configure public website
> - Set storage quota for site collection
> - Manage site collections

Understanding site collection administrators

Site collection administrators are users who have permission to manage SharePoint Online at the top of a specified site collection. A site collection administrator has permissions over all content in the site collection, including all subsites. Each site collection is a separate permissions root. For example, a site collection that has the URL *http://contoso2017er.sharepoint.com/sites/Research* does not have the same permissions as the site collection http://contoso2017er.sharepoint.com.

A site collection has only one primary administrator, but can have multiple site collection administrators. A primary site collection administrator receives administrative email alerts for the site collection.

To configure site collection administrators for a site collection, perform the following steps:

1. Sign in to the Office 365 Admin Center with a user account that has SharePoint Online administrator privileges.
2. Under Admin, click SharePoint. This opens the SharePoint Admin Center.
3. Ensure that Site Collections is selected.
4. In the list of Site Collections, select the site for which you wish to configure the site collection administrators. Figure 2-16 shows the site collection *https://mstnd667627.sharepoint.com/sites/ExampleSiteCollection* selected.

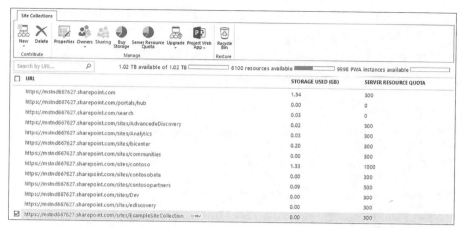

FIGURE 2-16 Site Collections

5. In the Site Collections section, click Owners, and then click Manage Administrators, as shown in Figure 2-17.

FIGURE 2-17 Manage Administrators

6. On the Manage Administrators dialog box, you can change the name of the Primary Site Collection Administrator, which is set when the site collection is created, and add the names of additional Site Collection Administrators. Figure 2-18 shows ExamRef Administrator set as the Primary Site Collection Administrator with Kim Akers and Don Funk set as Site Collection Administrators.

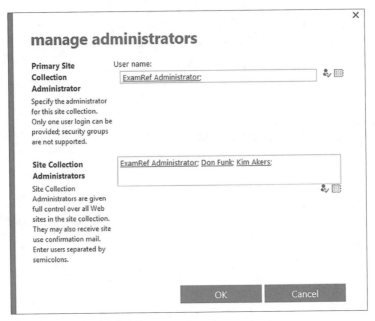

FIGURE 2-18 Manage Administrators

7. You can use the Check Names button to verify that the names entered are correct. When entering more than one name in the Site Collection Administrators text box, separate each name using a semicolon.

8. Click OK to assign the site collection administrator settings to the site collection.

> *MORE INFO* **SITE COLLECTION ADMINISTRATORS**
>
> You can learn more about site collection administrators at: *https://support.office.com/ en-au/article/Manage-administrators-for-a-site-collection-9a7e46f9-3fc4-4297-955a-82cb292a5be0.*

Understanding resource quotas

Server resources are a numerical way of representing server hardware capacity consumption, including RAM and CPU utilization. Each SharePoint Online deployment is allocated a server resource figure based on the number of user licenses. This server resource figure is shared across all site collections. You can view the amount of resources available for a collection on the Site Collections page. Figure 2-19 shows a tenancy where 6,100 resources are available.

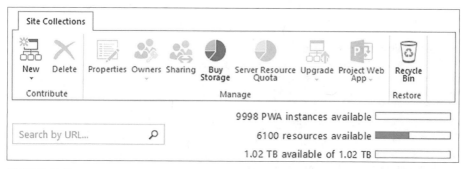

FIGURE 2-19 Resource quotas

Organizations that have customized site collections or sandboxed solutions can use re-source quotas to ensure that resources, such as server CPU and RAM aren't exhausted across the tenancy. If the number of resources used in a 24-hour period exceeds the resources available, SharePoint Online turns off the sandbox. When the sandbox is turned off, custom code does not run. The sandbox is turned back on when the 24-hour period expires and the resource number is reset.

By applying resource quotas to specific collections, administrators can ensure that custom code running in specific site collections does not deplete all server resources assigned to the tenancy. Purchasing extra user licenses increases the overall resource allocation to the tenancy.

To configure a resource quota for a specific site collection, perform the following steps:

1. Sign in to the Office 365 Admin Center with a user account that has SharePoint Online administrator privileges.

2. Under Admin, click SharePoint. This opens the SharePoint Admin Center.

3. Click Site Collections.

4. Select the site collection for which you wish to configure the resource quota and then click Server Resource Quota.

5. On the Set Server Resource Quota page, specify the number of server resources to be assigned to the collection. You can also configure an email to be sent to the primary site collection administrator when the resource utilization reaches a specific percentage of the assigned quota. Figure 2-20 shows a quota set to 300 and an email alert configured to be sent when the quota reaches 95 percent.

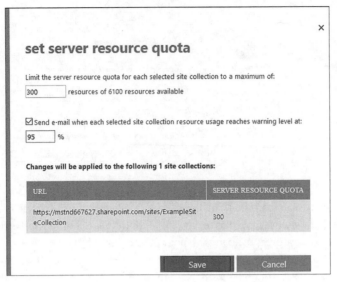

FIGURE 2-20 Server Resource Quota

6. Click Save to apply the new quota to the site collection.

You can configure resource quotas for SharePoint site collections using the Set-SPOSite cmdlet with the `ResourceQuota` and `ResourceQuotaWarningLevel` parameters.

> **MORE INFO** **RESOURCE QUOTAS**
>
> You can learn more about resource quotas at *https://support.office.com/en-us/article/Manage-SharePoint-Online-server-resource-quotas-for-sandboxed-solutions-90e4e-aaa-899a-48d6-b850-f272366bf8cc.*

Setting storage quota for site collection

Storage quotas determine how much storage space can be used. Office 365 tenancies are allocated an amount of storage space for SharePoint Online based on the number of users associated with the tenancy. It's possible for organizations to purchase additional storage on top of this initial allocation, as needed. Additional storage is allocated and on a GB per month basis. A site collection can be allocated a maximum of 25 TB of storage.

You can view the current amount of storage allocated to the tenancy by performing the following steps:

1. Sign in to the Office 365 Admin Center with a user account that has SharePoint Online administrator privileges.

2. Under Admin, click SharePoint. This opens the SharePoint Admin Center.

3. Click Site Collections. In the Site Collections area, you are able to see the resources available as well as the remaining storage available. Figure 2-21 shows 1.02 TB available out of 1.02 TB.

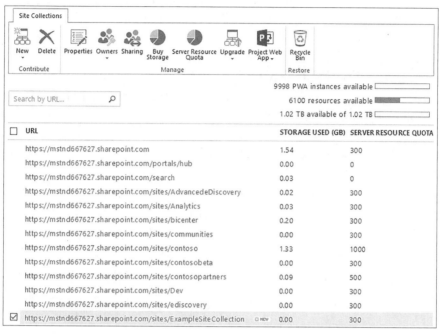

FIGURE 2-21 Storage use

This storage allocation is available to all site collections associated with the tenant. It functions as a central storage pool from which all SharePoint Online storage can be allocated.

You can purchase additional storage for a tenancy by performing the following steps:

1. Sign in to the Office 365 Admin Center with a user account that has SharePoint Online administrator privileges.

2. Under Admin, click SharePoint. This opens the SharePoint Admin Center.

3. In the Site Collections area, click Buy Storage.

4. You need to re-sign in to Office 365 with an account with tenancy Administrator permissions or Billing Administrator permissions.

5. On the Manage Subscription page, select the subscription that you would like to add additional storage to, and click the Add More link next to the text that indicates the number of current licenses.

6. In the section named Optional Add-Ons, enter the additional storage in GB that you wish to add to the tenancy. It is not necessary to enter information in the user license field, though you can also use this section of the Manage Subscription page to add additional user licenses to a subscription.

7. Click Add Licenses, and then click Place Order.

There are two ways of allocating storage:

- **Automatically**   You can choose to use the pooled storage model.
- **Manually**   You can manually configure storage allocations on a per-site collection basis.

Setting site collection storage limits

You can configure storage limits on a per site-collection basis if you use the manual rather than pooled storage model. To set the storage management option to manual, perform the following steps:

1. Sign in to the Office 365 Admin Center with a user account that has SharePoint Online administrator privileges.

2. Under Admin, click SharePoint. This opens the SharePoint Admin Center.

3. Click Settings.

4. Next to Site Collection Storage Management, select Manual, as shown in Figure 2-22, and then click OK.

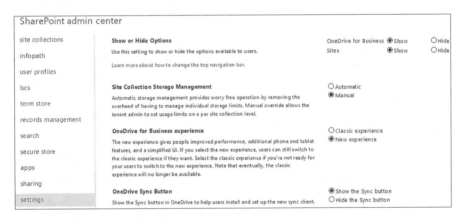

FIGURE 2-22 Storage management

Once you have set Site Collections Storage Management to manual, you are able to manually set storage quotas for site collections. To do this, perform the following steps:

1. Sign in to the Office 365 Admin Center with a user account that has SharePoint Online administrator privileges.

2. Under Admin, click SharePoint. This opens the SharePoint Admin Center.

3. Select the Site Collections area.

4. Select the site collection for which you want to configure the quota.

5. On the Site Collections toolbar, click Storage Quota.

6. On the Set Storage Quota dialog box, shown in Figure 2-23, configure the following options and then click Save:

- **Limit Storage Quota For Each Selected Site Collection To A Maximum Of** This option allows you to configure the maximum amount of storage allocated to each site collection. A figure of 0 indicates that no quota is set for the site collection.

- **Send Email To Site Collection Administrators When A Site Collection's Storage Reaches** Allows you to configure an email to be automatically sent after the storage allocated to the site collection reaches the specified percentage.

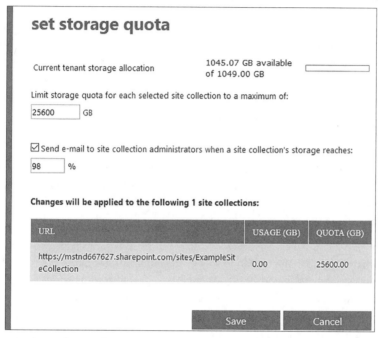

FIGURE 2-23 Storage Quota

> **MORE INFO** **STORAGE QUOTAS FOR SITE COLLECTIONS**
>
> You can learn more about storage quotas for site collections at *https://support.office.com/en-us/article/Manage-site-collection-storage-limits-77389c2c-8e7e-4b16-ab97-1c7103784b08*.

Managing site collections

A user with SharePoint Online Administrator permissions is able to create, delete, and restore deleted site collections.

Creating site collections

To create a site collection, perform the following steps:

1. Sign in to the Office 365 Admin Center with a user account that has SharePoint Online administrator privileges.

2. Under Admin, click SharePoint. This opens the SharePoint Admin Center.

3. In the site collections area, click New, and then click Private Site Collection.

4. On the New Site Collection page, shown in Figure 2-24, provide the following information, and click OK:

   - **Title**   The name of the site collection.

   - **Website Address**   Allows you to specify the address of the website. Drop-down menus allow you to select the domain name and the URL path. The URL path can either have /sites/ or /teams/ after the domain name.

   - **Template Selection**   Allows you to select which template to use for the site collection. Available templates are separated across the following categories: Collaboration, Enterprise, Publishing, and Custom. You also use this section to select a language from a drop-down list. Choosing the correct language at this stage of the process is critical because it is not possible to alter the language selection for the site collection after the collection is created. You can enable the SharePoint multiple language interface on a site collection, but the primary language is always the one selected during site collection creation.

   - **Time Zone**   Allows you to specify the time zone for the site collection.

   - **Administrator**   Use this option to specify the administrator of the site collection. You can type the user name, or browse for a site collection administrator. You can alter the site collection administrator after the creation of the site collection.

   - **Storage Quota**   Use this option to specify the storage quota in GB for the site collection up to a maximum value of 1 TB.

   - **Server Resource Quota**   Use this option to specify the resources you want to allocate to this collection in terms of available resources. Resources are a combination of performance metrics related to the execution of code for sandboxed solutions.

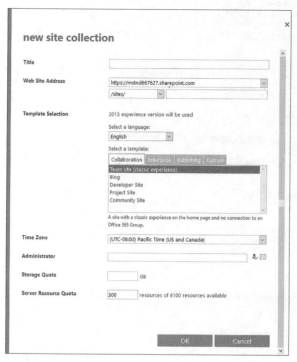

FIGURE 2-24 New Site Collection

Delete site collection

As part of ensuring that data stored on SharePoint Online is not retained past the point where no one is using it, you occasionally need to delete site collections. For example, you might wish to delete a site collection used for a specific project that has long since ended. Site collections that you delete are moved to the Recycle Bin. You read more about the Recycle Bin later in this chapter.

Deleting a site collection deletes the site hierarchy hosted within the collection. It also deletes the following user and content data stored within the site collection including:

- Documents and document libraries
- Lists and list data
- Site configuration settings
- Site and subsite role and security information
- Subsites of the top-level website
- Web parts
- Document workspaces
- Content types
- User associations

To delete a site collection, perform the following steps:

1. Sign in to the Office 365 Admin Center with a user account that has SharePoint Online administrator privileges.

2. Under Admin, click SharePoint. This opens the SharePoint Admin Center.

3. In the Site Collections area, select the site collection that you want to delete.

4. In the Site Collections area click Delete.

5. On the Delete Site Collections page, shown in Figure 2-25, click Delete.

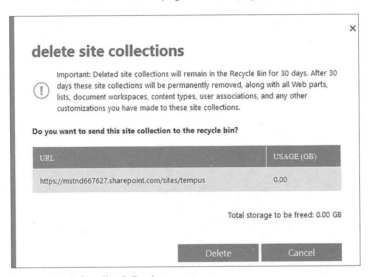

FIGURE 2-25 Delete Site Collections

MORE INFO   **CREATING AND DELETING SHAREPOINT ONLINE SITE COLLECTIONS**

You can learn more about creating and deleting SharePoint Online site collections at *https://support.office.com/en-us/article/Create-or-delete-a-site-collection-3a3d7ab9-5d21-41f1-b4bd-5200071dd539*.

Restore deleted site collection

When you delete a SharePoint Online site collection, it is moved to the Recycle Bin for 30 days before it is purged. If you need a site collection restored after this 30-day period has elapsed, you have an additional 14 days in which you can have Microsoft perform the restoration through a Service Request.

You can view the site collections in the Recycle Bin and the number of days remaining before being purged by performing the following steps:

1. Sign in to the Office 365 Admin Center with a user account that has SharePoint Online administrator privileges.

2. Under Admin, click SharePoint. This opens the SharePoint Admin Center.

3. In the Site Collections area click Recycle Bin.

4. In the Recycle Bin, you can see the list of site collections that have been deleted, and also when deleted, along with the number of days before being purged from the Recycle Bin. Figure 2-26 shows the Recycle Bin.

FIGURE 2-26 Recycle Bin contents

You can restore a deleted site collection under the following circumstances:

- The site collection has been in the Recycle Bin for less than 30 days.
- The usage quota for the SharePoint Online tenancy has not been exceeded.
- The storage quota for the SharePoint Online tenancy has not been exceeded.

Site collection URLs must be unique. This means that an active site collection cannot have the same URL as a deleted site collection that is still in the Recycle Bin. Should you need to create a new site with the same URL as a site in the Recycle Bin, the interface prompts you to permanently delete the site collection. This removes the site from the Recycle Bin.

To restore a deleted site collection, perform the following steps:

1. Sign in to the Office 365 Admin Center with a user account that has SharePoint Online administrator privileges.

2. Under Admin, click SharePoint. This opens the SharePoint Admin Center.

3. In the Site Collections area, click Recycle Bin.

4. In the Recycle Bin area, select the site collection that you wish to restore, and click Restore Deleted Items

5. On the Restore Site Collections page, shown in Figure 2-27, click Restore.

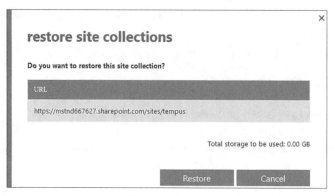

FIGURE 2-27 Restore Site Collections

> **MORE INFO** **RESTORE DELETED SITE COLLECTION**
>
> You can learn more about restoring deleted SharePoint Online site collections at *https:// support.office.com/en-us/article/Restore-a-deleted-site-collection-91c18651-c017-47d1-9c27-3a22f325d6f1*.

> **EXAM TIP**
>
> Remember the amount of time that a site collection remains in the Recycle Bin before being purged.

Skill 2.3: Plan a collaboration solution

This skill deals with using a variety of Office 365 tools for collaboration and coauthoring. To master this skill you'll need to understand the differences between Yammer and SharePoint newsfeeds, the settings related to coauthoring, the functionality of OneDrive For Business, the SharePoint App Store, and Enterprise eDiscovery.

This skill covers the following topics:

- Yammer
- Coauthoring
- Project Online
- Excel Services
- Visio Services
- OneDrive for Business
- App Store
- Enterprise eDiscovery

Yammer

Yammer is a private social network that has features similar to many of the larger social networks. Yammer allows people in your organization to collaborate with one another. Only people with company email addresses are able to join a company Yammer network.

To use Yammer with SharePoint Online, you need to configure Yammer as the SharePoint social collaboration option. To configure Yammer as the SharePoint social collaboration option, perform the following steps:

1. Sign in to the Office 365 Admin Center with a user account that has SharePoint Online administrator privileges.

2. Under Admin, click SharePoint. This opens the SharePoint Admin Center.

3. Click Settings. Next to Enterprise Social Collaboration, click Use Yammer.com Service, as shown in Figure 2-28.

FIGURE 2-28 Enterprise Social Collaboration

4. Click Save.

Switching to Yammer doesn't disable Newsfeed functionality, though it does disable the ability to make posts to everyone in the organization. Newsfeeds associated with specific sites remain in place after you have enabled Yammer.

Documenting coauthoring

The coauthoring feature of SharePoint Online allows multiple users to work on a document. This occurs in such a way that the changes made by one user do not interfere with the changes made by another. The ability to coauthor documents is enabled by default for documents stored in SharePoint Online.

Office 365 ProPlus provides coauthoring support for Word, PowerPoint, OneNote, and Visio. Coauthoring is also possible through the Word, PowerPoint, Excel, and OneNote Online web apps. The only restriction is that the Excel client application supports a Shared Workbook feature rather than direct coauthoring of workbooks stored in SharePoint Online.

When planning for document coauthoring in SharePoint Online, take the following into account:

- **Correct permissions** Every user who will coauthor a document needs to have appropriate permissions to edit the document. One method of accomplishing this goal is to give all users who need to edit the document access to the SharePoint site where the document is stored. SharePoint permissions can also be used to limit which documents within a SharePoint site can be edited by particular users.

- **Versioning** This keeps track of documents and stores previous versions of a document. SharePoint Online supports major and minor versioning, with major versioning being the default value. Microsoft recommends that monitor versioning not be used for document libraries that are used with OneNote coauthoring because it can interfere with OneNote's built-in versioning functionality.

- **Number of versions** The number of versions kept doesn't directly impact coauthoring, but it impacts the amount of storage space consumed by versions. The default value for SharePoint Online is 500 versions.

- **Check out** if an author checks out a document, the document is locked until the check out is released. This blocks coauthoring. Check out is disabled by default in SharePoint Online, but users can manually check out documents using the More menu, as shown in Figure 2-29. You should warn users not to check out documents when engaging in the coauthoring process.

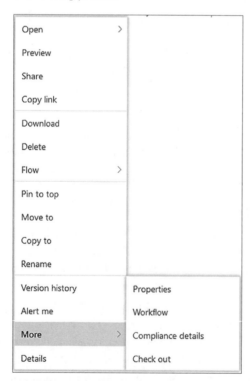

FIGURE 2-29 Check Out

To configure versioning and check out settings in a SharePoint Online document library, perform the following steps:

1. In the SharePoint Site, click Documents, and then click Library Settings under the gear menu, as shown in Figure 2-30.

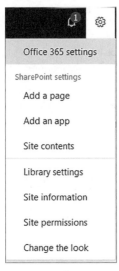

FIGURE 2-30 Documents

2. Under the General settings area, click Versioning Settings, as shown in Figure 2-31.

FIGURE 2-31 Library settings

3. Next to Content Approval, shown in Figure 2-32, choose whether you want to require content approval for submitted items.

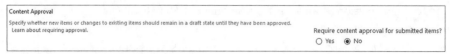

FIGURE 2-32 Content approval

4. Next to Document Version History, shown in Figure 2-33, choose whether you want to configure No Versioning, Create Major Versions, or Create Major And Minor (Draft) Versions. You can also specify the number of major and minor versions to be kept. The default is to use major versions and to keep 500 major versions of a document.

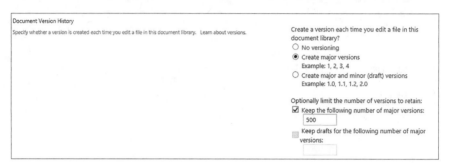

FIGURE 2-33 Version History

5. In the Draft Item Security Out section, shown in Figure 2-34, specify the options for draft items in the library. Options are that they are visible to any user who can read items, only users that can edit items, only users that can approve items (and the author of the item).

Draft Item Security

Drafts are minor versions or items which have not been approved. Specify which users should be able to view drafts in this document library.   Learn about specifying who can view and edit drafts.

Who should see draft items in this document library?
- Any user who can read items
- Only users who can edit items
- Only users who can approve items (and the author of the item)

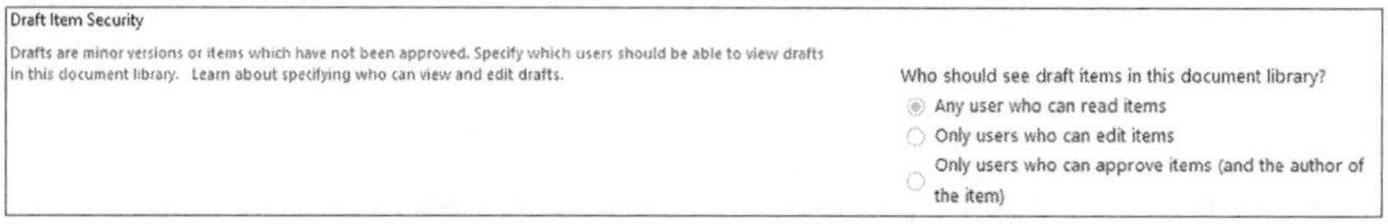

FIGURE 2-34 Draft item security

6. In the Require Check Out section, shown in Figure 2-35, specify whether documents should be checked out before editing. Remember that enabling this option disables coauthoring.

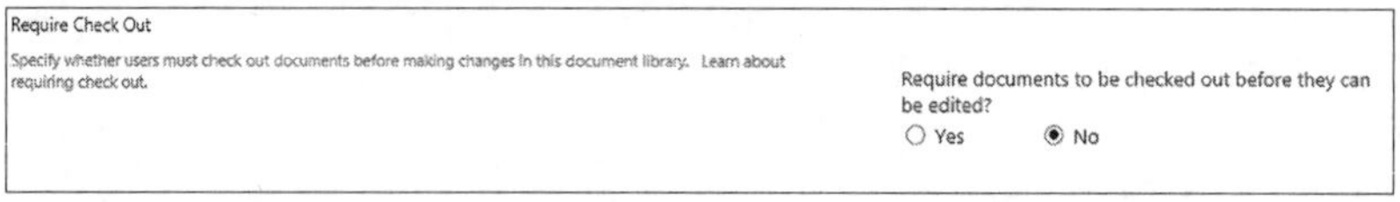

Require Check Out

Specify whether users must check out documents before making changes in this document library.   Learn about requiring check out.

Require documents to be checked out before they can be edited?
- Yes
- No

FIGURE 2-35 Require checkout

7. Click OK to apply the new settings.

Project Online

Project Online is a standalone web service that provides browser-based portfolio and project management tools. Project Online includes Project Web App. Depending on an organization's Office 365 subscription level it might also include Project Pro for Office 365. Project Pro for Office 365 is a desktop application that runs on client computers.

Excel Services

When you open an Excel file hosted in a SharePoint Online tenancy in a browser, the file opens in Excel Online. When you perform the same task with an Excel file hosted in an on-premises SharePoint 2013 deployment, the file might be opened either in Excel Services or in Excel Web App if an Office Web Apps server is present.

Visio Services

Visio Services is included with SharePoint 2013 and Office 365. It allows Visio diagrams stored in SharePoint 2013 or SharePoint Online to be viewed in a browser without requiring a full Visio client or Visio Viewer. Visio Services works with the .VSDX Visio file format. Older Visio files in .VDW format are also visible in a web browser through Visio Services.

Using OneDrive for Business

OneDrive for Business is a location that allows you to store, sync, and share work files. One-Drive for Business is separate from OneDrive, which was formerly known as SkyDrive. OneDrive for Business differs from OneDrive in the following ways:

- OneDrive is associated with a personal Microsoft account. People in your organization cannot access or manage OneDrive.

- OneDrive for Business is managed by an organization and is made available through an Office 365 subscription. This means that Office 365 administrators can access files stored in OneDrive for Business. OneDrive for Business allows Office 365 users to share files with each other for the purposes of collaboration. OneDrive for Business can also be used with an on-premises SharePoint deployment. Because this is an Office 365-related exam, using OneDrive for Business is not covered.

Accessing OneDrive for Business

A user can access OneDrive for Business by performing the following steps:

1. Sign in to Office 365 with your user account.

2. On the list of apps, shown in Figure 2-36, click OneDrive.

FIGURE 2-36 App list

3. The OneDrive for Business site, which is a SharePoint Online personal site, will be opened. Documents can be uploaded to this site or created and added to this location. It is also possible to create a folder hierarchy in this location. Figure 2-37 shows an OneDrive page.

FIGURE 2-37 OneDrive Documents

Collaborating with OneDrive for Business

Collaborating with someone using OneDrive for Business is very similar to collaborating using SharePoint Online. This makes sense considering OneDrive for Business stores data in Share-Point Online. The main difference is that an administrator usually manages the sharing done through SharePoint Online directly. The sharing done through OneDrive for Business is usually managed directly by an end user.

An end user can choose to share individual files or can create and share folders. As is the case with SharePoint Online, it's possible to share with people using a Microsoft account, or by sending an external link. Sharing settings are dependent on the sharing settings configured in the SharePoint Online tenancy.

- If the Don't Allow Sharing Outside Your Organization option is selected at the tenancy level, users will only be able to share with other users in the tenancy. If the users attempt to share with external users, they will see the message shown in Figure 2-38, explaining that sharing with external users is not possible.

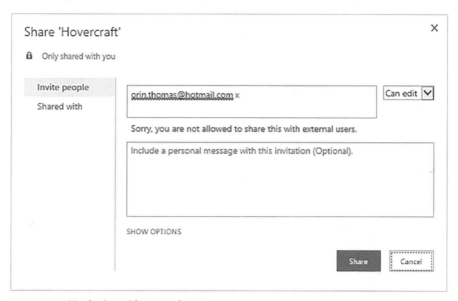

FIGURE 2-38 No sharing with external users

- If the Allow External Users Who Accept Sharing Invitations And Sign In As Authenticated Users option is selected at the tenancy level, sharing with external users is possible as long as those users have a Microsoft account or an Office 365 account.
- If the Allow Both External Users Who Accept Sharing Invitations And Anonymous Guest Links option is selected at the tenancy level, it is possible to share with external users with Office 365 or Microsoft accounts. It is also possible to forward links to shared documents or folders to users so that they can access content without having to authenticate.

To share an individual document, perform the following steps:

1. Sign in to Office 365 with your user account.

2. On the list of apps, click OneDrive.

3. In the OneDrive for Business site, select the document that you want to share.

4. Click the Share icon. If the Allow Both External Users Who Accept Sharing Invitations And Anonymous Guest Links option is selected at the tenancy level, users will be able to share to external users and generate links. To share with external users, enter the user's email address and determine if the users have read-only or edit access. Figure 2-39 shows the user orin.thomas@outlook.com is granted the edit permission.

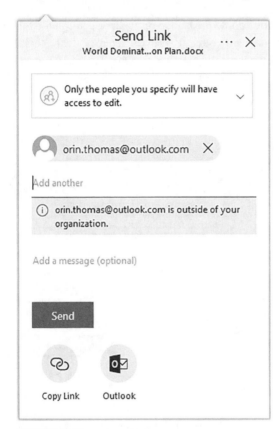

FIGURE 2-39 Share document

You can view whom a document is shared with on the document's Share page. Note that if you've invited someone to a document and they haven't accepted the invitation, their account will not be listed on the Shared With section of the Share page. Invitations remain valid for seven days.

To view who a document is shared with, perform the following steps:

1. Sign in to Office 365 with your user account.

2. On the list of apps, click OneDrive.

3. In the OneDrive for Business site, select the document of which you want to view the sharing properties.

4. On the toolbar, click Share, click the Ellipsis (...) on the Send Link dialog box, and then click Manage Access.

5. The Manage Access page shows you who the document has been shared with. You can choose to remove someone's permission to access a document from this page.

You can share folders from OneDrive for Business. All of the content in a folder inherits the sharing settings of the parent folder. This makes sharing documents a matter of placing them in the appropriately configured folder.

To share a folder, perform the following steps:

1. Sign in to Office 365 with your user account.

2. On the list of apps, click OneDrive.

3. In the OneDrive for Business site, select the Folder you want to share. Figure 2-40 shows the Hovercraft folder selected.

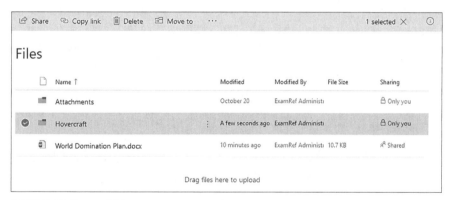

FIGURE 2-40 Share a folder

4. On the toolbar, click Share.

5. On the Invite People page, enter the email addresses of people who you want to invite to the folder and specify their permissions, either Read Only or Edit.

You can't create links for anonymous users to folders. Anonymous links can only be created for documents.

Administering OneDrive for Business

Administrators are able to view files and folders stored in OneDrive for Business. To access a user's OneDrive for Business content, perform the following steps:

1. In the Admin area of the Office 365 Admin Center, click SharePoint.

2. In the SharePoint Admin Center, click User Profiles.

3. In the User Profiles setting, click Manage User Profiles, as shown in Figure 2-41.

FIGURE 2-41 User Profiles

4. In the Find User Profiles box, enter part of the account name. Figure 2-42 shows a search for the name Don.

FIGURE 2-42 Find Profiles

5. Select the user whose OneDrive for Business content you wish to examine, and then click Manage Site Collection Owners, as shown in Figure 2-43.

FIGURE 2-43 Manage Site Collection Owners

6. Add an administrator account to the list of Site Collection Administrators, as shown in Figure 2-44, and then click OK.

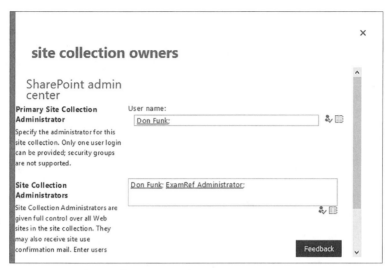

FIGURE 2-44 Add Site Collection Administrator

7. Select the user again, and this time select Manage Personal Site.

8. On the Site Settings page, click Documents.

9. The user's OneDrive for Business content will be visible.

> **MORE INFO   ONEDRIVE FOR BUSINESS**
>
> You can learn more about OneDrive for Business at *https://support.office.com/en-us/article/What-is-OneDrive-for-Business--187f90af-056f-47c0-9656-cc0ddca7fdc2.*

Understanding Enterprise eDiscovery

Enterprise eDiscovery is the process of locating content that serves as evidence in litigation or an official investigation. SharePoint Online has a special site collection called the eDiscovery Center. This site collection allows you to create special SharePoint sites named cases that you can use to locate, hold, search, and export content from Exchange online, SharePoint Online, and OneDrive for Business.

Creating a case

To create an eDiscovery case, perform the following steps:

1. In the Admin area of the Office 365 Admin Center, click Security & Compliance.

2. In the Security and Compliance Center, click Search & Investigation, and then click eDiscovery.

3. In the list of eDiscovery Cases, shown in Figure 2-45, click the Create A Case button to create a new case.

FIGURE 2-45 eDiscovery Cases

4. On the Site Contents, New SharePoint Site page, provide the following information, as shown in Figure 2-46, ensuring that you select the eDiscovery Case template:

   ■ Title: Title for the eDiscovery case

   ■ Description: Description for the case

FIGURE 2-46 New eDiscovery case

Add sources and place them on hold

Adding sources to an eDiscovery case allows information to be added to the case. To add sources to an eDiscovery case, perform the following steps:

1. In the Admin area of the Office 365 Admin Center, click Security & Compliance.

2. Under Search & Investigation, click eDiscovery.

3. In the list of eDiscovery Cases, shown in Figure 2-47, click the case that you wish to add a source to, and then click Open, which allows you to edit the case.

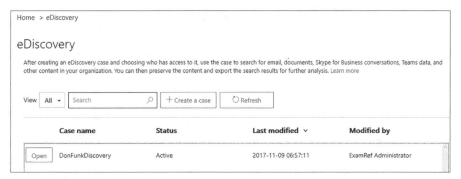

FIGURE 2-47 eDiscovery Cases

4. On the eDiscovery case page, click Hold. Click the (+) plus icon to create a new hold.

5. On the Create A New Hold page, shown in Figure 2-48, provide a name, specify mailboxes, and specify SharePoint sites related to the hold, and click Next

FIGURE 2-48 eDiscovery Case page

6. In the What Do You Want To Look For text box, enter keywords and conditions for the hold. Figure 2-49 shows the keyword hovercraft and the dates 3 November to 11 November 2017. Click Finish.

FIGURE 2-49 Hold Details

MORE INFO **ENTERPRISE EDISCOVERY**

You can learn more about Enterprise eDiscovery at *https://support.office.com/en-us/article/Plan-and-manage-eDiscovery-cases-d955aeb8-0d48-4291-a8e2-f3b84f17943f.*

Data Loss Prevention (DLP)

Data Loss Prevention (DLP) policies allow you to ensure that sensitive information is not inadvertently disclosed by someone using Office 365 to transmit it outside your organization. You can use DLP policies to accomplish the following:

- Locate sensitive information stored in Exchange Online, SharePoint Online, and OneDrive for Business.
- Prevent sensitive information from being accidentally shared.
- Ensure that members of your organization remain compliant with relevant data regulations.
- Monitor and protect sensitive information in the desktop versions of Word 2016, Excel 2016, and PowerPoint 2016.
- View DLP reports that locate content that matches applied DLP policies.

DLP policies contain the following elements:

- Location where content should be protected. This can include Exchange Online, SharePoint Online, and OneDrive for Business.
- Rules that consist of Conditions and Actions.
  - A condition determines which content the rule needs to match before it is enforced.
  - An action is the steps that the rule executes when a condition match is found.

DLP policies can assist in protecting sensitive information. Sensitive information is string of characters in a particular format, such as a credit card number, passport number, or social security number. A large number of sensitive information types are included with DLP policies so that Office 365 administrators don't need to configure regular expressions to identify specific sensitive information string formats.

To create a DLP policy, perform the following steps:

1. In the Admin area of the Office 365 Admin Center, click Security & Compliance.
2. Under Search & Investigation, click Policy under Data Loss Prevention.
3. On the Data Loss Prevention page, shown in Figure 2-50, click Create A Policy.

FIGURE 2-50 DLP policies

4. On the New DLP Policy page, select an existing template or create a custom policy. Figure 2-51 shows the Australia Financial Data template selected. Click Next.

FIGURE 2-51 DLP template

5. Provide a name for the policy and a description, and then click Next.

6. On the Choose Locations page, select whether all areas of Office 365 will be protected or if you wish to protect specific locations. Figure 2-52 shows the Choose Locations page. You can use this page to select specific Exchange email mailboxes, specific Share-Point sites, and specific OneDrive accounts.

FIGURE 2-52 DLP locations

7. On the policy settings page, specify whether the DLP policy applies to information being shared with people outside or within the organization.

8. On the What Do You Want To Do If We Detect Sensitive Information page, shown in Figure 2-53, specify what actions will be taken when sensitive information is being shared. Actions include sending incident reports and restricting who can access the content.

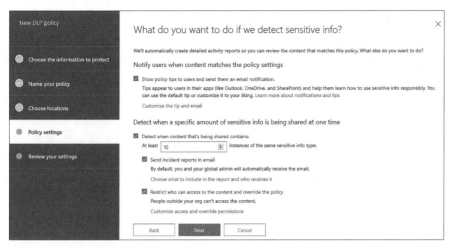

FIGURE 2-53 DLP policy settings

9. On the Do You Want To Turn On The Policy Or Test Things Out First? Page, shown in Figure 2-54, select whether you want to enable the policy immediately, test the policy out, or disable the policy so that it can be enabled later.

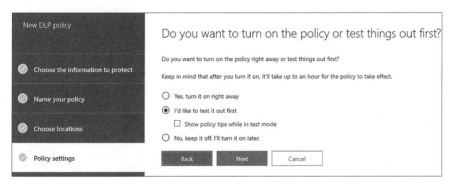

FIGURE 2-54 Test or enable DLP policy

10. On the Review Your Settings page, review the settings, and then click Create to create the policy.

MORE INFO **DATA LOSS PREVENTION**

You can learn more about DLP policies at *https://support.office.com/en-us/article/Overview-of-data-loss-prevention-policies-1966b2a7-d1e2-4d92-ab61-42efbb137f5e.*

Delve for collaboration

Delve uses Office Graph to show Office 365 users relevant content based on what they are working on and who they work with. Delve tailors information to each user and Delve will only present information to users that they already have the requisite permissions to.

Access to Delve is enabled if you have enabled the Allow access to the Office Graph permission through Settings in SharePoint Admin Center, as shown in Figure 2-55.

Office Graph	⦿ Allow access to the Office Graph (default)
Control access to the Office Graph for everyone in your organization. The Office Graph is a representation of the relationships and interactions between objects in Office 365 such as people and documents. Not allowing access to the Office Graph also disables solutions that are built on top of it such as Delve.	○ Don't allow access to the Office Graph

FIGURE 2-55 Enable access to Office Graph

> **MORE INFO** **DELVE**
>
> You can learn more about Delve at *https://support.office.com/en-us/article/Office-Delve-for-Office-365-admins-54f87a42-15a4-44b4-9df0-d36287d9531b?ui=en-US&rs=en-US&ad=US.*

EXAM TIP

Remember that document Check Out should be disabled if coauthoring is to take place with documents stored in SharePoint Online.

Thought experiment

After performing an audit of how content was being shared from your organization's Share-Point Online tenancy, management has decided that it will no longer allow users to share content with users anonymously. In the future, all content shared with external users can only be shared if the user has a Microsoft or an Office 365 account. Management is also concerned about one external user, Kim, who has had content shared with her across multiple site collections. Kim has recently started working for a competitor and management wants to remove her current access to information in your organization's SharePoint Online site collections.

Additionally, you have recently deleted a number of site collections from your organization's SharePoint Online tenancy. Several of these collections are still present in the Recycle Bin and others have been removed after exceeding the Recycle Bin retention period.

Your organization has also purchased several SharePoint apps to increase user productivity. You are in the process of training an assistant to manage how these apps are used.

With this information in mind, answer the following questions:

1. What's the quickest method of stopping anonymous users from accessing SharePoint Online content?

2. What steps need to be taken to remove the external user's access from site collections?

3. One of the site collections disappeared from the Recycle Bin yesterday. What steps could you take to recover it?

4. You want to create a new site collection with the URL of a recently deleted site collection. What steps must you take before you can perform this task?

5. Which part of the apps section of the SharePoint Admin Center should be used to determine application usage and errors?

6. Which part of the apps section of the SharePoint Admin Center should be used to view license utilization?

7. Which part of the apps section of the SharePoint Admin Center should be used to control, which SharePoint apps interact with the tenant?

Thought experiment answers

This section contains the solutions to the thought experiment.

1. Change the sharing settings at the SharePoint Online tenancy level.

2. It will be necessary to modify the sharing settings of each site collection to remove the external user's access.

3. Microsoft support can recover site collections up to 14 days after being removed from the Recycle Bin.

4. You need to remove the site from the Recycle Bin because site collection URLs must be unique.

5. You use the Monitor Apps section to determine application usage and review errors.

6. You use the Manage Licenses section to view SharePoint app license utilization.

7. You use the App Permissions section to configure which apps can access the SharePoint Online tenant.

Chapter summary

- External users are people with whom Office 365 SharePoint Online content can be shared.

- External users can authenticate with a Microsoft account, including an Office 365 account that is not part of the organization's tenancy.

- At the global level, you can configure an option for block sharing to external users, allow external users who have authenticated with Microsoft, or allow users who have authenticated with a Microsoft account and who have been provided with an anonymous link.

- Site owners and users who have Full Control permissions on a site are able to share sites with external users.

- Invitations sent to external users remain valid for seven days.

- Sharing settings configured at the SharePoint Online tenancy level determine the sharing options available at the site collection level. If sharing is blocked at the tenancy level, it is not available at the site collection level.

- Sharing settings configured at the site collection level determine the sharing options available at the document level.

- Site collection administrators are users who have permission to manage SharePoint Online at the top of a specified site collection.

- A site collection administrator has permissions over all content in the site collection, including all subsites.

- Server resources are a numerical way of representing server resources, including RAM and CPU utilization.

- Each SharePoint Online deployment is allocated a server resource figure based on the number of user licenses.

- If the number of resources used in a 24-hour period exceeds the resources available, the sandbox turns off and custom code will not run.

- SharePoint Online Public Websites is a functionality not available in new Office 365 subscriptions and only available in some existing subscriptions until March 2017.

- Office 365 tenancies are allocated an amount of storage space for SharePoint Online based on the number of users associated with the tenancy.

- You can assign storage quotas on a per-site collection basis to limit the amount of storage space consumed by individual site collections.

- When creating a site collection, you configure the name, URL, primary site collection administrator, template, storage quota, and server resource quota.

- A deleted site collection can be recovered from the Recycle Bin for 30 days.

- Newsfeeds in SharePoint Online function as an organizational blog where members of the organization can post and reply to posts.

- A newsfeed exists at the SharePoint Online tenancy level. Newsfeeds also exist at the team site level.

- Yammer is a private social network that has features similar to many of the larger social networks.

- To use Yammer with SharePoint Online, you need to configure Yammer as the SharePoint social collaboration option.

- Every user who will coauthor a document needs to have appropriate permissions to edit the document.

- If a document is checked out by an author, the document is locked until the check out is released, which blocks coauthoring.

- Project Online is a stand-alone web service that provides browser-based portfolio and project management tools.

- Excel Services is used when a file hosted in an on-premises SharePoint deployment is opened in a browser.

- Visio Services allows Visio diagrams stored SharePoint Online to be viewed in a browser without requiring a full Visio client or Visio Viewer.

- OneDrive for Business allows users to store, sync, and share work files.

- Whether users can share OneDrive for Business documents with external users depends on the settings in the SharePoint Online tenancy.

- eDiscovery allows you to configure search and hold for the purposes of litigation and investigation.

CHAPTER 3

Configure Exchange Online and Skype for Business Online for end users

Exchange Online and Skype for Business Online are the primary communications tools available to Office 365 subscribers. Exchange Online includes many of the features of an on-premises Exchange 2013 deployment, and administrators of Exchange Online need to perform many of the same tasks, including managing email addresses, configuring mailbox permissions, managing resource and shared mailboxes, as well as configuring retention policies and archives. Similarly, many of the tasks that need to be performed by Skype for Business administrators, such as configuring presence settings and external communication options, need to be configured by Skype for Business Online.

Skills covered in this chapter:

- Skill 3.1: Configure additional email addresses for users
- Skill 3.2: Create and manage external contacts, resources, and groups
- Skill 3.3: Configure personal archive policies
- Skill 3.4: Configure Skype for Business Online end-user communication settings

Skill 3.1: Configure additional email addresses for users

This skill deals with managing email addresses for Exchange Online mailboxes, including the SIP addresses used by Skype for Business Online.

> **This skill covers how to:**
> - Manage email addresses
> - Manage SIP addresses

Manage email addresses

The default address, also known as the primary address and as the reply-to address, is the address that users use to sign in to Office 365, and which recipients reply to when they receive an email message from a user. You can view the primary email address for a user in the Office 365 Admin Center on the user's properties page, as shown in Figure 3-1.

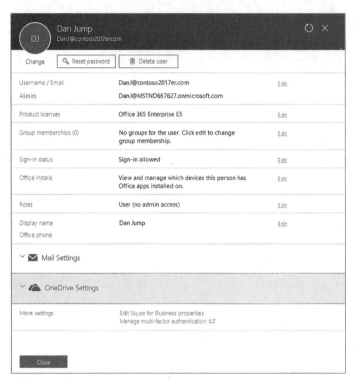

FIGURE 3-1 Primary Email Address

It's possible to change the primary email address once you have added an additional email address to an Office 365 user. It is important to note that changing the primary email address also changes the user name. For example, the warning in Figure 3-2 indicates that by changing the primary email address associated with the Dan Jump user account, the user name will also be changed. The email suffix for the primary address must be configured as an accepted domain for the Office 365 tenancy.

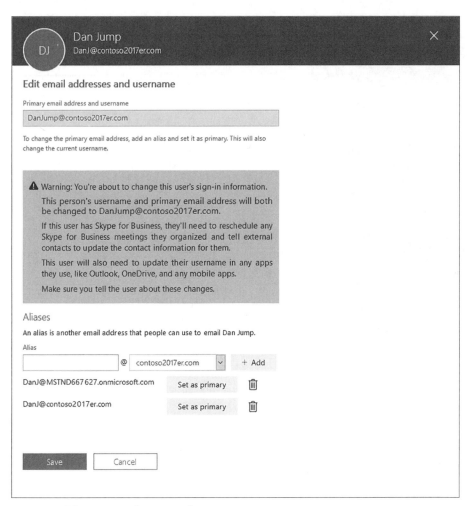

FIGURE 3-2 Primary name change warning

Additional email addresses

You can add additional email addresses to an Office 365 account's Exchange Online mailbox using a variety of methods. To add an additional email address to an Exchange Online mailbox using Exchange Admin Center, perform the following steps:

1. Sign in to the Office 365 Admin Center with a user account that has Tenant Administrator permissions.

2. In the Office 365 Admin Center, click Exchange under Admin Centers, as shown in Figure 3-3.

FIGURE 3-3 Admin menu

3. In Exchange Admin Center, click Recipients and then click Mailboxes. Select the recipient to which you wish to add an additional email address. Figure 3-4 shows the Dan Jump mailbox selected.

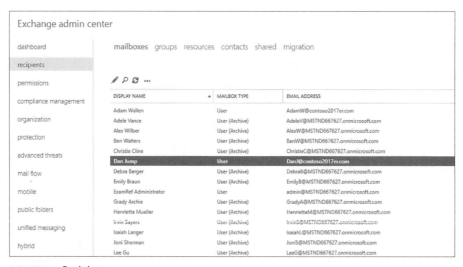

FIGURE 3-4 Recipients

4. Click the Edit (Pencil) icon.

5. On the User Mailbox properties page, click Email Address, as shown in Figure 3-5.

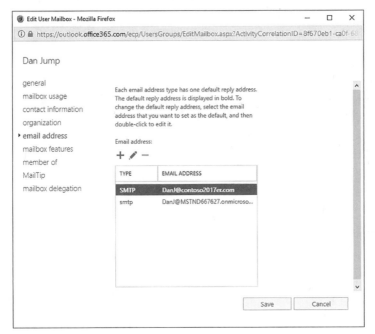

FIGURE 3-5 Email addresses

6. Click the Plus (+) icon

7. On the New Email Address page, ensure that SMTP is selected, as shown in Figure 3-6, and then enter the new email address. You can also specify the new email address as the default reply-to address.

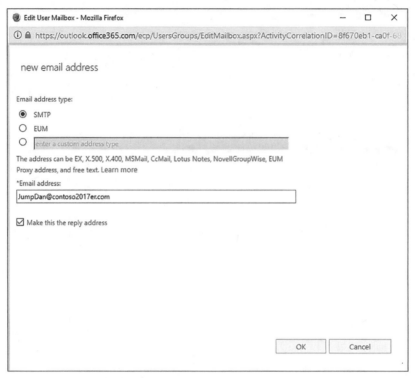

FIGURE 3-6 New Email Address

8. Click OK to save changes.

To add an additional email address to an Exchange Online mailbox using the Office 365 Admin Center, perform the following steps:

1. In the Office Admin Center, select Active Users under Users.

2. Select the user for which you want to configure the primary email address. Figure 3-7 shows Betsy Drake selected.

FIGURE 3-7 Betsy Drake user account

3. On the More menu, click Edit email addresses and username.

4. In the Alias box, shown in Figure 3-8, type the new email address and click Add.

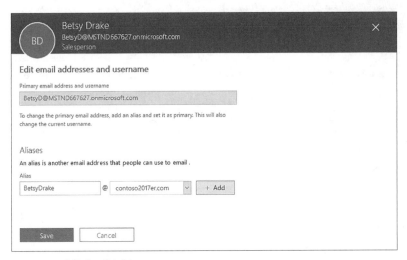

FIGURE 3-8 Edit Email Address

5. To set the new email address as the new primary email address, as shown in Figure 3-9, click Set as Primary.

FIGURE 3-9 Other Email Addresses

You can use the Set-Mailbox cmdlet to add additional email addresses. For example, to add the email address funk.don@contoso2017er.com to Don Funk's Exchange Online mailbox, issue the following command:

```
Set-Mailbox "Don Funk" -EmailAddresses @{Add=funk.don@contoso2017er.com}
```

Manage reply-to address

When a user has more than one email address, you will need to specify which is the default address. This address is also known as the primary or reply-to email address. You can use multiple methods to set the reply-to address.

To use Exchange Admin Center to manage the reply-to address, perform the following steps:

1. Sign in to the Office 365 Admin Center with a user account that has Tenant Administrator permissions.

2. In the Office 365 Admin Center, click Exchange under Admin Centers.

3. In Exchange Admin Center, click Recipients and then click Mailboxes. Select the recipient to which you wish to configure the reply-to address.

4. Click the Edit (Pencil) icon. On the Mailbox properties page, click email address.

5. On the email address page, the primary email address is designated with the acronym SMTP in capitals, with secondary email addresses having smtp in lowercase, as shown in Figure 3-10.

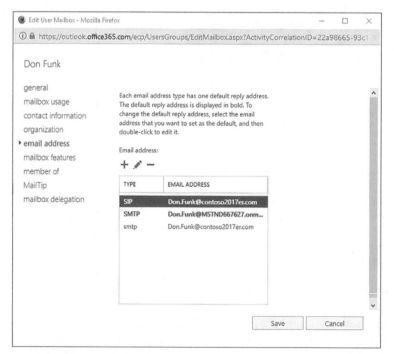

FIGURE 3-10 New email address

6. To set another email address as the primary, select the email address and click the Pencil icon.

7. On the Email Address page, select the Make This The Reply Address checkbox, as shown in Figure 3-11, click OK, and then click Save.

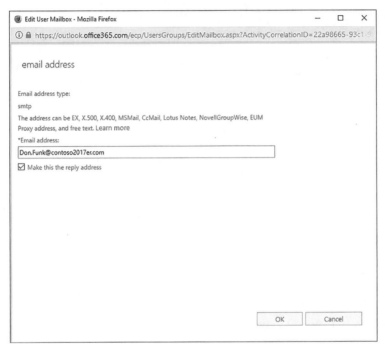

FIGURE 3-11 Set reply address

To configure the primary email address using the Office 365 Admin Center, perform the following steps:

1. In the Office Admin Center, select Active Users under Users.

2. Select the user for which you want to configure the primary email address. Figure 3-12 shows Don Funk selected.

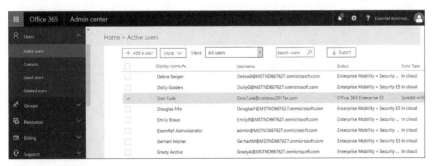

FIGURE 3-12 Don Funk selected

3. Click More and then click Edit Email Address and Username

4. On the dialog box shown in Figure 3-13, click Set As Primary next to the appropriate email address to configure a new primary email address.

FIGURE 3-13 Edit Email Address

5. Review the Warning dialog box, and click Save.

6. Review the dialog box to ensure that the correct email address is now set as the primary address, as shown in Figure 3-14.

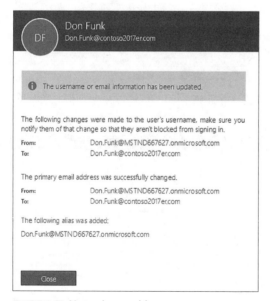

FIGURE 3-14 New primary address

Bulk add for new domain

In some cases, it might be necessary to add email addresses to a large number of existing Office 365 accounts. You can do this using Windows PowerShell and a CSV file containing mailbox names and the new email addresses.

For example, you might have the file c:\import\NewEmailAddress.csv that contains the following contents:

```
Mailbox,NewEmailAddress
Dan Jump,danj@adatum347er.onmicrosoft.com
Don Funk,donf@adatum347er.onmicrosoft.com
Kim Akers,kima@adatum347er.onmicrosoft.com
Janet Schorr,janets@adatum347er.onmicrosoft.com
Jeffrey Zeng,jeffreyz@adatum347er.onmicrosoft.com
Spencer Low,spencerl@adatum347er.onmicrosoft.com
Toni Poe,tonip@adatum347er.onmicrosoft.com
```

You can use the following command to use the data in the CSV to add the email address to each appropriate mailbox.

```
Import-CSV "C:\import\NewEmailAddress.csv" | ForEach {Set-Mailbox $_.Mailbox
-EmailAddresses @{Add=$_.NewEmailAddress}}
```

Manage SIP addresses

Session Initiation Protocol (SIP) addresses are used by Skype for Business to route incoming calls and send voicemail to an Office 365 user. Users are assigned SIP addresses automatically when you create their accounts using the Office 365 console.

Add an SIP address

When a user is created in Office 365, they will be assigned an SIP address. Should this address be removed, you can add an SIP address to an Exchange Online user, performing the following steps:

1. In the Office 365 Admin Center, click Exchange under Admin Centers.

2. In Exchange Admin Center, click Recipients and then click Mailboxes. Select the recipient to which you wish to add an SIP address, as shown in Figure 3-15.

FIGURE 3-15 Dan Jump selected

3. On the toolbar, click the Edit icon, which is shown as a pencil. This will open the user's properties dialog box, as shown in Figure 3-16.

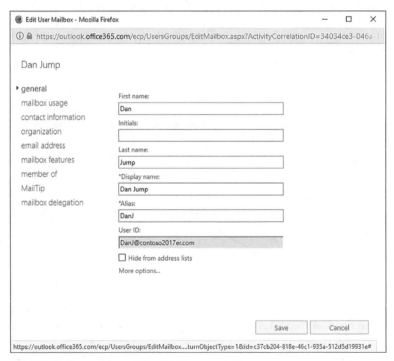

FIGURE 3-16 General page of User Mailbox properties

4. Click Email Address and then click the Plus (+) icon, as shown in Figure 3-17.

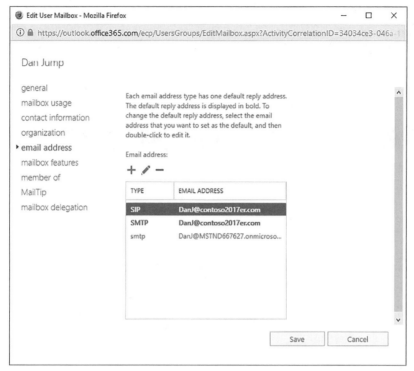

FIGURE 3-17 SIP address selected

5. On the New Email Address page, under email address type, select EUM. In the Address/Extension box, type the new SIP address, in the Dial Plan (Phone Context) box, click Browse, and select the SIP URI plan. Note that you will need to have a SIP URI plan configured to add an SIP address.

You can use the Set-Mailbox cmdlet to add an SIP address. For example, to add the SIP address djump@contoso2017er.com to the Dan.Jump mailbox using the dial plan mydialplan.contoso2017er.com, use the following PowerShell code when a PowerShell session is established to the Office 365 tenancy:

```
$mbx=Get-Mailbox Dan.Jump
$mbx.EmailAddress +="eum:djump@contoso2017er.com;phone
-context=mydialplan.contoso2017er.com"
Set-Mailbox Dan.Jump -EmailAddresses $mbx.EmailAddresses
```

> **MORE INFO** **ADD AN SIP ADDRESS**
>
> You can learn more about adding an SIP address at: *https://technet.microsoft.com/en-us/library/jj662760(v=exchg.150).aspx.*

Change an SIP address

To alter an SIP address, perform the following steps:

1. Sign in to the Office 365 Admin Center with a user account that has Tenant Administrator permissions.

2. In the Office 365 Admin Center, click Exchange under Admin Centers.

3. In the list of Recipients, select the recipient whose SIP address you wish to modify. Figure 3-18 shows the Kim Akers recipient selected.

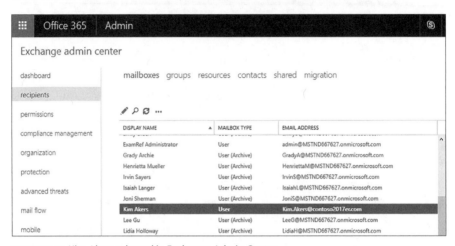

FIGURE 3-18 Kim Akers selected in Exchange Admin Center

4. On the toolbar, click the Edit icon, which is shown as a pencil. This will open the user's properties dialog box, as shown in Figure 3-19.

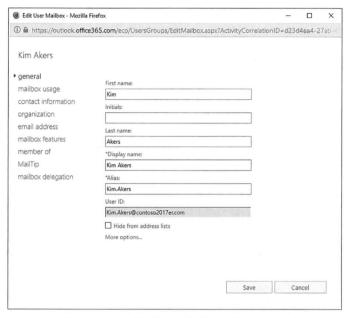

FIGURE 3-19 General page of Exchange Online mailbox properties

5. Click Email address and then select the current SIP address, as shown in Figure 3-20.

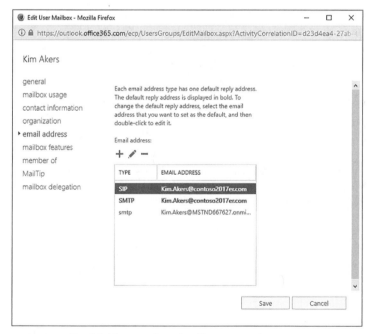

FIGURE 3-20 Email Address section of mailbox properties

6. Click the Edit icon. On the Email Address page, shown in Figure 3-21, change the SIP address to the new SIP address that you want to use and click OK.

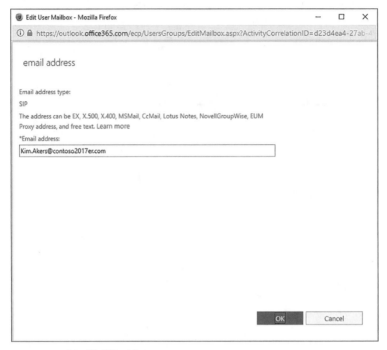

FIGURE 3-21 Modify SIP address

7. On the User Mailbox properties page, click Save to save the change.

You can use the Set-Mailbox cmdlet to modify an SIP address. For example, to change the SIP address to kakers@contoso2017er.com for the Kim.Akers mailbox using the dial plan mydialplan.contoso2017er.com, use the following PowerShell code when a PowerShell session is established to the Office 365 tenancy:

```
$mbx=Get-Mailbox Kim.Akers
$mbx.EmailAddress.Item(1)="eum:kakers@contoso2017er.com;phone-
context=MySIPDialPlan.contoso2017er.com"
Set-Mailbox Kim.Akers -EmailAddresses $mbx.EmailAddresses
```

> **MORE INFO**   **CHANGE AN SIP ADDRESS**
>
> You can learn more about changing an SIP address at: *https://technet.microsoft.com/en-us/ library/dd335189(v=exchg.150).aspx.*

Remove an SIP address

You can remove an SIP address by performing the following steps:

1. Sign in to the Office 365 Admin Center with a user account that has Tenant Administrator permissions. `
2. In the Office 365 Admin Center, click Exchange under Admin Centers.
3. In the list of Recipients, select the recipient whose SIP address you wish to modify and click the Edit (Pencil) icon.
4. In the email addresses section, shown in Figure 3-22, select the SIP address that you want to remove and then click the Minus (-) icon.

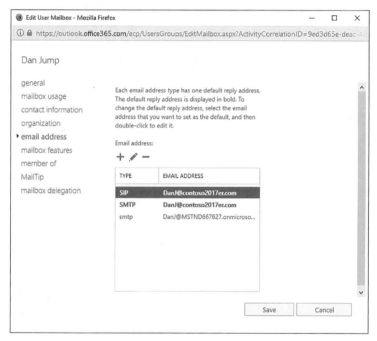

FIGURE 3-22 Remove SIP address

5. Click Save to remove the SIP address.

> **MORE INFO   REMOVE AN SIP ADDRESS**
>
> You can learn more about removing an SIP address at: *https://technet.microsoft.com/en-us/ library/jj662761(v=exchg.150).aspx*.

EXAM TIP

Remember the PowerShell commands required to manipulate recipient email addresses.

Skill 3.2: Create and manage external contacts, resources, and groups

This skill deals with delegating permissions on mailboxes, the creation of shared and resource mailboxes, how to create external contacts, and how to create and manage Exchange Online distribution groups.

> **This skill covers how to:**
> - Delegate permissions
> - Create shared mailboxes
> - Manage resource mailboxes
> - Manage external contacts
> - Manage distribution groups

Delegate permissions

Through delegating permissions, you can allow one user to access another's mailbox, send email as that user, or send email on behalf of that user. For example, you can use the delegation functionality in Exchange Online to grant Dan the ability to access the content of Kim's mailbox, but to not allow Dan to send messages as Kim or on behalf of Kim. Or you can allow Kim to send messages as Dan, but block Kim from accessing Dan's Exchange Online mailbox. The key to understanding permissions delegation is to understand the difference between the Send As, Send On Behalf, and Full Access permissions.

> **MORE INFO   DELEGATING PERMISSIONS**
> You can learn more about managing recipient permissions at: *https://technet.microsoft.com/en-us/library/jj919240(v=exchg.160).aspx.*

Send As

The Send As permission allows the person delegated the permission to send messages as though they were sent by the mailbox owner. For example, if Don Funk is delegated the Send As permission to Kim Aker's Exchange Online mailbox, then Don will be able to send messages that appear to have been sent by Kim. If you delegate this permission to a group, the message will appear to be from the group. For example, if you delegate Don Funk the Sent As permission to the HelpDesk group, Don will be able to send message that appear to have been sent by the HelpDesk group.

To delegate the Send As permission for a mailbox, perform the following steps:

1. In the Office 365 Admin Center, click Exchange under Admin Centers. This will open the Exchange Admin Center.

2. Click Recipients. In the list of mailboxes, select the Exchange Online mailbox to which you wish to delegate the Send As permission. Figure 3-23 shows the Don Funk mailbox selected.

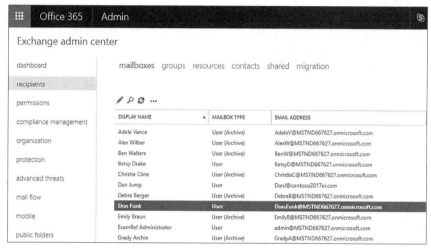

FIGURE 3-23 Don Funk selected

3. With the mailbox selected, click the Edit (Pencil) icon.

4. On the Mailbox Delegation tab, click the Plus (+) icon under Send As, as shown in Figure 3-24.

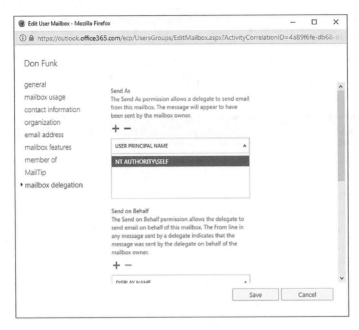

FIGURE 3-24 Mailbox Delegation

5. On the Select Send As dialog box, select the user to whom you want to delegate Send As permission. Figure 3-25 shows the Dan Jump user delegated the Send As permission. Click OK.

FIGURE 3-25 Select Send As user

6. Verify that the delegate is listed. Figure 3-26 shows Dan Jump delegated the Send As permission. Click Save to have the permission assigned.

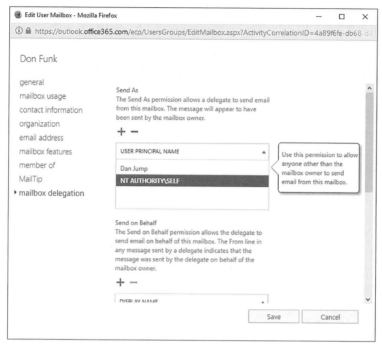

FIGURE 3-26 Dan Jump with Send As permission

You can use the Add-RecipientPermission cmdlet to assign the Send As permission using Windows PowerShell. For example, to assign Dan Jump the Send As permission to the Don Funk mailbox, run the command:

```
Add-RecipientPermission –Identity "Don Funk" –Trustee "Dan Jump" –AccessRights SendAs
```

You can use the Remove-RecipientPermission cmdlet to remove the Send As permission using Windows PowerShell. For example, to remove the Send As permission from Dan Jump to the Don Funk mailbox, run the command:

```
Remove-RecipientPermission –Identity "Don Funk" –Trustee "Dan Jump" –AccessRights SendAs
```

Send on Behalf

The Send on Behalf permission allows the person delegated the permission to send messages on behalf of the mailbox owner. The From address of a message sent by the delegate will indicate that the message was sent by the person delegated the permission on behalf of the mailbox owner.

To delegate the Send on Behalf permission for a mailbox, perform the following steps:

1. In the Office 365 Admin Center, click Exchange under Admin Centers. This will open the Exchange Admin Center.

2. Click Recipients. In the list of mailboxes, select the Exchange Online mailbox to which you wish to delegate the Send As permission. Figure 3-27 shows the Kim Akers mailbox selected.

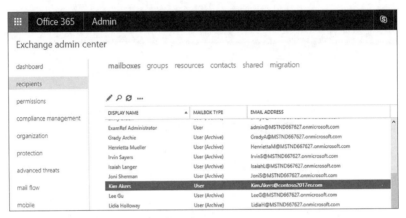

FIGURE 3-27 Kim Akers recipient selected

3. With the mailbox selected, click the Edit (Pencil) icon.

4. On the Mailbox Delegation tab, click the Plus (+) icon under Send on Behalf, as shown in Figure 3-28.

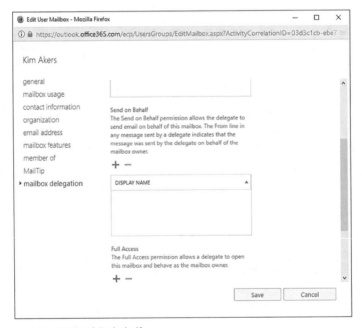

FIGURE 3-28 Send On behalf

5. On the Select Send On Behalf page, select the user to whom you wish to assign the Send on Behalf permission, click Add and then click OK. Figure 3-29 shows Don Funk selected.

FIGURE 3-29 Select Send On Behalf

6. Verify that the correct user has been delegated the Send On Behalf permission, as shown in Figure 3-30, and then click Save.

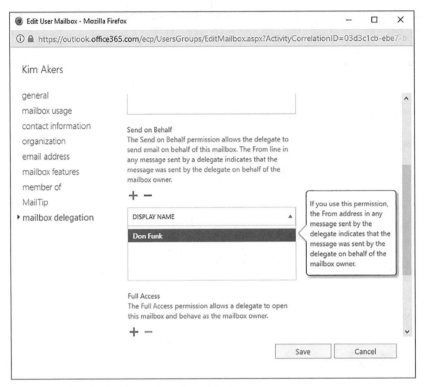

FIGURE 3-30 Don Funk delegated Send On Behalf

You can use the Set-Mailbox cmdlet to assign the Send on Behalf permission. For example, to assign the Send on Behalf permission to the kim.akers@contoso2017er.com mailbox to don.funk@contoso2017er.com, issue the following command:

```
Set-Mailbox -Identity kim.akers@contoso2017er.com -GrantSendOnBehalfTo don.funk@
contoso2017er.com
```

You also use the Set-Mailbox cmdlet to remove the Send on Behalf permission. For example, to remove the Send on Behalf permission from Don Funk for the Kim Akers mailbox, issue the command:

```
Set-Mailbox -Identity kim.akers@contoso2017er.com -GrantSendOnBeahlfTo @{Remove="don.
funk@contoso2017er.com}
```

Full Access

The Full Access permission allows the person delegated the permission the ability to open and access the contents of an Exchange Online mailbox. While the permission is named Full Access, being delegated the permission does not allow a delegate to send mail from the mailbox. The Send As or Send on Behalf permissions must be delegated for this to occur.

To delegate the Full Access permission for a mailbox, perform the following steps:

1. In the Office 365 Admin Center, click Exchange under Admin Centers. This will open the Exchange Admin Center.

2. Click Recipients. In the list of mailboxes, select the Exchange Online mailbox to which you wish to delegate the Send As permission. Figure 3-31 shows the Dan Jump mailbox selected.

FIGURE 3-31 Dan Jump mailbox

3. With the mailbox selected, click the Edit (Pencil) icon.

4. In the Mailbox Delegation section, click the Plus (+) icon, next to Full Access, as shown in Figure 3-32.

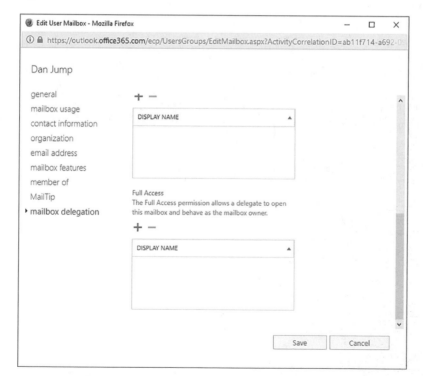

FIGURE 3-32 Full Access

5. On the Select Full Access page, select the user to whom you want to assign full access, click Add and then click OK. Figure 3-33 shows the Kim Akers user being assigned full access.

FIGURE 3-33 Delegate full access

6. On the mailbox properties page, verify that the appropriate user is assigned access, as shown in Figure 3-34, and then click Save.

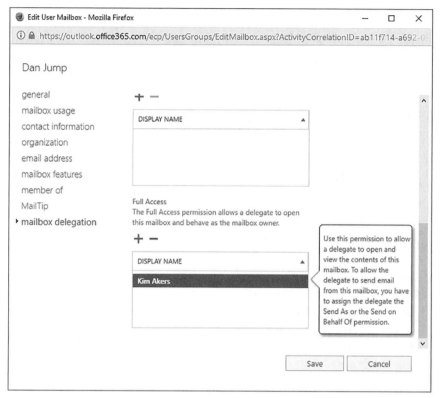

FIGURE 3-34 Kim Akers granted Full Access

You can use the Add-MailboxPermission cmdlet to assign the Full Access permission to a user mailbox. For example, to assign Kim Akers the Full Access permission on the Dan Jump mailbox, use the command:

```
Add-MailboxPermission –Identity "Dan Jump" –User "Kim Akers" –AccessRights FullAccess
 –InheritanceType all
```

You use the Remove-MailboxPermission cmdlet to remove the Full Access permission on a user mailbox. For example, to remove the Full Access permission from Kim Akers on Dan Jump's mailbox, use the command:

```
Remove-MailboxPermission –Identity "Dan Jump" –User "Kim Akers" –AccessRights FullAccess
 –InteritanceType All
```

Create shared mailboxes

Shared mailboxes allow multiple users to view, respond to, and send email messages. Shared mailboxes also allow a group of users to have a common calendar. Users don't sign in to a shared mailbox, but are granted permissions on the shared mailbox. Shared mailboxes use the following permissions:

- **Full Access**   Allows a user to act as an owner of the mailbox. The user is able to create calendar items, read, view, and delete email messages and perform the same mailbox tasks as they can with their own Exchange Online mailbox. Users assigned the Full Access permission cannot send email from the shared mailbox unless assigned additional permissions.

- **Send As**   Allows the user to send email as the shared mailbox. For example, if you assign Kim Akers the Send As permission on the Accounting shared mailbox, Kim will be able to send email that appears to come from the email address assigned to the accounting mailbox.

- **Send on Behalf**   Allows a user to send email on behalf of the shared mailbox. Whereas Send As allows the user to impersonate the shared mailbox, the Send on Behalf permission provides an indication that the mail is sent on behalf of the shared mailbox. For example, if you assigned Kim Akers the Send on Behalf permission on the Accounting shared mailbox, and she sent an email from this mailbox, the email from her would be designated "Kim Akers on behalf of Accounting."

Shared mailboxes do not need to be assigned licenses until they exceed the storage quota of 50 GB. A shared mailbox that exceeds its 50 GB quota will be locked after a month if no license has been assigned.

To create a Shared Mailbox, perform the following steps:

1.   In the Office 365 Admin Center, click Exchange under Admin Centers. This will open the Exchange Admin Center.

2.   Click Recipients and then click Shared.

3.   On the toolbar shown in Figure 3-35, click the Plus (+) icon. This will open the New Shared Mailbox page.

FIGURE 3-35 Shared Mailboxes

4. On the New Shared Mailbox dialog box, shown in Figure 3-36, provide the display name, the email address, and users who have permission to view and send email from the shared mailbox. Adding users here grants them both the Full Access and Send As permissions.

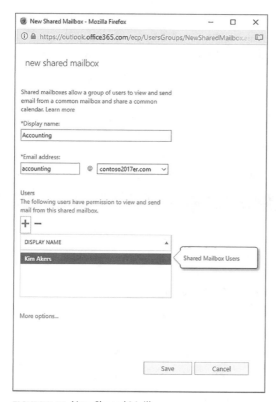

FIGURE 3-36 New Shared Mailbox

5. Click Save to create the shared mailbox.

You can create a New Shared Mailbox using the New-Mailbox Windows PowerShell cmdlet using the Shared parameter. For example, to create a New Shared Mailbox named Accounting, issue the command:

```
New-Mailbox -Shared -Name "Accounting" -DisplayName "Accounting" -Alias Accounting
```

> **MORE INFO**   **SHARED MAILBOXES**
>
> You can learn more about shared mailboxes at: *https://technet.microsoft.com/en-us/library/jj966275(v=exchg.150).aspx.*

Manage resource mailboxes

Resource mailboxes represent organizational facilities and equipment. Users are able to book the facilities and equipment by including the resource mailbox in a meeting request. Users are also able to view existing bookings of facilities and equipment by viewing the resource mailbox's calendar. Exchange Online supports two types of resource mailbox: room mailboxes and equipment mailboxes.

Equipment mailboxes

Equipment mailboxes are a type of resource mailbox that represents a piece of equipment such as a projector, camera, drone, or company hovercraft. Users reserve the equipment that corresponds to the mailbox by including it in a meeting request. To create an equipment mailbox, perform the following steps:

1. In the Office 365 Admin Center, click Exchange under Admin Centers. This will open the Exchange Admin Center.

2. Click Recipients and then click Resources.

3. Click the Plus icon (+) and then click Equipment Mailbox, as shown in Figure 3-37.

FIGURE 3-37 New Equipment Mailbox

4. On the new equipment mailbox page, shown in Figure 3-38, specify the following:
 - Equipment name
 - Email address

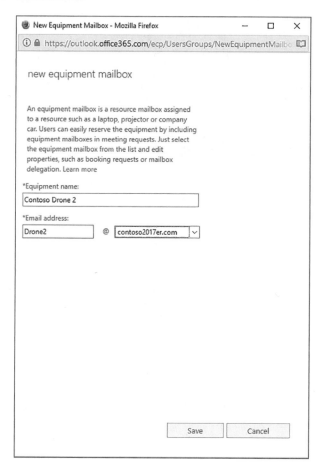

FIGURE 3-38 New Equipment Mailbox

5. Click Save to create the equipment mailbox.

Once the equipment mailbox is saved, you can edit the properties of the mailbox to configure additional options, including:

- **Booking Delegates** On the Booking Delegates page, you can configure whether booking requests are accepted automatically, or whether delegates can accept or decline booking requests. Figure 3-39 shows Don Funk configured as a delegate.

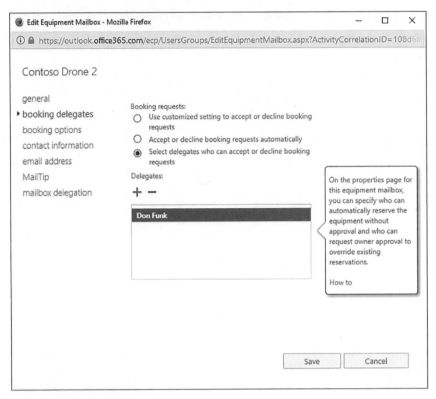

FIGURE 3-39 Booking Delegates

- **Booking Options** On the Booking Options page, shown in Figure 3-40, you can configure whether repeat bookings are allowed, whether bookings can only occur during working hours, how far in advance bookings can occur, and the maximum booking duration.

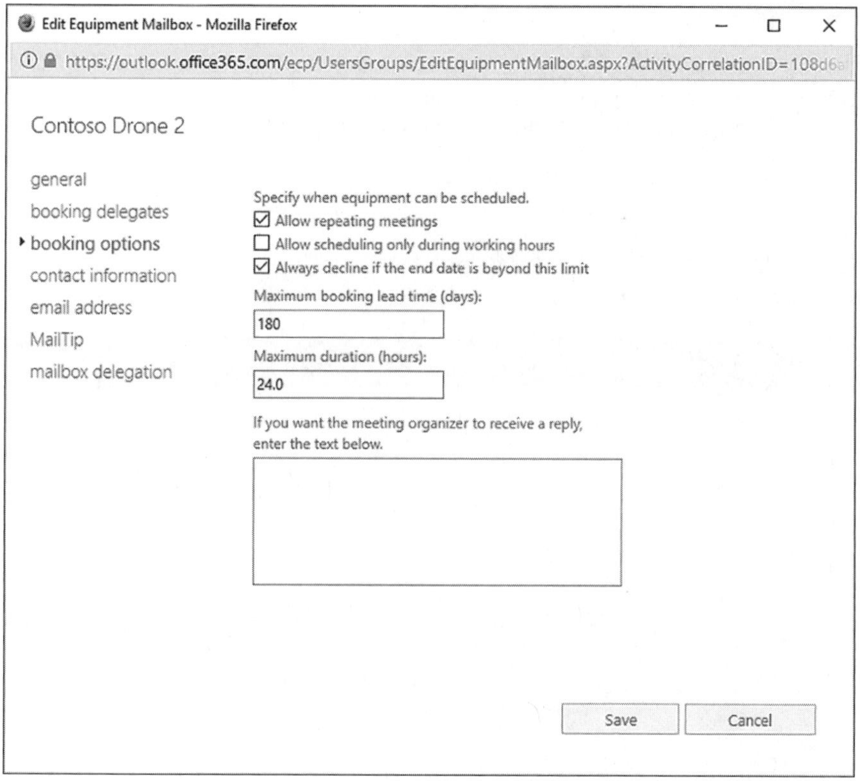

FIGURE 3-40 Booking Options

- **Contact Information** Allows you to set contact information about the resource.
- **Email Address** Allows you to configure email addresses for the resource.
- **MailTip** Allows you to configure a MailTip for the resource
- **Mailbox Delegation** Allows you to delegate permissions on the resource.

You can create an equipment mailbox using the New-Mailbox cmdlet and the Equipment parameter. For example, to create a new equipment mailbox named CompanyHovercraft, issue the command:

```
New-Mailbox -Name "CompanyHovercraft" -Equipment
```

> **MORE INFO** **EQUIPMENT MAILBOXES**
>
> You can learn more about equipment mailboxes at: *https://technet.microsoft.com/en-us/library/jj215770(v=exchg.160).aspx.*

Room mailboxes

Room mailboxes allow users to book rooms for meetings and to view room availability. One of the differences between a room mailbox and an equipment mailbox is the ability to specify the room capacity. To create a room mailbox, perform the following steps:

1. In the Office 365 Admin Center, click Exchange under Admin Centers. This will open the Exchange Admin Center.

2. Click Recipients and then click Resources.

3. Click the Plus (+) icon and then click Room Mailbox, as shown in Figure 3-41.

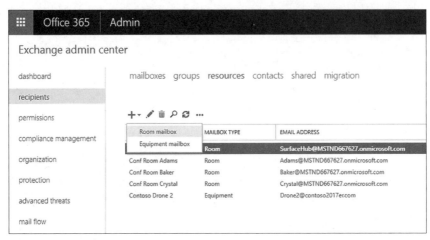

FIGURE 3-41 New Room Mailbox

4. On the New Room Mailbox page, shown in Figure 3-42, specify the following information:

- **Room Name**   The name of the room as it will appear in the address list.
- **Email Address**   The email address associated with the room.
- **Location**   Room location (optional).
- **Phone**   A phone number allocated to the room (optional).
- **Capacity**   The room capacity (optional).

FIGURE 3-42 New Room Mailbox

5. Click Save to create the room mailbox.

Once the room mailbox is created, you can edit the mailbox to configure the following additional settings:

- **Booking Delegates** Allows you to configure whether the room can be booked automatically or whether bookings must be approved by a delegate.

- **Booking Options** Allows you to configure whether repeat meetings can be scheduled, whether meetings can only be scheduled during working hours, how far in advance bookings can be made, and the maximum booking duration.

- **Contact Information** Allows you to set contact information about the resource.

- **Email Address** Allows you to configure email addresses for the resource.

- **MailTip** Allows you to configure a MailTip for the resource.

- **Mailbox Delegation** Allows you to delegate permissions on the resource.

You can create a new room mailbox using the New-Mailbox Windows PowerShell cmdlet with the Room parameter. For example, to create a mailbox named Sydney Conference Room, use the following command:

```
New-Mailbox -Name SydConf -DisplayName "Sydney Conference Room" -Room
```

> **MORE INFO MANAGE ROOM MAILBOXES**
>
> You can learn more about managing room mailboxes at: *https://technet.microsoft.com/en-us/library/jj215781(v=exchg.160).aspx.*

Manage external contacts

External contacts allow you to add people with email addresses from outside your organization to your internal address books. For example, if you want to add the address of someone at Adatum Corporation to the Contoso address book, you can do so using an external contact.

To create an external contact, perform the following steps:

1. In the Office 365 Admin Center, click Exchange under Admin Centers. This will open the Exchange Admin Center.

2. Click Recipients. Click Contacts. Click the Plus (+) icon, and then click Mail Contact.

3. On the Mail Contact page, shown in Figure 3-43, provide the following information:
   - First Name
   - Initial
   - Last Name
   - Display Name
   - Alias
   - External Email Address

FIGURE 3-43 New Mail Contact

4. Click Save to save the contact.

You use the New-MailContact Windows PowerShell cmdlet to create a mail contact. For example, to create a mail contact for Thomas Andersen, issue the following command:

```
New-MailContact -Name "Thomas Andersen" -ExternalEmailAddress tandersen@adatum.com
```

You can add additional email addresses to a mail contact using the Set-MailContact Windows PowerShell cmdlet. For example, to add an addition email address to the Thomas Andersen contact for an email address in the tailspintoys.com email domain, issue the command:

```
Set-MailContact -Name "Thomas Andersen" -EmailAddresses "SMTP:tandersen@adatum.
com","smtp:tandersen@tailspintoys.com"
```

The uppercase SMTP defines the primary email address. There can only be one primary email address.

> **MORE INFO EXTERNAL CONTACTS**
>
> You can learn more about external contacts at: *https://technet.microsoft.com/library/ aa998858(v=exchg.150).aspx.*

Manage Distribution Groups

Distribution Groups allow users to send email messages to a single address and have those messages forwarded to all members of the Distribution Group. Exchange Online supports the following types of distribution group, as shown in Figure 3-44:

- **Distribution Group** Also termed a distribution list, this type of group allows you to distribute messages to groups of users.
- **Security Group** Also termed a mail-enabled security group, it allows you to distribute messages to groups of users, as well as allowing permissions to be configured for resources.
- **Dynamic Distribution Group** A distribution list where the list of recipients is calculated each time a message is sent. Membership of the list is determined based on group settings and conditions.

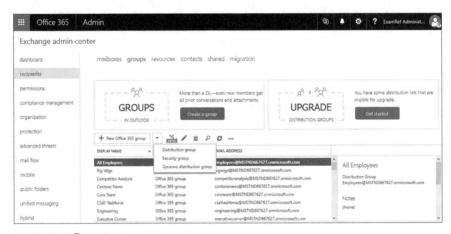

FIGURE 3-44 Group types

MORE INFO   **DISTRIBUTION GROUP TYPES**

You can learn more about Exchange Online Distribution Groups at: *https://support.office.com/en-us/article/Create-edit-or-delete-a-security-group-55c96b32-e086-4c9e-948b-a018b44510cb #__groups_in_exchange.*

Distribution Group

To create a Distribution Group that can be used to forward messages to users but cannot be used to assign security permissions, perform the following steps:

1. In the Office 365 Admin Center, click Exchange under Admin Centers. This will open the Exchange Admin Center.

2. Click Recipients. Click Groups. Click the Plus (+) icon and then click Distribution Group.

3. On the New Distribution Group dialog box, provide the following information, as shown in Figure 3-45:

- **Display Name**   The name of the security group as it appears in the address book.
- **Alias**   The group alias.
- **Email Address**   The prefix name. The group email address.
- **Owners**   Users who have permission to manage the group.

FIGURE 3-45 New Distribution Group

- **Members**   Allows you to specify members of the group.
- **Join settings**   Specify whether approval is required to join the group. You can configure the group to be open, which means anyone can join, Closed. This means group owners control membership, or owner approval, which allows people to request group membership subject to group owner approval. These options are shown in Figure 3-46.

FIGURE 3-46 Joining settings

- **Leave settings** Specify whether approval is required to leave the group. These options are shown in Figure 3-47.

FIGURE 3-47 Leaving group settings

- Click Save to create the distribution group.

You use the New-DistributionGroup Windows PowerShell cmdlet to create Distribution Groups. For example, to create a new Distribution Group named ExampleDistGroup that allows members to join, issue this command:

```
New-DistributionGroup –Name "ExampleDistGroup" –Alias ExampleDG –MemberJoinRestriction
 Open
```

You can use the Set-DistributionGroup Windows PowerShell cmdlet to modify the properties of an existing distribution group. For example, to modify the distribution group Example-DistGroup so that new members must be approved by the group owner, issue the command:

```
Set-DistributionGroup –Identity "ExampleDistGroup" –MemberJoinRestriction
 'ApprovalRequired'
```

MORE INFO **MANAGE DISTRIBUTION GROUPS**

You can learn more about managing Exchange Online Distribution Groups at: *https://tech-net.microsoft.com/library/bb124513.aspx.*

Mail-enabled security group

Mail-enabled security groups are groups that allow you to send messages to multiple people and which can also be used to assign permissions. To create a mail-enabled security group, perform the following steps:

1. In the Office 365 Admin Center, click Exchange under Admin Centers. This will open the Exchange Admin Center.

2. Click Recipients and click the arrow and select Security group.

3. On the New Distribution Group dialog box, provide the following information, as shown in Figure 3-48:

   - **Display Name** The name of the security group as it appears in the address book.

   - **Alias** The group alias.

   - **Email Address** The prefix name and the group email address.

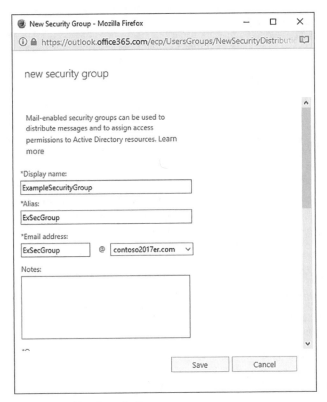

FIGURE 3-48 New Security Group

- **Owners** Users who have permission to manage the group.
- **Members** Allows you to specify members of the group. Owners and Members settings are shown in Figure 3-49.

FIGURE 3-49 New Security Group Owners and Members

- **Join settings** Specify whether approval is required to join the group. You can configure the group to be open, which means anyone can join Closed, which means group owners control membership; or owner approval, which allows people to request group membership subject to group owner approval.
- **Leave settings** Specify whether approval is required to leave the group.

4. Click Save to create the mail-enabled security group.

You use the New-DistributionGroup Windows PowerShell cmdlet with the Type parameter set to Security to create a mail-enabled security group. For example, to create a new security group named ExampleSecurityGroup, use the command:

```
New-DistributionGroup –Name "ExampleSecurityGroup" –Alias ExSecGroup –Type Security
```

You can use the Set-DistributionGroup Windows PowerShell cmdlet to modify the properties of a mail-enabled security group.

Dynamic Distribution Group

Dynamic Distribution Groups differ from Distribution Groups and mail-enabled security groups in that membership of the group is generated dynamically rather than including list of users who have chosen to join or have been added to the group. You configure the membership by first specifying what types of recipients will be members, as shown in Figure 3-50, and then by adding rules. Recipient types that you can select include:

- Users With Exchange mailboxes
- Mail Users With External Email Addresses
- Resource Mailboxes
- Mail Contacts With External Email Addresses
- Mail-Enabled Groups

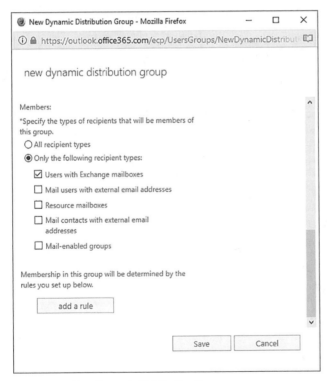

FIGURE 3-50 New Dynamic Distribution Group

You can use the following attributes when creating a rule for a dynamic distribution group:

- State or province
- Company
- Department
- Custom attributes 1 through 15

To create a rule, select the attribute and then specify the words or phrases that match the attribute. Figure 3-51 shows the word Accounting configured as the word that should be matched for a specific attribute.

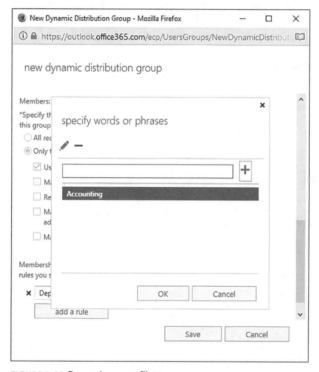

FIGURE 3-51 Dynamic group filter

Figure 3-52 shows a Distribution Group where only users with Exchange Mailboxes whose Department attribute matches the word Accounting.

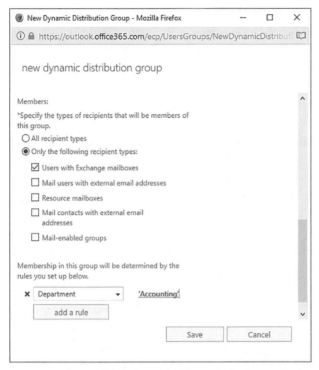

FIGURE 3-52 Users With Exchange Mailboxes in the Accounting Department

To create a dynamic Distribution Group, perform the following steps:

1. In the Office 365 Admin Center, click Exchange under Admin Centers. This will open the Exchange Admin Center.

2. Click Recipients. Click Groups. Click the Plus (+) icon, and then click Dynamic distribution group.

3. Provide the following information:

   ■ **Display Name** Name of the group that will be displayed.

   ■ **Alias** Group alias, which will also be the name used for the email address prefix.

   ■ **Owner** Allows you to specify a group owner. Group owners are able to change the properties of the dynamic distribution group and to perform moderation tasks on messages sent to the group. If not configured, the user that created the group will be set as the owner.

   ■ **Members** Specify the recipient types to be included.

   ■ **Membership rules** Specify the rules that will filter the recipient types selected.

4. Click Save to save the group properties.

You can also use the New-DynamicDistributionGroup Windows PowerShell cmdlet to create dynamic distribution groups. For example, to create a new dynamic distribution group named AccountingDDG that includes only mailbox users from the Accounting department, issue the following command:

```
New-DynamicDistributionGroup -Name "AccountingDDG" -Alias "AccountingDDG"
-IncludedRecipients MailboxUsers -ConditionalDepartment "Accounting"
```

> **MORE INFO** **DYNAMIC DISTRIBUTION GROUPS**
>
> You can learn more about dynamic distribution groups at: *https://technet.microsoft.com/library/bb123722.aspx.*

EXAM TIP

Remember the difference between Send As, Send on Behalf, and Full Access recipient permissions.

 Quick check

Which Windows PowerShell cmdlet would you use if you wanted to assign the Full Access permission to Kim Akers over Don Funk's Exchange Online mailbox?

Quick check answer

You would use the Add-MailboxPermission cmdlet to assign Full Access permission over an Exchange Online mailbox.

Skill 3.3: Configure personal archive policies

This skill deals with configuring personal archives, retention tags, and retention policies. These features control which information is kept and which information is discarded from Exchange Online mailboxes on a long-term basis.

This skill covers how to:

- Enable personal archive for mailboxes
- Retention tags and retention policies

Enable personal archive for mailboxes

Archive mailboxes, which are termed in-place archives in Exchange Online, allow for extra email storage. Once you enable an archive, messages that are in a user's Exchange Online mailbox that exceed two years of age will automatically be transferred to the archive by the default retention policy. Users are also able to manually move messages to the archive or can create inbox rules that automatically move messages that match the rules to the archive. If an archive isn't enabled for a user, messages that exceed two years of age remain in the Exchange Online mailbox.

Archives also allow you to alleviate the need for personal store (.pst) files on local computers. There are several advantages to using archives, including simplifying the process of managing retention and eDiscovery requests as all mail will be stored in a location accessible to administrators. For example, if you are in the process of responding to an eDiscovery request involving an executive's email, you need to be able to search all locations where that email is stored. If the executive stores email on their personal laptop computer in a .pst file, you will need to search that file as well as the user's Exchange Online mailbox. Once you have configured an archive, you can use other tools to import the contents of any .pst files into an Exchange Online mailbox and then block the utilization of .pst files on client computers.

You can see which users have an archive enabled by noting the archive designation in the mailbox type column in the list of recipients. Figure 3-53 shows that the Dan Jump mailbox is configured with an archive.

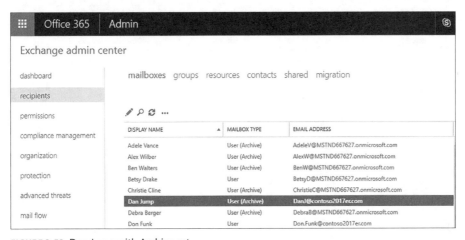

FIGURE 3-53 Dan Jump with Archive set

To enable the personal archive for an existing Exchange Online mailbox, perform the following steps:

1. In the Office 365 Admin Center, click Exchange under Admin Centers. This will open the Exchange Admin Center.

2. In the Exchange Admin Center, click Recipients.

3. Click Mailboxes.

4. In the list of mailboxes, select the mailbox for which you wish to enable the archive. Figure 3-54 shows the Dan Jump mailbox selected.

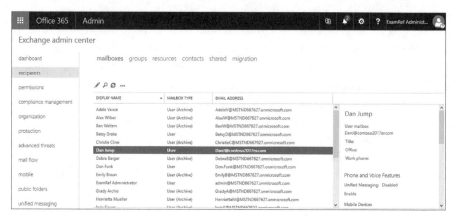

FIGURE 3-54 Dan Jump selected

5. Click the Edit (Pencil) Icon.

6. Click Mailbox features. Under Archiving, shown in Figure 3-55, click Enable.

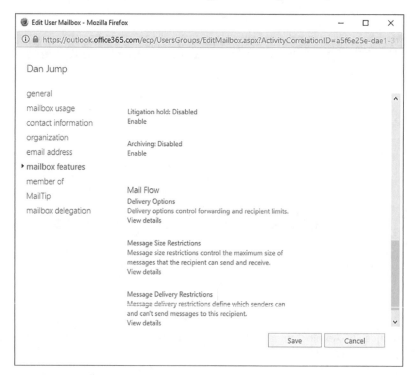

FIGURE 3-55 Mailbox Features

7. Once archiving is enabled, click View Details, as shown in Figure 3-56, to configure archive details.

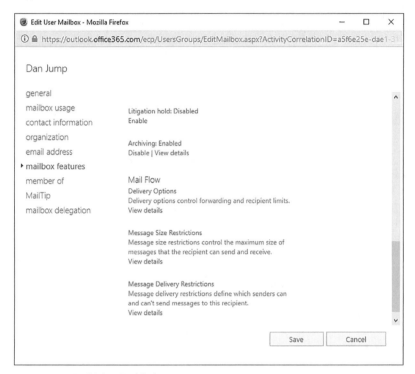

FIGURE 3-56 Archiving Enabled

8. On the Archive Mailbox dialog, you can specify the name of the folder in the user's mailbox for the archive. Depending on the Exchange Online plan, you will be able to configure the Archive Quota and the warning threshold. Figure 3-57 shows the Archive Mailbox dialog with the name set to Archive. Click OK to save changes.

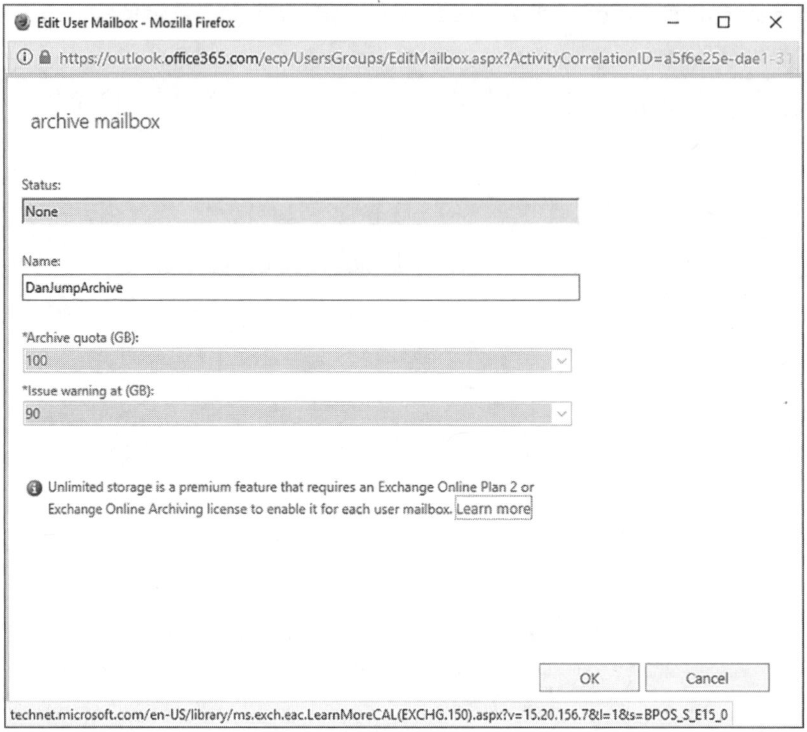

FIGURE 3-57 Archive Mailbox settings

9. Click Save on the User Mailbox dialog to save settings.

You can use the Enablemailbox Windows PowerShell cmdlet to enable an archive on a specific mailbox. For example, to enable an archive on Kim Akers mailbox, issue the following command:

```
Enablemailbox "Kim Akers" -Archive
```

When you use this command, the mailbox will be assigned the name "Personal Archive - <display name>" by default. For example, for Kim Akers, the archive will be named "Personal Archive – Kim Akers."

To enable archives on all mailboxes that do not currently have archives enabled, run the following command:

```
Get-Mailbox -Filter {ArchiveStatus -Eq "None" -AND RecipientTypeDetails -eq
 "UserMailbox"} | Enablemailbox -Archive
```

> **MORE INFO   ARCHIVES**
>
> You can learn more about archives at: *https://technet.microsoft.com/en-us/library/ JJ984357(v=EXCHG.150).aspx.*

Retention tags and retention policies

Messaging Records Management (MRM) allows organizations to manage how email messages are treated so that the legal risks associated with the long-term storage of messages and other communication is minimized. For example, when properly configured, MRM allows organizations to ensure that messages that they must keep for a certain period of time due to regulation or legal requirement are kept while other messages that are not subject to these restrictions are automatically removed if no longer required. Without MRM, you might have some users who delete email messages that should legally be stored and others that never delete anything, meaning that they are constantly at risk of exceeding their Exchange Online mailbox quota.

> **MORE INFO** **RETENTION TAGS AND RETENTION POLICIES**
>
> You can learn more about retention tags and retention policies at: *https://technet.microsoft.com/en-us/library/dd297955(v=exchg.160).aspx.*

Create retention tags

Retention tags include a retention action and a retention period. A retention action specifies whether the tag deletes and allows recovery of a message, permanently deletes a message, or moves the message to the archive. The retention period defines the number of days that must pass before the tag is triggered.

To create a retention tag, perform the following steps:

1. In the Office 365 Admin Center, click Exchange under Admin Centers. This will open the Exchange Admin Center.

2. In the Exchange Admin Center, click Compliance Management.

3. In Compliance Management, click Retention Tags, as shown in Figure 3-58.

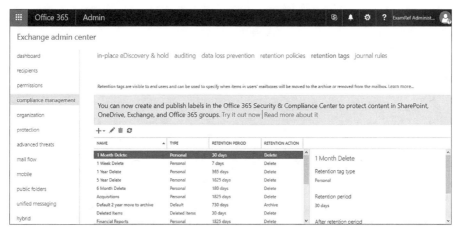

FIGURE 3-58 Retention Tags

4. On the toolbar, click the Plus (+) icon and select between the following options, as shown in Figure 3-59:

- Applied automatically to entire mailbox
- Applied automatically to a default folder
- Applied by users to items and folders (personal)

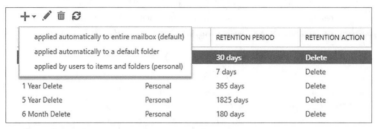

FIGURE 3-59 New Retention Tag

5. On the New Tag dialog box, shown in Figure 3-60, provide the following information:

- **Tag Name**   The name of the retention tag.
- **Retention Action**   Specify if the tag deletes and allows recovery, permanently deletes, or moves the message to the archive.
- **Retention Period**   The number of days that must pass before the tag is triggered.

FIGURE 3-60 New Tag for Entire Mailbox

You create retention tags using the New-RetentionPolicyTag Windows PowerShell cmdlet. For example, to create a retention tag of the default type named Research-Default that permanently deletes messages after 180 days, issue the following command:

```
New-RetentionPolicyTag "Research-Default" -Type All -RetentionEnabled $true
-AgeLimitForRetention 180 -RetentionAction PermanentlyDelete
```

> **MORE INFO** **RETENTION TAGS**
>
> You can learn more about creating retention tags in Windows PowerShell at: *https://technet.microsoft.com/en-us/library/dd335226(v=exchg.160).aspx.*

Create custom retention policy

A retention policy is a collection of retention tags that can be applied to a mailbox. To create a new retention policy, perform the following steps:

1. In the Office 365 Admin Center, click Exchange under Admin Centers. This will open the Exchange Admin Center.

2. In the Exchange Admin Center, click Compliance Management and click Retention policies. These are displayed in Figure 3-61.

FIGURE 3-61 Retention Policies

3. On the toolbar, click the Plus (+) button.

4. On the New Retention Policy page, shown in Figure 3-62, provide a name for the retention policy. Click the Plus (+) icon to add retention tags.

FIGURE 3-62 New Retention Policy

5. On the Select Retention Tags page, shown in Figure 3-63, select the tags that you want to add to the policy and click Add. Click OK to close the Select Retention Tags dialog box.

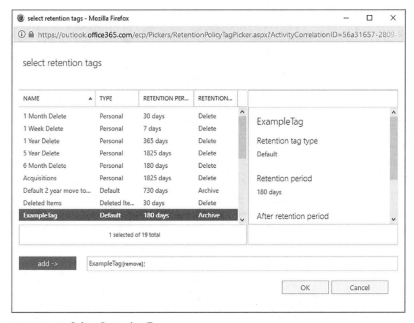

FIGURE 3-63 Select Retention Tags

6. On the New Retention Policy dialog box, shown in Figure 3-64, click Save to create the new retention policy.

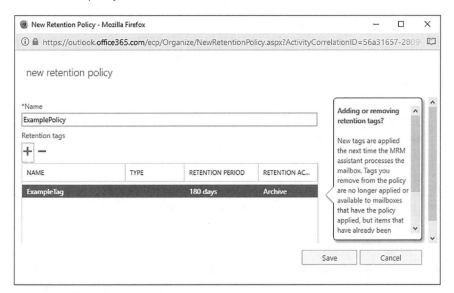

FIGURE 3-64 Example policy and tag

To create a new retention policy that includes the Research and Accounting retention policy tags, issue the following command:

```
New-RetentionPolicy "Contoso General" –RetentionPolicyTagLinks "Research","Accounting"
```

> **MORE INFO** **RETENTION POLICIES**
>
> You can learn more about creating retention policies using Windows PowerShell at: *https://technet.microsoft.com/en-us/library/dd297970(v=exchg.160).aspx.*

Review and modify default retention policy

The name of the default retention policy is Default MRM Policy. The Default MRM Policy is always the default retention policy applied automatically to new users. Even if you create other retention policies, it is the default that is applied automatically. While you cannot change the fact that the Default MRM Policy is automatically applied to new users, you can modify which retention tags are contained in the policy, as well as modifying the retention tags themselves.

- The Default MRM Policy contains the retention tags listed in Table 3-1.

TABLE 3-1 Retention tags in Default MRM Policy

Name	Type	Retention period	Action
Default 2 years move to archive	Default Policy Tag (DPT)	730	Move to Archive
Recoverable Items 14 days move to archive	Recoverable Items folder	14	Move to Archive
Personal 1 year move to archive	Personal tag	365	Move to Archive
Personal 5 year move to archive	Personal tag	1825	Move to Archive
Personal never move to archive	Personal tag	Not applicable	Move to Archive
1 Week Delete	Personal tag	7	Delete and Allow Recovery
1 Month Delete	Personal tag	30	Delete and Allow Recovery
6 Month Delete	Personal tag	180	Delete and Allow Recovery
1 Year Delete	Personal tag	365	Delete and Allow Recovery
5 Year Delete	Personal tag	1825	Delete and Allow Recovery
Never Delete	Personal tag	Not applicable	Delete and Allow Recovery

To alter the default retention policy, perform the following steps:

1. In the Office 365 Admin Center, click Exchange under Admin Centers. This will open the Exchange Admin Center.

2. In the Exchange Admin Center, click Compliance Management and click Retention policies.

3. In the list of retention policies, select the Default MRM Policy, as shown in Figure 3-65, and then click the Pencil (Edit) icon.

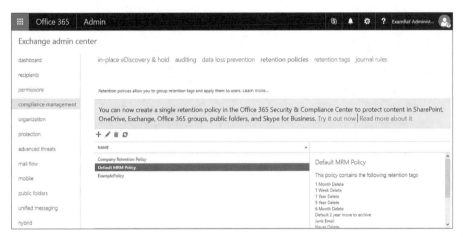

FIGURE 3-65 Default MRM Policy

4. On the Default MRM Policy page, shown in Figure 3-66, make the changes that you want to make to the policy by adding and removing retention tags.

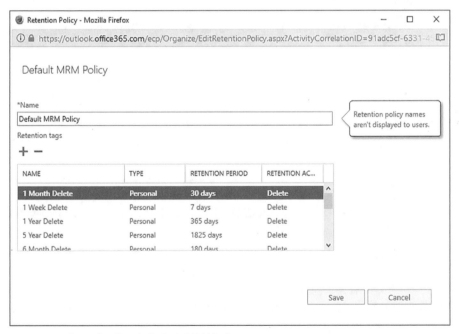

FIGURE 3-66 Retention Tags in Default MRM Policy

5. Click Save to save the modifications to the MRM policy.

You can use the Set-RetentionPolicy Windows PowerShell cmdlet to modify the default retention policy.

MORE INFO **DEFAULT RETENTION POLICY**

You can learn more about the default retention policy at: *https://technet.microsoft.com/en-us/library/Dn775046(v=EXCHG.150).aspx.*

Apply retention policy to mailboxes

While the default retention policy is automatically applied to mailboxes and Exchange Online mailboxes, and can only have a single retention policy applied, it is possible to replace the default retention policy with a custom retention policy.

To apply a custom retention policy to a single mailbox, perform the following steps:

1. In the Office 365 Admin Center, click Exchange under Admin Centers. This will open the Exchange Admin Center.

2. Click Recipients. In the list of mailboxes, select the Exchange Online mailbox to which you wish to apply the retention policy. Figure 3-67 shows the Dan Jump mailbox selected.

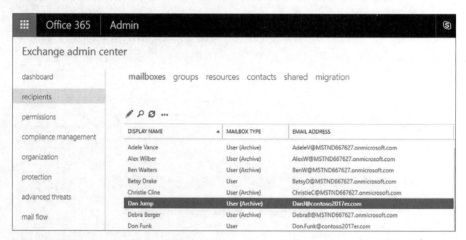

FIGURE 3-67 Dan Jump mailbox selected

3. Click the Edit (Pencil) icon. This will bring up the mailbox properties page.

4. Click Mailbox Features. Use the Retention Policy drop down list to select the retention policy that you want to apply to the mailbox. Figure 3-68 shows the ExamplePolicy retention policy applied to the mailbox.

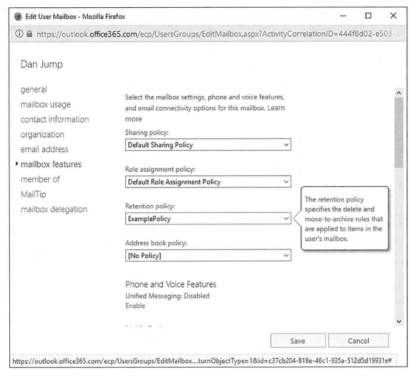

FIGURE 3-68 Retention Policy set

5. Click Save to apply the policy to the mailbox.

You don't have to apply retention policies on a per-mailbox basis. It is possible to apply the same retention policy to multiple Exchange Online mailboxes. To apply a custom retention policy to multiple mailboxes, perform the following steps:

1. In the Office 365 Admin Center, click Exchange under Admin Centers. This will open the Exchange Admin Center.

2. Click Recipients. In the list of mailboxes, use the Shift or Ctrl keys to select the Exchange Online mailboxes to which you wish to apply the retention policy. Figure 3-69 shows the Don Funk and Kim Akers mailboxes selected.

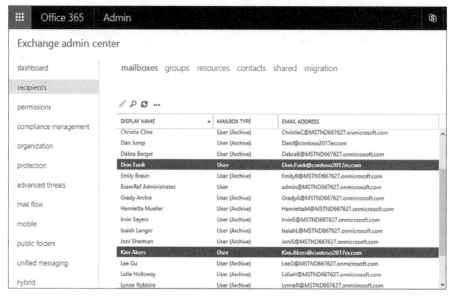

FIGURE 3-69 Multiple users selected

3. With the multiple mailboxes selected, click More Options, as shown in Figure 3-70.

FIGURE 3-70 More Options

4. Under Retention Policy, shown in Figure 3-71, click Update.

FIGURE 3-71 Update multiple users retention policy

5. On the Bulk Assign Retention Policy page, select the retention policy that you want to assign to the selected mailboxes. Figure 3-72 shows the ExamplePolicy selected.

FIGURE 3-72 Bulk Assign Retention Policy

6. Click Save to apply the policy to the selected mailboxes.

You use the Set-Mailbox Windows PowerShell cmdlet to apply retention policies to mailboxes. For example, to apply the ExamplePolicy retention policy to Don Funk's mailbox, issue the command:

```
Set-Mailbox "Don Funk" -RetentionPolicy "ExamplePolicy"
```

MORE INFO   APPLY RETENTION POLICY

You can learn more about applying retention policies at: *https://technet.microsoft.com/en-us/library/dd298052(v=exchg.160).aspx.*

EXAM TIP

Remember that unless you apply a different retention policy, the default retention policy will apply to all newly created Exchange Online mailboxes.

Skill 3.4: Configure Skype for Business Online end-user communication settings

This skill deals with configuring end-user communication settings for Skype for Business Online. To master this skill, you'll need to understand how to configure user settings, including presence, external communication, whether meetings are recorded, and disabling features that cannot be recorded to ensure that compliance obligations are met.

> **This skill covers how to:**
> - Configure presence
> - Configure per user external communication
> - Configure user settings

Configure presence

Presence settings determine who is able to see when a user is available, in a meeting, or out of office in Skype for Business Online. You can configure the following options:

- **Automatically Display Presence Information**   When you choose this option, any user that does not belong to the External or Blocked privacy group can view the user's presence information.

- **Display Presence Information Only To A User's Contacts**   When you choose this option, presence information is visible only to people in the user's Contacts list who are not in the External or Blocked privacy group.

To configure presence settings for Skype for Business Online, perform the following steps:

1. In the Office 365 Admin Center, click Skype for Business under Admin Centers.

2. In the Skype for Business Admin Center, click Organization.

3. Under Presence Privacy Mode, shown in Figure 3-73, select the appropriate privacy mode.

FIGURE 3-73 Presence Privacy Mode

Configure external communication

External communication settings allow you to configure whether users can add Skype for Business or Skype users external to your organization to their list of business contacts. You can configure these settings across the tenancy or on a per-user basis.

When configuring external communications settings across the tenancy, you can choose between the following options:

- **Off Completely**   This blocks access to users from outside the tenancy.
- **On Except For Blocked Domains**   This allows communications with users except those who come from blocked domains.
- **On Only For Allowed Domains**   This allows communications with users who are from the list of allowed domains.

Separately from this, you can also allow connectivity with Skype users and other public IM service providers. This option is disabled if you select the Off Completely option. To configure external communications settings across the tenancy, perform the following steps:

1. In the Office 365 Admin Center, click Skype for Business under Admin Centers.
2. In the Skype for Business Admin Center, click Organization.
3. Click External communications.
4. On the external access page, select the external access option and whether you want to allow communication with Skype users and other public IM providers. These options are shown in Figure 3-74.

FIGURE 3-74 External Access

5. To add a blocked or allowed domain, click the Plus (+) icon.

6. On the Add A Domain page, shown in Figure 3-75, enter the domain name and click Add. If the setting is configured for blocked domains, the added domain will be blocked. If the setting is configured for allowed domains, the added domain will be allowed.

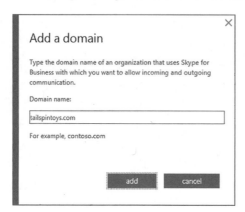

FIGURE 3-75 Add A Domain

To configure external communication settings on a per-user basis, perform the following steps:

1. In the Office 365 Admin Center, select the user that you want to configure external communication settings for from the list of Active Users. Figure 3-76 shows the Dan Jump user selected.

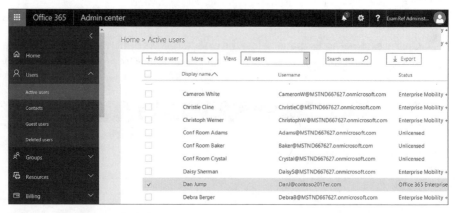

FIGURE 3-76 Dan Jump selected

2. Double-click the user.

3. At the bottom of the user properties page, shown in Figure 3-77, click Edit Skype for Business properties.

Sign-in status	Sign-in allowed	Edit
Office installs	View and manage which devices this person has Office apps installed on.	Edit
Roles	User (no admin access)	Edit
Display name	Dan Jump	Edit
Office phone		
∨ ✉ Mail Settings		
∨ ☁ OneDrive Settings		
More settings	Edit Skype for Business properties Manage multi-factor authentication ⤤	

FIGURE 3-77 Details page

4. Click External Communications. On the Options page, shown in Figure 3-78, specify whether the user can communicate with Skype for Business Users outside the organization and/or users on public IM networks.

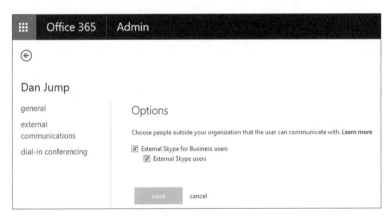

FIGURE 3-78 Skype For Business Options

5. Click Save to save changes.

MORE INFO   **CONFIGURING EXTERNAL COMMUNICATIONS**

You can learn more about configuring external communications at: *https://support.office. com/en-us/article/Let-Skype-for-Business-Online-users-communicate-with-external-Skype-for-Business-or-Skype-contacts-b414873a-0059-4cd5-aea1-e5d0857dbc94.*

Configure user options

You can configure which features you wish a user to have access to in the General setting of the options page shown in Figure 3-79.

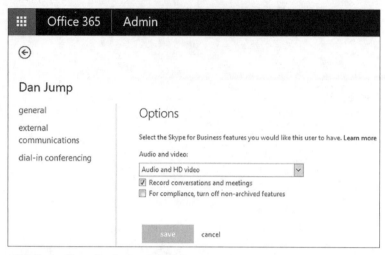

FIGURE 3-79 Skype For Business Options

You can configure the following Audio and video settings:

- **None**   Blocks use of audio and video when using Skype for Business. Online   Text-based messaging is available.

- **Audio Only**   Allows use of audio and text based messaging, but not video.

- **Audio And Video**   Allows use of audio, standard-definition video, and text based messaging.

- **Audio And HD Video**   Allows use of audio, high-definition video- and text-based messaging.

You can configure the following additional options:

- **Record Conversations And Meetings**   When the Record Conversations And Meetings option is selected, conversations and meetings are recorded. This allows conversations and meetings to be reviewed at a later point in time.

- **Allow Anonymous Attendees To Dial-Out**   When the Allow Anonymous Attendees To Dial-Out option is selected, it is possible for anonymous attendees to connect to meeting audio by having the conferencing service call them. If this option is not enabled, anonymous attendees must call in to the conferencing service.

- **For Compliance, Turn Off Non-Archived Features**   When you enable this option, features that are not recorded when an in-place hold is enacted are unavailable. This includes file transfers through instant messaging, shared OneNote pages, and annotations made to PowerPoint presentations conducted across Skype for Business.

EXAM TIP

Remember what functionality is disabled if the For Compliance, Turn Off Non-Archived Features option is enabled in Skype for Business Online.

Thought experiment

In this thought experiment, demonstrate your skills and knowledge of the topics covered in this chapter. You can find answers to this thought experiment in the next section.

You are the Office 365 administrator at Adatum. You have a number of tasks that you need to complete, first of which relates to modifying the SIP address configuration. The organization also has recently purchased several HoloLens devices that will be used by the company's research team to interact with several computer-aided design applications. As there are only a small number of devices, you want to allow people to book these devices using Outlook.

It will also be necessary to send email messages to members of the research team. Currently there is no security group associated with this team, but each member of the team has their user account's department attribute in Active Directory set to Research. The distribution group used for this purpose should not need to be maintained manually.

One challenge you are also facing is that a large number of users at Adatum have very large inbox folders. These inbox folders have grown large because users are not deleting old messages. Unfortunately, some users are approaching their quota and you'd like to implement a solution to resolve the situation before this occurs.

Finally, you also need to configure the presence settings for Skype for Business Online. You want to only allow presence information to be seen by users who are in a person's contact list.

With all of this information in mind, answer the following questions:

1. What must you have in place before you can add an additional SIP address?
2. Which Windows PowerShell cmdlet allows you to alter the SIP address of an Office 365 user?
3. What type of resource mailboxes should you create for the HoloLens devices?
4. What type of distribution list should you create for the research team?
5. What feature can you enable to allow users to keep old messages as long as they want?
6. What can you do to ensure that messages over 180 days are not stored in the user's inbox folder?

7. Which presence option should you configure for users at Adatum?

8. When this setting is configured, which users who are in the user's contacts list will be unable to view presence information?

Thought experiment answers

This section contains the solutions to the thought experiment.

1. You will need to have a SIP URI plan configured to add an SIP address.

2. You use the Set-Mailbox cmdlet to alter the SIP address of an Office 365 user.

3. You should create equipment mailboxes for the HoloLens devices.

4. You should create a dynamic distribution list for the research team. This will use the Research department setting on each account when calculating group membership.

5. You can enable the archive to allow users to keep messages as long as they want.

6. You can configure retention tags and retention policies to deal with messages that are over 180 days old.

7. You would configure the Display presence information only to a user's contacts option.

8. Any users in the External or Blocked privacy group will be unable to view presence information.

Chapter summary

- The default email address is also known as the primary email address and the reply-to address.

- You can add additional email addresses to an Office 365 Exchange Online mailbox.

- Once you add an additional email address to a mailbox, you can configure that as the primary email address.

- You can bulk add additional email addresses to existing Office 365 accounts using Windows PowerShell.

- SIP addresses are used to route Skype for Business calls.

- The default SIP address has the same format as the primary email address.

- The Send As permission allows the person delegated the permission to send messages as though they were sent by the mailbox owner.

- The Send on Behalf permission allows the person delegated the permission to send messages on behalf of the mailbox owner.

- The Full Access permission allows the person delegated the permission the ability to open and access the contents of an Exchange Online mailbox.

- Being delegated the Full Access permission does not allow a delegate to send mail from the mailbox.

- Shared mailboxes allow multiple users to view, respond to, and send email messages. Shared mailboxes also allow a group of users to have a common calendar.

- Resource mailboxes represent organizational facilities and equipment.

- Exchange Online supports two types of resource mailbox, room mailboxes and equipment mailboxes.

- External contacts allow you to add people with email addresses from outside your organization to your internal address books.

- Distribution groups allow users to send email messages to a single address and have those messages forwarded to all members of the distribution group.

- Exchange Online supports distribution groups, mail-enabled security groups, and dynamic distribution groups.

- In-place archives allow for extra email storage.

- Once you enable an archive, messages that are in a user's Exchange Online mailbox that exceed two years of age will automatically be transferred to the archive by the default retention policy.

- Users are able to manually move messages to the archive or can create inbox rules that automatically move messages that match the rules to the archive.

- Retention tags include a retention action and a retention period.

- Retention action specifies whether the tag deletes and allows recovery, permanently deletes, or moves the message to the archive.

- Retention period defines the number of days that must pass before the tag triggers.

- The Default MRM Policy is always the default retention policy applied automatically to new users.

- Presence settings determine who is able to see when a user is available, in a meeting, or out of office in Skype for Business Online.

- You can allow presence information to be displayed to any user not in the external or blocked privacy group or choose to have presence information only displayed to a user's contacts.

- External communication settings allow you to configure whether users can add Skype for Business or Skype users external to your organization to their list of business contacts.

- You can configure audio and video and conversation recording settings on a per-user basis.

- You can configure whether Skype for Business Online non-archived features are disabled to meet compliance requirements.

CHAPTER 4

Plan for Exchange Online and Skype for Business Online

For many organizations, the default settings for Exchange Online and Skype for Business Online within an Office 365 tenancy don't require much attention or modification. This is because the default configuration of these services does what the tenants needs them to do. For other users, it is necessary to tune the settings on these services to better meet organizational requirements. In this chapter, you'll read about configuring anti-spam and anti-malware policies, determining an appropriate mailbox migration strategy, performing compliance operations, and managing settings at a tenancy level for Skype for Business Online.

Skills in this chapter:

- Skill 4.1: Manage anti-malware and anti-spam policies
- Skill 4.2: Recommend a mailbox migration strategy
- Skill 4.3: Plan for Exchange Online
- Skill 4.4: Manage Skype for Business global external communications settings

Skill 4.1: Manage anti-malware and anti-spam policies

This skill deals with the Exchange Online anti-malware and anti-spam functionality. You manage this functionality through the configuration of anti-malware and spam filter policies. These policies determine what action Exchange Online will take with spam and malware as it passes through the service.

> **This skill covers the following topics:**
> - Anti-malware policies
> - Spam filter policies
> - Outbound spam policy
> - Release quarantine
> - Advanced threat protection

Anti-malware policies

Anti-malware policies allow you to block incoming malware from reaching user inboxes. Anti-malware policies also allow you to stop your own users from inadvertently sending malware to other people in your organization or others on the Internet. Anti-malware policies are part of an in-depth defense strategy. Users in your organization are far less likely to be infected by malware transmitted through email messages if malware is being purged by Exchange Online, as well as by an anti-malware solution installed on the client computer.

> *MORE INFO* **ANTI-MALWARE POLICIES**
>
> You can learn more about anti-malware policies at *https://technet.microsoft.com/en-us/library/jj200745(v=exchg.150).aspx*.

Malware detection response

The malware detection response settings determine what happens when malware is detected in a message attachment on inbound and outbound messages. When malware is detected, the message is automatically quarantined. Only an administrator can release a message from quarantine. Because the malware engine occasionally generates false positives, you may wish to notify users if a message sent to them is flagged as containing malware. You can do this with the Malware Detection Response settings shown in Figure 4-1.

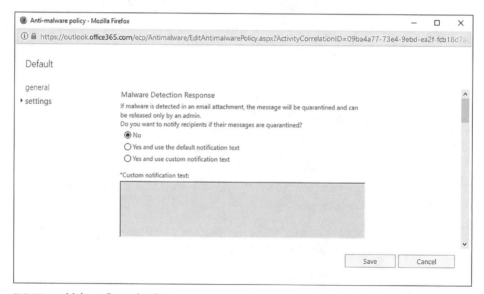

FIGURE 4-1 Malware Detection Response

You can configure the following options:

- **No** No notification is sent to the recipient.

- **Yes And Use The Default Notification Text** A notification using the default notification text is sent to the recipient.
- **Yes And Use Custom Notification Text** A notification using custom notification text is sent to the recipient.

Anti-malware notifications

Notifications allow you to configure whether the sender of the message in which malware is detected is notified and whether administrators are notified. Notifications are only sent when the entire message is deleted. The notification language is dependent on the location of the message being processed. You can choose the following options, shown in Figure 4-2:

- **Notify Internal Senders** Sends a message to a sender from within your organization who sends a message in which malware is detected.
- **Notify External Senders** Sends a message to a sender external to your organization who sends a message to someone inside your organization in which malware is detected.
- **Notify Administrators About Undelivered Messages From Internal Senders** Allows you to have an administrator sent a message about messages from internal senders in which malware is detected. You need to provide the administrator email address.
- **Notify Administrators About Undelivered Messages From External Senders** Allows you to have an administrator sent a message about messages from external senders in which malware is detected. You need to provide the administrator email address.

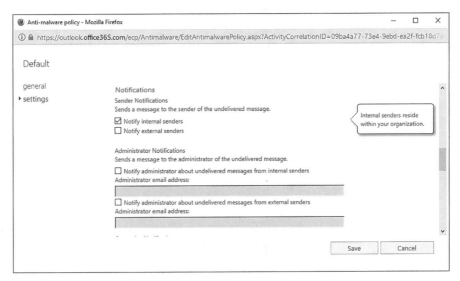

FIGURE 4-2 Notifications Settings

The default notification text is as follows "This message was created automatically by mail delivery software. Your email message was not delivered to the intended recipients because malware was detected." If you don't want to use the default notification text, you can create your own custom notification text by configuring the following settings, shown in Figure 4-3. These settings are only available if the relevant notifications are configured.

- **From Name** The name that the email message appears to be from.
- **From Address** The email address the message appears to originate from.
- **Messages From Internal Senders** The subject and the message sent to internal senders who have messages deleted by the anti-malware policy.
- **Messages From External Senders** The subject and the message sent to external senders who have messages deleted by the anti-malware policy.

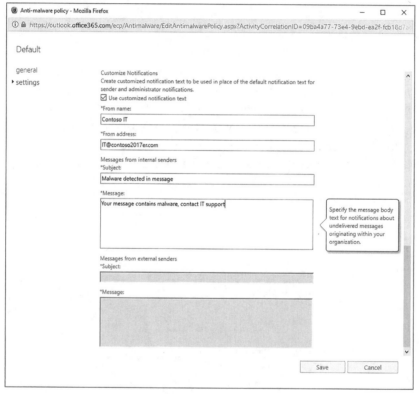

FIGURE 4-3 Customized notifications

Review default anti-malware policy

To review the default anti-malware policy, perform the following steps:

1. In the Office 365 Admin Center, click Exchange under Admin Centers.

2. In Exchange Admin Center, click Protection, and then click Malware Filter. Figure 4-4 shows the Default anti-malware policy selected.

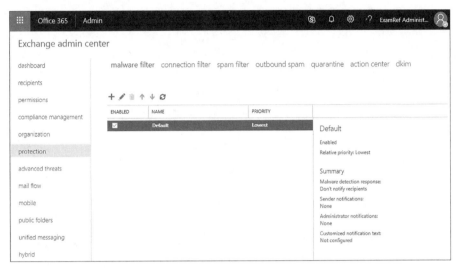

FIGURE 4-4 Default Malware Filter policies

3. With the Default policy selected, click the edit (Pencil) icon on the toolbar. This opens the Anti-Malware Policy properties page. The General section, shown in Figure 4-5, shows the policy Name and Description.

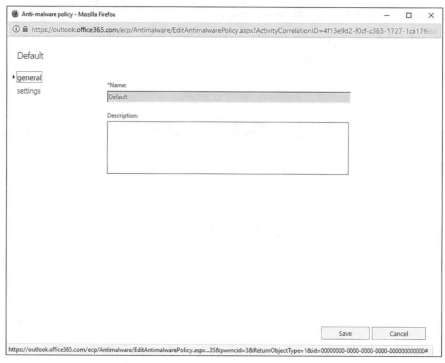

FIGURE 4-5 Default Policy

4. On the Settings page, you can configure the following settings:

- Malware Detection Response
- Notifications
- Administrator Notifications
- Customize Notifications

Create an anti-malware policy

You can create different anti-malware policies and then apply them to different groups of mail users. For example, you might wish to have an anti-malware policy for one group of users that provides notifications to the user if malware is detected and a message is purged, and another policy that sends notifications to an administrator if malware is detected and the message purged.

When creating a new custom anti-malware policy, you need to configure the Applied To setting. This setting takes the form of an If statement with a condition and exceptions. As Figure 4-6 shows, the If conditions can include:

- **The Recipient Is**   Use this to specify a specific recipient.
- **The Recipient Domain Is**   Use this to specify the recipient's mail domain.

- **The Recipient IS A Member Of** Use this to specify a recipient group.

FIGURE 4-6 Select condition

The exceptions are the same and include:

- **The Recipient Is** Use this to specify a specific recipient.
- **The Recipient Domain Is** Use this to specify the recipient's mail domain.
- **The Recipient Is A Member Of** Use this to specify a recipient group.

You can create as many conditions as you want, as long as those conditions are unique. For example, Figure 4-7 shows a set of conditions that apply if the recipient is a member of the Accounting group, the recipient domain is contoso2017er.com, and if the recipient is Dan Jump or Don Funk.

FIGURE 4-7 Policy conditions

To create a new anti-malware policy, perform the following steps:

1. In the Office 365 Admin Center, click Exchange under Admin Centers.
2. In Exchange Admin Center, click Protection, and then click Malware Filter.

3. Click the Plus (+) icon. This opens the New Anti-Malware Policy page, shown in Figure 4-8. Provide the following information:

- Policy Name
- Policy Description
- Malware Detection Response
- Notification Settings
- Applies To Settings

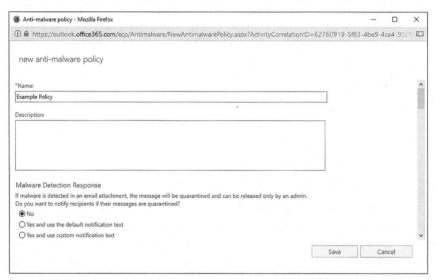

FIGURE 4-8 New anti-malware policy

When you have multiple policies, you can use the Malware Filter list to determine which apply and in which order they apply. The policy with the number closest to zero applies first. If the conditions of a message don't match the first policy, it moves to the next policy until it encounters the Default policy. If any malware filter policies are configured, as shown in Figure 4-9, Example Policy is applied first, and then Another Example Policy, and then finally the Default policy. You can use the arrows to change the priority assigned to each policy.

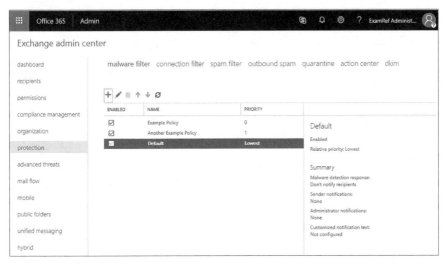

FIGURE 4-9 Policy priorities

Windows PowerShell anti-malware policy cmdlets

There are a number of Windows PowerShell cmdlets that you can use to manage filter policies and malware filter rules. Filter rules determine the conditions under which a malware filter policy applies. For example, you might have one malware filter policy that applies to recipients in one recipient domain and another malware filter policy that applies to recipients in another recipient domain. The Windows PowerShell anti-malware policy cmdlets are as follows:

- **Get-MalwareFilterPolicy**   This cmdlet allows you to view malware filter policy settings.
- **Set-MalwareFilterPolicy**   This cmdlet allows you to modify malware filter policy settings.
- **New-MalwareFilterPolicy**   Allows you to create a new custom malware filter policy. This includes configuring an action, either blocking a message, replacing attachments with the default alert, or with a custom alert, and configuring notification settings.
- **Remove-MalwareFilterPolicy**   This cmdlet allows you to remove a custom filter policy.
- **New-MalwareFilterRule**   Use this cmdlet to create a new filter rule that can be applied to a custom policy. For example, you could use this cmdlet to apply a specific malware filter policy named ContosoExamplePolicy when the email recipient is in the contoso.com domain.
- **Set-MalwareFilterRule**   Use this cmdlet to edit an existing malware filter rule. For example, to change a rule so that it applies a specific policy to recipients in more than one email domain.
- **Enable-MalwareFilterRule**   Use this cmdlet to turn on a malware filter rule.
- **Disable-MalwareFilterRule**   Allows you to turn off a malware filter rule.

Connection filter policies

Connection filter policies let you always allow email from trusted senders and always block email from known spammers. Exchange Online only supports the default connection filter policy. You configure connection filters by configuring an IP Allow list and an IP block list, as shown in Figure 4-10.

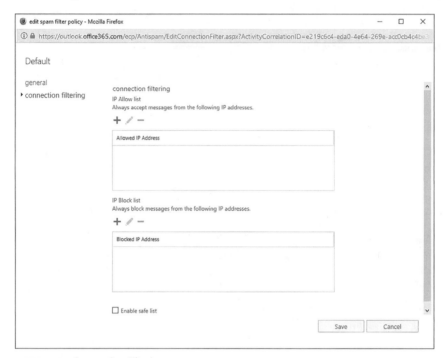

FIGURE 4-10 Connection Filtering

When configuring connection filters, you can also enable the Safe List check box. When you enable this check box, your connection filter allows messages from a list of third-party sources of trusted senders to which Microsoft subscribes.

When adding an IP address list, you can either specify the IP address directly, or use CIDR notation in the form xxx.xxx.xxx.xxx/yy, where yy is a number between 24 and 32. You can specify a maximum of 1,273 separate entries, where an entry is either a single IP address or a CIDR range. IPv6 addresses are supported for TLS encrypted messages. You enter allowed IP addresses on the Allowed IP Address WebPage Dialog, shown in Figure 4-11.

FIGURE 4-11 Allowed IP address

You enter blocked IP address ranges on the Blocked IP Address webpage dialog box, as shown in Figure 4-12.

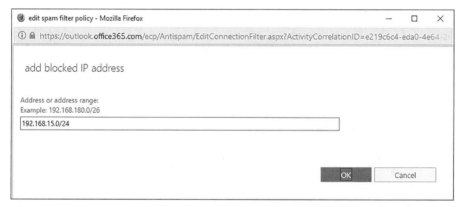

FIGURE 4-12 Add Blocked IP Address

If an IP address is added to both the allow list and the block list, email from that IP address will be allowed.

To edit the default connection filter policy, perform the following steps:

1. In the Office 365 Admin Center, click Exchange under Admin Centers.

2. In Exchange Admin Center, click Protection, and then click Connection Filter.

3. With the Default policy selected, click the Edit (Pencil) icon.

4. Click the Connection Filtering tab to access the IP Allow list, the IP Block list, and the Enable Safe List option, as shown in Figure 4-13.

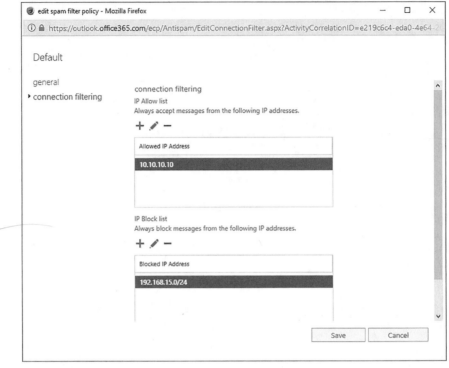

FIGURE 4-13 IP Allow and block lists

You can use the following Windows PowerShell cmdlets to managed the connection filter policy:

- **Get-HostedConnectionFilterPolicy**   Use this cmdlet when you want to review the default policy settings.

- **Set-HostedConnectionFilterPolicy**   Use this cmdlet to configure the connection filter policy settings. This cmdlet includes the `IPAllowLIst` and `IPBlockList` parameters.

> **MORE INFO**   **CONNECTION FILTER POLICIES**
>
> You can learn more about connection filter policies at: *https://technet.microsoft.com/en-us/library/jj200718(v=exchg.150).aspx*.

Spam filter policies

Spam filter policies allow you to configure how incoming messages are categorized, including which characteristics a message might have that means you want flagged as spam. The default policy applies to all users in the company. You can also configure custom policies that apply to specific users, groups, and domains within the organization.

You configure spam filter policies on the Spam Filter tab of the Protection section in Exchange Admin Center, as shown in Figure 4-14. You can have multiple policies as long as each policy has a different set of conditions. The highest priority policy that has conditions that match a message will apply. When there are multiple custom policies, you can adjust their priority using the arrow buttons in the Exchange Admin Center.

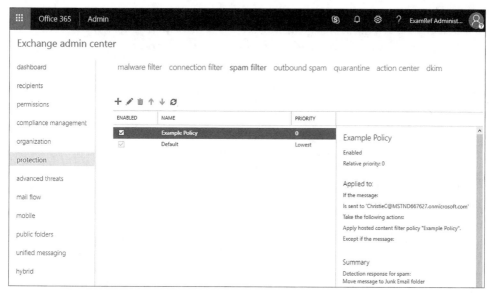

FIGURE 4-14 Policy priority

MORE INFO **SPAM FILTER POLICIES**

You can learn more about spam filter policies at: *https://technet.microsoft.com/en-us/library/jj200684(v=exchg.150).aspx.*

Spam and bulk actions

When configuring the default policy or creating a custom policy, you need to configure which actions to take for messages that are likely to be spam and messages that are almost certainly spam.

You can choose from the following options for messages that are likely to be spam and for messages that are almost certainly spam:

- **Move Message To Junk Email Folder**   This is the default, with messages moved to each user's junk email folder.
- **Quarantine Message**   When this setting is chosen, messages are moved to a quarantine folder for up to 15 days before being deleted. Being moved to quarantine allows someone to review the message so that they can determine whether or not it is actually

spam. For example, you might choose to quarantine messages that are likely to be spam and delete messages that are almost certainly spam.

- **Delete Message**   When this setting is chosen, the message and any attachments are simply deleted.

You can also configure whether bulk email is marked as spam and the threshold that should be applied to bulk email. Setting the threshold as 1 will have almost all bulk email treated as spam and a setting of 9 will allow almost all bulk email to be delivered. A setting of 7 is the default. The Spam And Bulk Actions tab of a spam filter policy is shown in Figure 4-15.

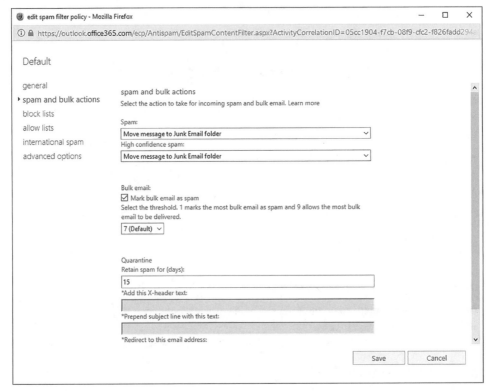

FIGURE 4-15 Spam And Bulk Actions

Spam filter block lists

The block lists setting of a spam filter policy, shown in Figure 4-16, allows you to block email messages from specific email addresses or specific email domains. When a message comes from a blocked sender or a blocked domain, it is subject to the high confidence spam action configured in the spam and bulk actions section of the policy.

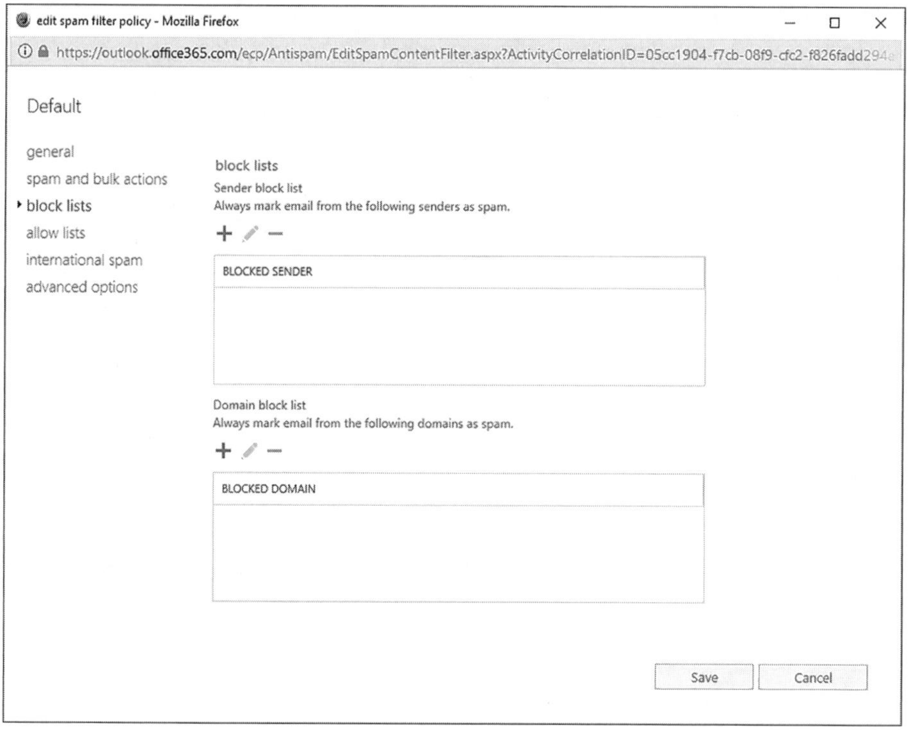

FIGURE 4-16 Block Lists

If you want to block all messages from a specific email address, you can add that email address to the blocked sender list. Figure 4-17 shows the email address don.funk@adatum.com being added to this list. The owner of the email address added to the list will not be notified that their email messages are being categorized as spam.

FIGURE 4-17 Block sender

You can add entire mail domains to a block list using the Add Blocked Domain dialog box shown in Figure 4-18. You should be as specific as possible when adding domains. If you add a top level domain, such as .com or .org to this list, all email messages that come from .com or .org addresses are marked as spam.

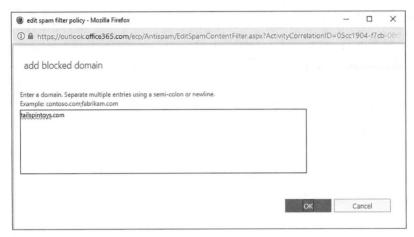

FIGURE 4-18 Blocked Domain

Spam filter allow lists

Spam filter allow lists provide you with a way of ensuring that email messages from specific users or from specific domains will always be delivered to users in your organization. When configuring Allow Lists in a spam filter policy, you configure the Sender Allow List for specific email addresses and the Domain Allow List for specific email domains. The Allow Lists section of the spam filter policy is shown in Figure 4-19.

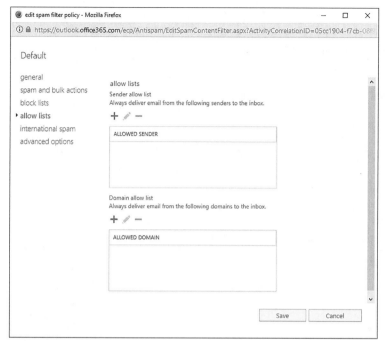

FIGURE 4-19 Allow Lists

You add users to the Allow List using the Add Allowed Sender dialog box, as shown in Figure 4-20. To separate email address entries, use a semicolon.

FIGURE 4-20 Allowed Sender

You Add Allowed Domains on the Add Allowed Domain dialog box, shown in Figure 4-21. You should be as specific as possible and not add generic top-level domains such as .com or .org because this allows email from all .com and .org domains.

FIGURE 4-21 Allowed Domain

International spam

The International Spam settings, shown in Figure 4-22, allow you to filter messages based on the message language and the country or region from which the message is sent.

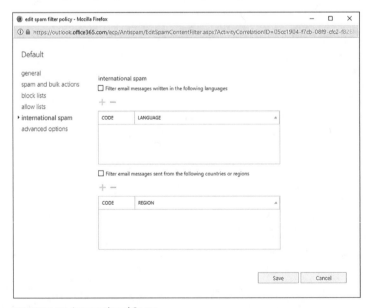

FIGURE 4-22 International Spam

When blocking message content on the basis of language, you enable the Filter Email Messages Written In The Following Languages option, and then specify the languages you want to filter on the Select Language dialog box, as shown in Figure 4-23.

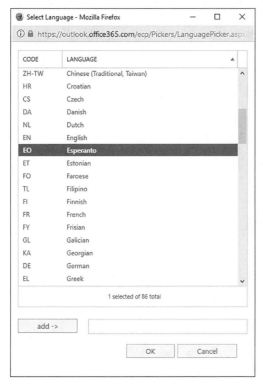

FIGURE 4-23 Select language

To block messages from specific regions, enable the Filter Email Messages Sent From The Following Countries Or Regions option, and then specify the countries or regions that you want to filter out on the Select Region dialog box, as shown in Figure 4-24.

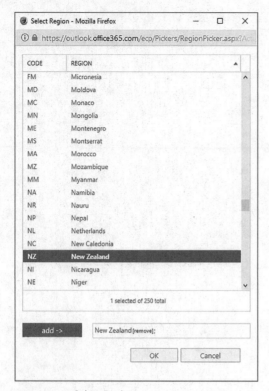

FIGURE 4-24 Select Region

Advanced policy options

Advanced policy options, shown in Figure 4-25, allow you to toggle specific options that either increase the spam score, making it more likely that Exchange Online will recognize the message as spam, or simply mark the message as spam directly.

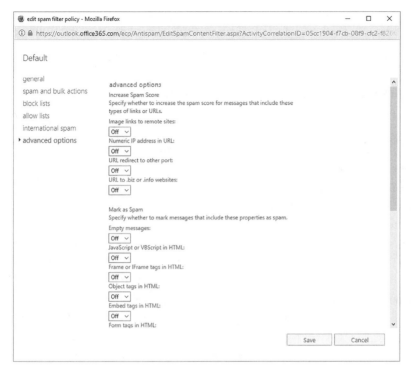

FIGURE 4-25 Advanced Options

You can configure the policy to increase the spam score if the message includes the following types of links or URLs:

- **Image Links To Remote Sites**   Triggered if the message contains HTML content with an IMG tag linked to an image on a remote site.

- **Numeric IP Address In URL**   Triggered if the message has an URL with a numeric IP address.

- **URL Redirect To Other Port**   Triggered if the message contains a hyperlink that redirects to a port other than port 80, port 8080, or port 443.

- **URL To .Biz Or .Info Websites**   Triggered if the message contains a URL that includes the .biz or .info suffix.

You can configure the policy to mark a message as spam under the following conditions:

- **Empty Messages**   Triggered if the body and subject line are both empty and there is no attachment.

- **JavaScript Or VBScript In HTML**   Triggered if either JavaScript or VBScript is present in the HTML included in the message.

- **Frame Or IFrame Tags In HTML**   Triggered if the HTML code in the message includes the Frame or IFrame tags.

- **Object Tags In HTML**   Triggered if the HTML code in the message contains the <Object> tag.

- **Embed Tags In HTML**   Triggered if the HTML code in the message contains the <Embed> tag.

- **Form Tags In HTML**   Triggered if the HTML code in the message contains the <Form> tag.

- **Web Bugs In HTML**   Triggered if the message contains a web bug. Web bugs are small, usually one pixel by one pixel graphic images that are used to determine whether an email message has been read.

- **Apply Sensitive Word List**   Triggered if a word on the sensitive word list is present in the message. These words are associated with messages that are likely to be offensive. Administrators cannot edit the sensitive word list.

- **SPF Record: Hard Fail**   Triggered if the message fails a Sender Protection Framework (SPF) check. This means that the message was received from an IP address not listed in the SPF record. Used by organizations concerned about phishing messages.

- **Conditional Sender ID Filtering: Hard Fail**   Triggered if the message fails a conditional sender ID check, which combines an SPF check with a Sender ID check to protect against messages where the sender header is forged.

- **NDR Backscatter**   If you don't enable this setting, Non Delivery Reports (NDRs) go through spam filtering.

> **MORE INFO   ADVANCED SPAM FILTERING OPTIONS**
>
> You can learn more about advanced spam filtering options at *https://technet.microsoft.com/ en-us/library/jj200750(v=exchg.150).aspx*.

Spam confidence levels

When a new message passes through the Exchange Online spam filtering algorithms, it is assigned a spam score. This spam score maps to a Spam Confidence Level (SCL) rating and is stamped in an X-Header for the message. Exchange Online performs actions on messages based on the SCL rating.

TABLE 4-1 SCL ratings

SCL rating	Meaning	Action
-1	Message coming from a sender, recipient, or IP address listed as trusted	Delivered to recipient
0,1	Message unlikely to be spam	Delivered to recipient
5,6	Message likely to be spam	Determined by filter policy setting for spam
7,8,9	Message very likely to be spam	Determined by filter policy setting for high confidence spam

You can have Exchange manually set an SCL rating for a message using a transport rule, but transport rules are not addressed by the 70-347 exam.

> **MORE INFO**   **SPAM CONFIDENCE LEVELS**
>
> You can learn more about spam confidence levels at: *https://technet.microsoft.com/en-us/ library/JJ200686(v=EXCHG.150).aspx*.

Applying spam filter policies

When creating a new custom spam filter policy, you need to configure the Applied To setting. This setting determines which recipients the policy applies. This setting takes the form of an If statement with a condition and exceptions. As is the case with anti-malware policies, the If conditions can include:

- The Recipient Is
- The Recipient Domain Is
- The Recipient Is A Member Of

The exceptions are the same and include:

- The Recipient Is
- The Recipient Domain Is
- The Recipient Is A Member Of

You can create as many conditions as you want, as long as those conditions are unique. For example, Figure 4-26 shows a set of condition that will apply if the recipient domain is conto-so2017er.com, the recipient is a member of the Accounting group, and the recipient is not Don Funk.

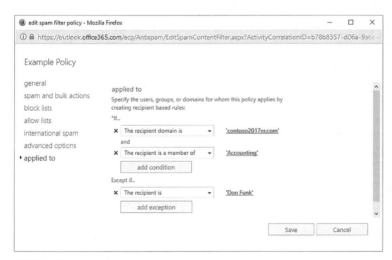

FIGURE 4-26   Applied To

Spam filter Windows PowerShell cmdlets

You can use the following PowerShell commands to configure spam filter policies:

- **Get-HostedContentFilterPolicy**   This allows you to view existing spam filter settings.
- **Set-HostedContentFilterPolicy**   Use this cmdlet to edit spam filter settings, including the recipients to which the spam filter policy applies.
- **New-HostedContentFilterPolicy**   Use this cmdlet to create a new custom spam filter policy.
- **Remove-HostedContentFilterPolicy**   This cmdlet allows you to remove a custom spam filter policy.

Outbound spam policy

The Outbound Spam policy blocks users inside of the organization from sending spam to recipients outside of the organization. If an outbound message is suspected to be spam, it is sent through the higher risk delivery pool. Using the higher risk delivery pool reduces the likelihood that the IP address of the normal outbound delivery pool will be added to a block list by real-time block list providers.

By configuring the default Outbound Spam policy, you can specify whether:

- A copy of all suspicious messages is forwarded to one or more email addresses for review.
- A notification is sent to one or more email addresses when a sender is blocked for sending outbound spam.

You can configure the default outbound spam policy by performing the following steps:

1. In the Office 365 Admin Center, click Exchange under Admin Centers.
2. In Exchange Admin Center, click Protection, and then click Outbound Spam.
3. Ensure that the Default policy is selected, as shown in Figure 4-27, and then click the Edit (Pencil) icon.

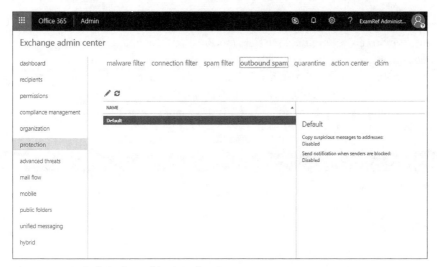

FIGURE 4-27 Default Outbound Spam policy

4. On the Outbound Spam Preferences page, shown in Figure 4-28, configure whether a copy of all suspicious messages is forwarded to one or more email addresses for review, and whether a notification is sent to one or more email addresses when a sender is blocked for sending outbound spam.

FIGURE 4-28 Outbound Spam Preferences

MORE INFO **OUTBOUND SPAM POLICY**

You can learn more about the outbound spam policy at: *https://technet.microsoft.com/en-us/library/jj200737(v=exchg.150).aspx.*

Quarantine

Content filtering can be configured to send messages to Quarantine rather than to a recipient's junk email folder, or to simply delete them. Messages sent to Quarantine can be viewed in the Quarantine section of the Exchange Admin Center, as shown in Figure 4-29. Messages in Quarantine remain there until released by an administrator or until they are automatically deleted when the Quarantine period expires. The maximum Quarantine period for messages recognized as spam is 15 days.

FIGURE 4-29 Quarantine

Administrators can use the Quarantine section of the Exchange Admin Center to search for quarantined messages and to release messages to their intended recipients. When releasing a message, an administrator can choose between the following options:

- **Release The Message Without Reporting It As A False Positive**   When you select this option, you can choose to release the message to some or all of the message's original recipients.

- **Release The Message And Report It As A False Positive**   If you choose this option, the message is released to all recipients. The message is also reported to the Microsoft Spam Analysis team, which might use the false positive result to adjust content filter rules across Exchange Online.

You can use the following Windows PowerShell cmdlets to manage quarantine:

- **Get-QuarantineMessage**   Allows you to search for messages in quarantine. For example use the following command to find all messages from the adatum.com email domain:

```
Get-QuarantineMessage | ? {$_.Senderaddress -like "*@adatum.com"}
```

- **Release-QuarantineMessage**   Allows you to release a message from quarantine. Use the `ReleaseToAll` parameter to allow the message.

Advanced Threat Protection

Advanced Threat Protection (ATP) provides Office 365 with the ability to protect your organization from attacks through email. ATP analyzes email messages and their attachments for malicious content. There are three primary methods through which ATP provides protection, safe links, safe attachments, and spoof intelligence. ATP is available for Office 365 Enterprise E5 subscriptions.

Safe links policies

Safe links policies allow you to protect your organization from URLs in messages or attached Office documents that might be used for phishing and other attacks. When you configure a safe link policy, URLs that Microsoft knows to be malicious are blocked as well as any custom URLs that you add to a safe link policy. To configure a safe links policy, the user creating the policy must be a member of the Hygiene Management or Organization Management role groups.

   To configure a safe link policy that applies to the entire organization, perform the following steps:

1. In the Office 365 Admin Center, click Security And Compliance under Admin Centers.

2. In the Security & Compliance Center, under Thread Management, choose Policy. Click Safe Links.

3. In the Safe Links policies area, select the Default policy, shown in Figure 4-30, and click the Edit (pencil) icon.

FIGURE 4-30 Safe links

4. In the Safe Links Policy For Your Organization dialog box, shown in Figure 4-31, choose from the following options:

FIGURE 4-31 Safe links policy

- **Block The Following URLS** Allows you to block a custom set of addresses in addition to URLs known to be malicious.
- **Office 365 ProPlus, Office For iOS And Android** ATP safe link policies apply to hyperlinks in documents open in Office 365 applications.
- **Do Not Track When Users Click Safe Links** Data about URLs that are encountered by ATP is not stored.
- **Don't Let Users Click Through Safe Links To Original URLs** Blocks users form clicking past the ATP warning to the URL that has been blocked.

5. Click Save.

You can also configure safe link policies that apply to specific users rather than to the entire organization. To configure a safe link policy that applies to a specific set of recipients, in the Policies that apply to specific recipients section, create a new policy and specify the recipients. Recipient policies override the default policy that applies to all recipients. You can choose from the following options shown in Figure 4-32:

FIGURE 4-32 Safe links policy for specific recipients

- **Off**   Will not scan links in email messages. Use when you want to exempt a user from a safe links policy.
- **On**   Rewrites URLs so that users are routed through ATP safe link protection. This service compares the URL with Microsoft's list of malicious URLs as well as the custom block list.
- **Use Safe Attachments To Scan Downloadable Content**   Hyperlinks in attachments are scanned and compared against ATP safe links.
- **Do Not Track When User Clicks Safe Links**   Click data for URLs is not stored.
- **Don't Let Users Click Through Safe Links To Original URLs**   Blocks users form clicking past the ATP warning to the URL that has been blocked.
- **Do Not Rewrite The Following URLs**   Leaves specific URLs as they presented in original message.
- **Applied To**   Allows you to specify conditions under which the safe links policy applies.

> *MORE INFO*   **SAFE LINKS POLICIES**
>
> You can learn more about safe links policies at *https://support.office.com/en-us/article/Set-up-Office-365-ATP-safe-links-policies-bdd5372d-775e-4442-9c1b-609627b94b5d.*

Safe attachments policies

Safe attachment policies allow Office 365 administrators to manage how attachments that may contain malware might be treated. Safe attachment policies are configured for specific recipients and take precedence over the default malware policies. Like safe link policies, safe attachments policies are only available with an Office 365 Enterprise E5 subscription. A safe attachment policy is shown in Figure 4-33.

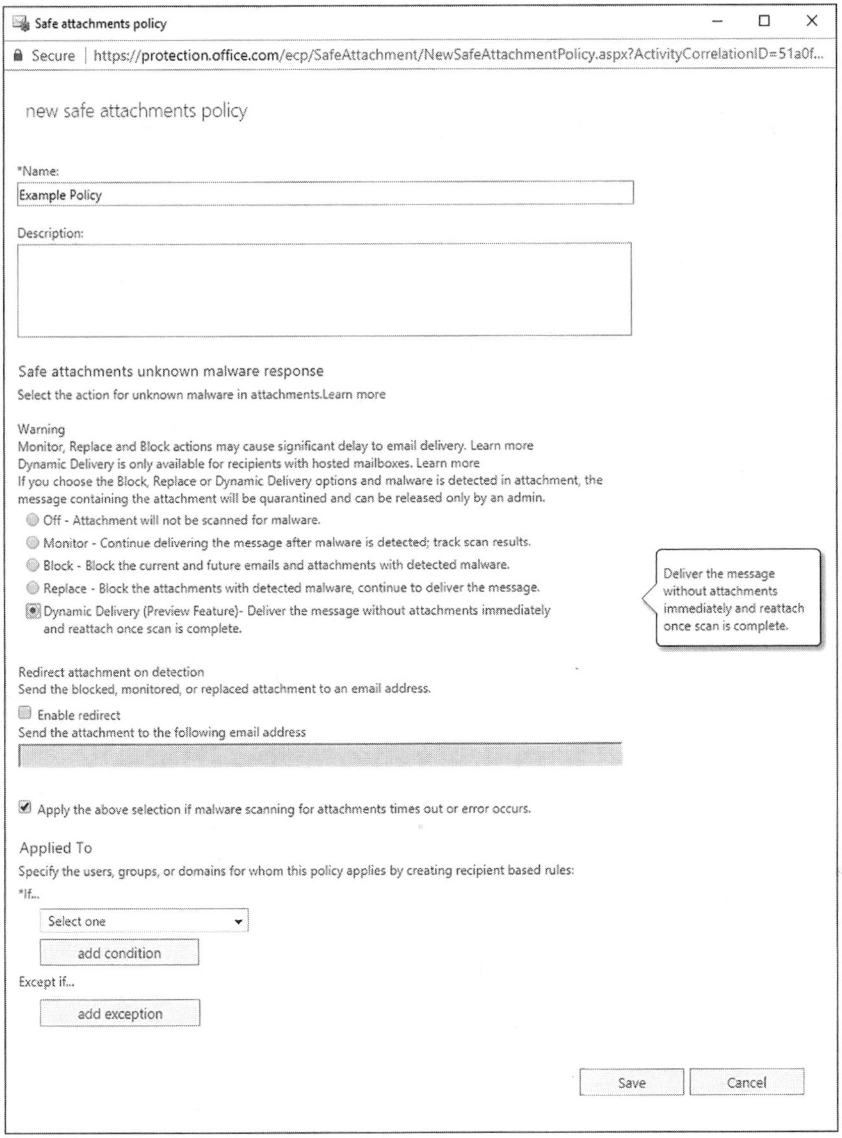

FIGURE 4-33 Safe attachments policy

The options in a safe attachment policy includes the following option:

- **Off**   Do not scan attachments from internal senders for malware.

- **Monitor**   Delivers messages that have attachments identified as containing malware. Monitors what happens next.

- **Block**   Blocks messages identified as containing malware. Malware is sent to quarantine for review. Future messages and attachments containing the same identified malware are automatically blocked.

- **Replace**   Removes attachments identified as containing malware. Message body is delivered.

- **Dynamic Delivery**   Message body is delivered immediately, attachments are delivered after being scanned and deemed safe.

- **Enable Redirect**   Forwards problematic attachments to a specific email address.

> **MORE INFO   SAFE ATTACHMENTS POLICIES**
>
> You can learn more about safe attachments policies at: *https://support.office.com/en-ie/article/Set-up-ATP-safe-attachments-policies-in-Office-365-078eb946-819a-4e13-8673-fe-0c0ad3a775.*

EXAM TIP

Remember the Windows PowerShell cmdlets used to manage anti-malware policies and spam settings.

Skill 4.2: Recommend a mailbox migration strategy

This skill deals with migrating mailboxes from an on-premises messaging solution, which in most cases will be Microsoft Exchange, to Exchange Online. To master this skill, you'll need to understand the different migration options and the conditions why you would choose one migration method over another.

> **This skill covers the following topics:**
> - Remote move migration
> - Staged migration
> - Cutover migration
> - IMAP migration
> - Migration comparison

Remote move migration method

You use a remote move migration when you have an Exchange hybrid deployment. A hybrid deployment is where you have coexistence between an on-premises Exchange deployment and an Exchange Online deployment. You have to use a hybrid deployment and use the remote move migration method when you need to migrate more than 2,000 Exchange Server 2010, Exchange Server 2013, or Exchange Server 2016 mailboxes to Exchange Online.

With a hybrid deployment, you get the following advantages:

- User accounts are managed through your on-premises tools.
- Directory synchronization connects your on-premises Exchange organization with Exchange Online.
- Users are able to use single-sign on to access their mailbox whether the mailbox is hosted in the on-premises Exchange organization or Exchange Online.
- Email is routed securely between the on-premises Exchange deployment and Exchange Online.
- Free/busy calendar sharing between users with mailboxes hosted in the on-premises Exchange organization and mailboxes hosted in Exchange Online.

Prior to performing a remote move migration you need to ensure the following prerequisites are met:

- A hybrid deployment has already been configured between your on-premises Exchange organization and Exchange Online.
- You need to have been assigned the appropriate permissions. For mailbox moves in a hybrid deployment, this means that you need to have an account that is a member of the Organization Management, or the Recipient Management role groups.
- You need to have deployed the Mailbox Replication Proxy Service (MRSProxy) on all on-premises Exchange 2013 or Exchange 2016 Client Access servers.

Once these prerequisites have been met, you can move mailboxes from your on-premises Exchange deployment to Exchange Online by performing the following steps:

1. **Create migration endpoint**   Migration endpoints host connection settings for an on-premises Exchange server running the MRS proxy service.

2. **Enable MRSProxy service**   The MRSProxy service is hosted on on-premises Client Access servers. This service can be enabled using Exchange Administration Console by selecting the Client Access server, editing the properties of the EWS virtual directory, and ensuring that the MRS Proxy enabled check box is selected.

3. **Move mailboxes**   You can move mailboxes using the Office 365 tab in EAC on the on-premises Exchange server by creating a new migration batch in Exchange Admin Console, or by using Windows PowerShell. When moving mailboxes, you move some, not all mailboxes, at a time in groups, which are termed batches.

4. **Remove completed migration batches**   Once migration of a batch is complete, remove the migration batch using Exchange Administration Center, or Windows Power-Shell.

5. **Re-enable offline access for Outlook Web App**   If users have been migrated from on-premises Exchange Server to Office 365, it is necessary to reset the offline access setting in their browser.

MORE INFO   **REMOTE MOVE MIGRATION**

You can learn more about remote move migrations at: *https://support.office.com/en-us/ article/Ways-to-migrate-multiple-email-accounts-to-Office-365-0a4913fe-60fb-498f- 9155-a86516418842?ui=en-US&rs=en-US&ad=US#remotemove.*

Staged migration method

In a staged migration, you migrate mailboxes from your on-premises Exchange organization to Office 365 in groups, termed batches. You would select a staged migration in the following circumstances:

- Your organization has more than 2,000 on-premises mailboxes hosted in Exchange 2007.

- Your organization intends to completely move its messaging infrastructure to Office 365.

- Your available migration period is in the timeframe of several weeks to several months.

- After migration completes, you still manage user accounts using on-premises manage- ment tools and have account synchronization performed with Azure Active Directory.

- The primary domain name used for your on-premises Exchange organization must be configured as a domain associated with the tenancy in Office 365.

Staged migration involves the following general steps:

1. You create a CSV file that includes a row for every user who has an on-premises mailbox that you want to migrate. This is not every user in the organization, just those who you will migrate in a particular batch.

2. Create a staged migration batch using Exchange Admin Center, or using Windows PowerShell.

3. Trigger the migration batch. Once the migration batch is triggered, Exchange Online performs the following steps:

    - Verify that directory synchronization is enabled and functioning. Directory synchro- nization migrates distribution groups, contacts, and mail enabled users.

    - Verifies that a mail-enabled user exists in Office 365 for every user listed in the batch CSV file.

    - Converts the Office 365 mail-enabled user to an Exchange Online mailbox for each user in the migration batch.

    - Configures mail forwarding for the on-premises mailbox.

4. Once these steps have been completed, Exchange Online sends you a status report informing you of which mailboxes have migrated successfully and which mailboxes have not migrated successfully. Successfully migrated users can start using Exchange Online mailboxes.

5. Once migration is successful, you convert the mailboxes of successfully migrated on-premises users to mail-enabled users in the on-premises Exchange deployment.

6. You configure a new batch of users to migrate and delete the current migration batch.

7. Once all users have been migrated, the administrator assigns licenses to Office 365 users, configures MX records to point to Exchange online, and creates an Autodiscover record that points to Office 365.

8. Decommission the on-premises Exchange deployment.

> **MORE INFO** **STAGED MIGRATION METHOD**
>
> You can learn more about staged migrations at *https://support.office.com/en-us/article/ What-you-need-to-know-about-a-staged-email-migration-to-Office-365-7e2c82be- 5f3d-4e36-bc6b-e5b4d411e207.*

Cutover migration method

In a cutover migration, all mailboxes in an on-premises Exchange deployment are migrated to Office 365 in a single migration batch. Cutover migrations migrate global mail contacts as well as distribution groups. Cutover migrations are suitable when:

- You intend all mailboxes to be hosted in Office 365 when the migration completes.

- You intend to manage user accounts using Office 365 tools.

- You want to perform the migration period in less than a week.

- Your organization has less than 2,000 mailboxes.

- Your on-premises messaging solution is Exchange Server 2007 or later. Exchange Server 2003 reached the end of extended support in April 2014 and Exchange Server 2007 on April 11, 2017.

- The primary domain name used for your on-premises Exchange organization must be configured as domain associated with the tenancy in Office 365.

You can perform a cutover migration using the Exchange Admin Center or by using Windows PowerShell.

The cutover migration method involves the following general steps:

1. An administrator creates empty mail-enabled security groups in Office 365.

2. An administrator connects Office 365 to the on-premises Exchange deployment. This is also termed creating a migration endpoint.

3. An administrator creates and starts a cutover migration batch using Exchange Admin Center or Windows PowerShell.

4. Once the migration batch is triggered, Exchange Online performs the following steps:

   - The address book of the on-premises Exchange deployment is queried to identify mailboxes, distribution groups, and contacts.

   - New Exchange Online mailboxes are provisioned.

   - Distribution groups and contacts are created within Exchange Online.

   - Mailbox data, including email messages, contacts, and calendar items, are migrated from each on-premises mailbox to the corresponding Exchange Online mailbox.

5. Exchange Online forwards the administrator a report providing statistics including the number of successful and failed migrations. The migration report includes automatically generated passwords for each new Exchange Online mailbox. Users are forced to change passwords the first time they sign in to Office 365.

6. Incremental synchronization occurs every 24 hours, updating Exchange Online with any new items created in the on-premises mailboxes.

7. Once migration issues have been resolved, the administrator changes the MX records to point to Exchange Online.

8. Once mail flow to Exchange Online has been successfully established, the administrator deletes the cutover migration batch. This terminates synchronization between the on-premises mailboxes and Office 365.

9. Administrator performs post migration tasks, including assigning Office 365 licenses, creating an Autodiscover DNS record, and decommissioning on-premises Exchange servers.

> **MORE INFO   CUTOVER MIGRATION**
>
> You can learn more about cutover migrations at: *https://support.office.com/en-us/article/ What-you-need-to-know-about-a-cutover-email-migration-to-Office-365-961978ef-f434- 472d-a811-1801733869da.*

IMAP migration

IMAP migrations use the IMAP protocol to move the contents of on-premises user mailboxes to Exchange Online. IMAP migrations are suitable where the on-premises mail server is not running Exchange Server, but is instead running an alternate mail server solution.

IMAP migration is supported for the following on-premises messaging solutions:

- Courier-IMAP
- Cyrus
- Dovecot
- UW-IMAP

IMAP migrations involve the following general steps:

1. A tenant administrator creates Office 365 user accounts and assigns them Exchange Online user licenses. This provisions the user accounts with Exchange Online mailboxes.

2. The tenant administrator creates a CSV file. This CSV file includes a row for each on-premises user who will be migrated to Exchange Online using IMAP. This CSV file needs to include the passwords used by each on-premises IMAP mailbox user. It is recommended that you reset user passwords for on-premises IMAP mailbox users to simplify this process.

3. The administrator creates and then triggers an IMAP migration batch. This can be done using the Migration dashboard, as shown in Figure 4-34, or through Windows Power-Shell.

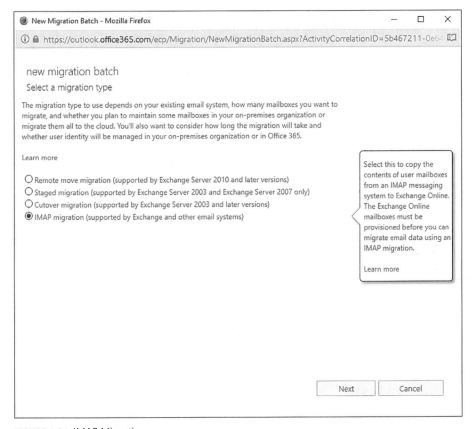

FIGURE 4-34 IMAP Migration

4. Once the migration batch is initiated, the following occurs:
   - Exchange Online creates a migration request for each user in the CSV file.
   - Each migration request includes the credentials for the user in the on-premises IMAP messaging system.

- Messages from each user's IMAP mailbox are copied to the corresponding Exchange Online mailbox until all data is migrated.

5. Exchange Online provides a status email to the administrator informing them of the status of the migration. This email contains statistics about the number of mailboxes successfully migrated, how many could not be migrated, and any error reports.

6. Exchange Online and the IMAP messaging system are synchronized every 24 hours to move any new messages from the on-premises environment to Exchange Online.

7. Once all migration issues have been resolved, the administrator updates MX records to point to Exchange Online. Once mail is flowing to Exchange Online, the administrator deletes the migration batches.

> **MORE INFO** **IMAP MIGRATIONS TO EXCHANGE ONLINE**
>
> You can learn more about IMAP migrations to Exchange Online at: *https://support.office. com/en-us/article/Migrate-other-types-of-IMAP-mailboxes-to-Office-365-58890ccd-ce5e-4d94-be75-560a3b70a706*

Import service

Network upload allows you to import PST files into Office 365. This can be done either by directly uploading the files or by shipping hard drives to Microsoft and having them import data directly.

To import PST files, perform the following steps:

1. In the Data governance section of the Security & Compliance center, use the Import section to create a Shared Access Signature (SAS) key, also known as the SAS URL. This key provides the necessary permission and location to upload PST files to an Azure storage location.

2. Download and install the Azure AzCopy tool. Use AzCopy with the SAS URL to upload one or more PST files to Azure.

3. Once uploaded, review the list of PST files that have been successfully transferred to Office 365. You can do this with Azure Storage Explorer.

4. Create a mapping file that maps uploaded PST files to Office 365 mailboxes. This file must be in CSV format.

5. Create a PST import job from the Data governance section of the Security & Compliance center. You specify the mapping file when creating this job.

6. Run the job to import the data into the appropriate Office 365 mailboxes.

Migration comparison

Table 4-2 lists the difference between the different methods you can use to migrate from an on-premises messaging environment to Exchange Online.

TABLE 4-2 Migration type comparison

On-premises messaging environment	Number of mailboxes	Will user accounts be managed on-premises	Migration method
Exchange 2007 to Exchange 2016	Less than 2,000	No	Cutover migration
Exchange 2007	Less than 2,000	No	Staged migration
Exchange 2007	More than 2,000	Yes	Staged migration or remote move migration in hybrid deployment
Exchange 2010 or Exchange 2016	More than 2,000	Yes	Remote move migration in hybrid deployment
Non-Exchange on-premises messaging system	No maximum	Yes	IMAP migration

Skill 4.3: Plan for Exchange Online

This skill deals with planning how to implement a variety of features in Exchange Online. This includes understanding what client prerequisites are required to ensure that users are able to access archive mailboxes, configuring in-place hold and litigation hold, allowing and blocking access to OWA, and allowing and blocking access to ActiveSync.

Plan client requirements for archive

In Chapter 3, "Configure Exchange Online and Skype for Business Online for end users," you read about archive mailboxes. Users can access archive mailboxes on a computer running Outlook or Outlook Web App through a browser, but are unable to access the archive mailbox when using Outlook on a mobile device or accessing Outlook Web App through a browser on a mobile device. Archive mailboxes can be used with the following versions of Outlook:

■ Outlook 2016

■ Outlook 2013

■ Outlook 2010

■ Outlook 2007

The archive mailbox appears in Outlook as a folder, as shown in Figure 4-35.

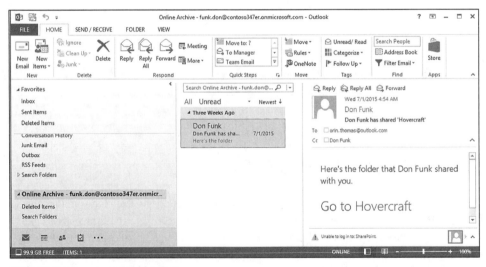

FIGURE 4-35 Move to archive mailbox

There are several methods that users can use to transfer items to the archive mailbox. These include:

- **Move messages manually** Users of clients that support archive mailboxes can manually move messages to the archive mailbox. This process is labor-intensive. Figure 4-36 shows moving an item to an archive mailbox.

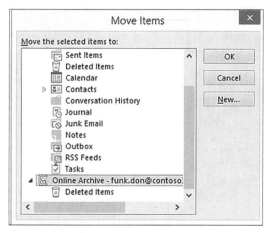

FIGURE 4-36 Move to archive mailbox

- **Use Inbox rules to move messages** Messages can be moved to the archive mailbox using inbox rules. This requires the user to configure the Inbox rule, as shown in Figure 4-37.

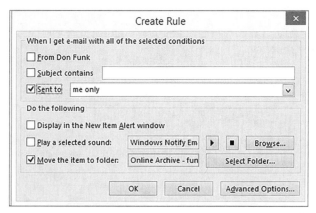

FIGURE 4-37 Create Rule

- **Have retention policies move messages** The default retention policy assigned to each Exchange Online mailbox automatically moves messages that are two years or older to the archive mailbox.
- **Importing messages from PST files** Users are able to manually import data from PST files on their local computers into the archive mailbox. Having the data stored centrally in Office 365, rather than on a specific computer, is also beneficial for users who

want to ensure that the message data in the .pst file is backed up and available on other computers.

Users can import PST files into their archive mailbox by performing the following steps:

1. In Outlook, select the Archive folder.

2. Click File, and then click Open & Export.

3. On the Open page, shown in Figure 4-38, click Import/Export.

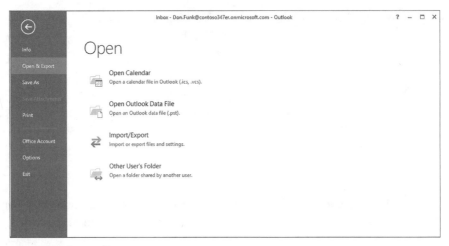

FIGURE 4-38 Import/Export

4. On the Import And Export Wizard, click Import From Another Program Or File, as shown in Figure 4-39, and then click Next.

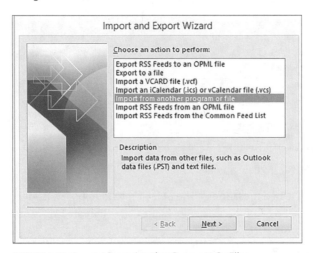

FIGURE 4-39 Import From Another Program Or File

5. On the Import A File page, select Outlook Data File (.pst), as shown in Figure 4-40, and click Next.

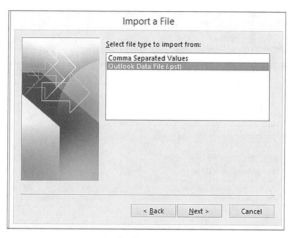

FIGURE 4-40 Import Outlook Data File

6. Select the .pst file that you will import.

7. Under Options, select between the following methods of dealing with duplicates, as shown in Figure 4-41.

   - Replace Duplicates With Items Imported

   - Allow Duplicates To Be Created

   - Do Not Import Duplicates

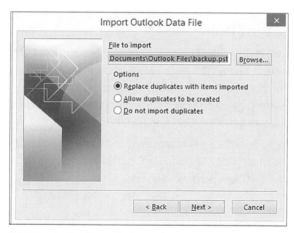

FIGURE 4-41 Duplicate Options

8. Click Next. On the Import Outlook Data File page, ensure that the option to Import items into the same folder is set to Online Archive, as shown in Figure 4-42.

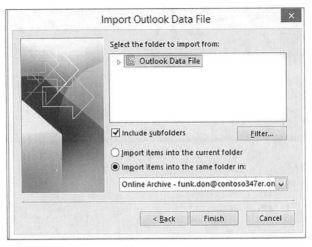

FIGURE 4-42 Import to archive

9. Click Finish.

> **MORE INFO** **ARCHIVE MAILBOXES**
>
> You can learn more about archive mailboxes at: *https://technet.microsoft.com/en-us/library/ dn922147(v=exchg.150).aspx.*

In-place hold and litigation hold

Litigation hold is a feature introduced in Exchange Server 2010 that allows preservation of data for eDiscovery. The feature is available in Exchange Server 2013, Exchange Server 2016, and Exchange Online. You apply litigation hold on a per-mailbox basis. For example, if you want to preserve the contents of all conversations between Don, Kim, and Dan, using the litigation hold functionality, you would need to place all three mailboxes on litigation hold.

In-place hold allows holds be applied on the basis of a query. For example, you could put an in-place hold on all conversations between Don, Kim, and Dan, but the hold would not apply to items outside the contents defined by the in-place hold query.

Enable litigation hold

Litigation hold, also termed legal hold, is used when one or more users at an organization is subject to an internal investigation, legal discovery, or other procedure that requires the organization to preserve the stage of their Exchange Online mailbox. Litigation hold is necessary to avoid tampering with evidence. For example, if a person has sent abusive email messages from the email account associated with their Exchange Online mailbox, placing the mailbox on litigation hold ensures that any potential email messages containing abusive content will not be deleted by the person subject to the investigation.

When a mailbox is placed on litigation hold, the following occurs:

- Content in the archive mailbox is preserved.
- Original and modified versions of items are preserved.
- Deleted items are preserved for a specified period or until the hold is removed.
- Items in the recoverable items are preserved.

When a mailbox is placed on litigation hold, its storage requirements increase dramatically. Not only are deleted items stored, but so are the original versions of modified items, as well as the modified versions. To ensure that all items are kept and the mailbox remains functional, the quota applied to the recoverable items folder is increased from 30 GB to 100 GB. Even though the quota on the recoverable items folder is increased, Microsoft recommends that administrators monitor mailboxes placed on litigation hold to ensure that issues related to the exhaustion of applied quotas do not arise.

When you place a mailbox on litigation hold you can specify the duration of the hold. The person requesting the litigation hold should specify whether the litigation hold will be of a specific duration or indefinite. You should also ensure that documentation requesting the implementation of the hold is in order because a company's human resources or legal department usually requests litigation hold. To leave the mailbox on litigation hold indefinitely, leave the litigation hold duration field empty, as shown in Figure 4-43.

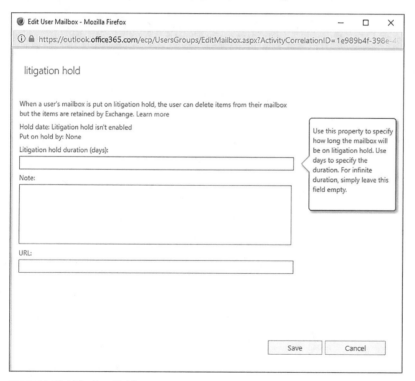

FIGURE 4-43 Litigation Hold

It is important to note that litigation hold can take up to 60 minutes to be enforced. You need to take this period into account in scenarios where you need to immediately preserve the contents of a mailbox and you suspect that the person subject to the litigation hold might attempt to scrub evidence. You should talk to your organization's human resources department about putting policies in place that provide enough time for a litigation hold to be enacted before the person subject to that hold is informed that this has occurred.

To put an Exchange Online mailbox on litigation hold, perform the following steps:

1. In the Recipients section of Exchange Admin Center, select the Mailboxes area, and then select the mailbox of the user for which you wish to configure a litigation hold. Figure 4-44 shows the Dan Jump mailbox selected.

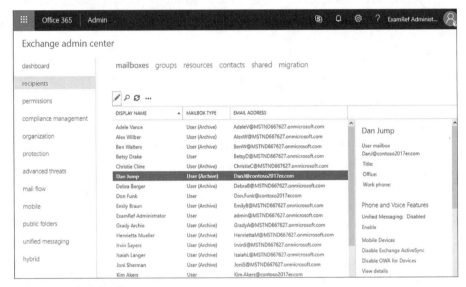

FIGURE 4-44 List of Mailboxes

2. Click the Edit (Pencil) icon to access the Mailbox Properties page.

3. On the Mailbox Properties page, click Mailbox Features.

4. Under Litigation Hold: Disabled, shown in Figure 4-45, click Enable.

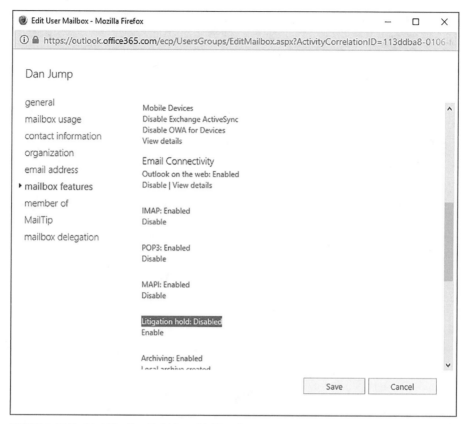

FIGURE 4-45 Enable Litigation Hold from Mailbox Features

5. On the Litigation Hold dialog box, shown in Figure 4-46, enter the litigation hold duration. If the litigation hold is to be indefinite, ensure that you do not enter a figure in this field. You can also provide a note about the litigation hold and a URL, which is used to inform the user that their mailbox has been placed on hold. You can also provide a URL to provide the user with more information. Click Save to enact the litigation hold.

FIGURE 4-46 180-day Litigation Hold

6. Click Save on the User Mailbox properties page to enact the litigation hold.

If the Office 365 user account associated with a mailbox that is placed on litigation hold is deleted, the mailbox is converted into an inactive mailbox. Inactive mailboxes store the contents of the deleted user's mailbox and retain all mailbox items for the duration of the hold at the time when the hold was applied. For example, if a 90-day hold is placed on a mailbox, and the Office 365 user account is deleted five days later, the contents of the inactive mailbox will be preserved for another 85 days. Inactive mailboxes are unable to receive new email messages and are not displayed in address books or other lists.

Remove litigation hold

Removing a user from litigation hold means that all deleted items that have exceeded their retention period will be purged. The original versions of items that have since been modified will also be deleted once litigation hold is removed. Once litigation hold is removed, the quota on the recoverable items folder will also return to 30 GB from 100 GB.

To remove a user from litigation hold, perform the following steps:

1. In the Recipients section of Exchange Admin Center, select the mailboxes area, and then select the mailbox of the user for which you wish to remove the litigation hold.

2. Click the Edit (Pencil) icon.

3. In the Mailbox Features section of the mailbox properties dialog box click Disable under Litigation Hold: Enabled.

4. On the Warning dialog box, warning you that you are about to disable litigation hold, click Yes.

5. Click Save to apply the change to the user's mailbox.

Manage litigation hold with PowerShell

You use the Set-Mailbox Windows PowerShell cmdlet to place a mailbox on litigation hold. For example, to place the mailbox don.funk@contoso2017er.com on indefinite litigation hold, issue the following command:

```
Set-Mailbox don.funk@contoso2017er.com -LitigationHold $True
```

You can use the LitigationHoldDuration parameter to configure a duration for the litigation hold. For example, to place the kim.akers@contoso2017er.com mailbox on litigation hold for 180 days, issue the following command:

```
Set-Mailbox kim.akers@contoso2017er.com -LitigationHold $True -LitigationDuration 180
```

You can use a combination of the Get-Mailbox and the Set-Mailbox cmdlets to put all of the mailboxes in the organization on litigation hold. You might need to do this if your organization is subject to litigation and the contents of all user mailboxes must be preserved. For example, to place all user mailboxes in the organization on hold for a period of 90 days, issue the following Windows PowerShell cmdlet:

```
Get-Mailbox -ResultSize Unlimited -Filter {RecipientTypeDetails -eq "UserMailbox"} |
Set-Mailbox -LitigationHoldEnabled $true -LitigationHoldDuration 90
```

You can remove a mailbox from litigation hold using the Set-Mailbox Windows PowerShell cmdlet. For example, to remove the litigation hold on the mailbox don.funk@contoso2017er.com, issue the following command:

```
Set-Mailbox don.funk@contoso2017er.com -LitigationHoldEnabled $False
```

MORE INFO **LITIGATION HOLD**

You can learn more about litigation hold at: *https://technet.microsoft.com/en-us/library/dn790612.aspx.*

Configure OWA access

Outlook Web App (OWA), also termed Outlook On The Web, allows users to access their Office 365 Exchange Online mailbox through a web browser. While a large number of Office 365 users access their Exchange Online mailbox through the Outlook client software on their computer or mobile device, in some scenarios, such as when they are using a kiosk computer in an airport, they will want to access their mailbox through a web browser.

Allowing access to Office 365 Exchange Online mailboxes through OWA does provide users with convenience, but also exposes the organization to risk. Many users do not exercise due care when using computers in airports or Internet cafés. There are many instances where user credentials have been captured by malware installed on these computers provided for public use. These credentials can be used at a later point in time by attackers to access organizational data because they can gain access to OWA or even a user's Office 365 subscription. For this reason, many organizations disable OWA. Because smartphone users are able to access Office 365 Exchange Online mailboxes through the Outlook app, available in each vendor's App Store, fewer users require access to OWA when away from their trusted computers.

To disable OWA, perform the following steps:

1. In the Recipients area of the Exchange Admin Center, select the user for which you wish to disable ActiveSync.

2. Click the Edit (Pencil) icon.

3. In the Mailbox Features section, click Disable under Outlook On The Web: Enabled, as shown in Figure 4-47.

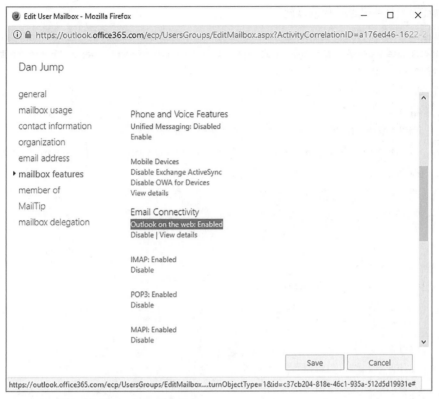

FIGURE 4-47 Disable Outlook On The Web

4. On the Warning dialog box, click Yes.

5. Click Save to save the changes to the Office 365 Exchange Online mailbox.

You use the Set-CASMailbox Windows PowerShell cmdlet to enable and disable OWA on a per user basis. For example, to disable OWA for the dan.jump@contoso2017er.com account, issue the command:

```
Set-CasMailbox dan.jump@contoso2017er.com –OwaEnabled $False
```

You can use the Get-Mailbox cmdlet with the Set-CasMailbox cmdlet to disable OWA for all mailbox users. To do this, issue the following command:

```
Get-Mailbox -ResultSize Unlimited -Filter {RecipientTypeDetails -eq "UserMailbox"} |
Set-CasMailbox –OwaEnabled $False
```

To enable OWA for the dan.jump@contoso2017er.com account, issue the command:

```
Set-CasMailbox dan.jump@contoso2017er.com –OwaEnabled $True
```

Configure ActiveSync

ActiveSync is a protocol, primarily used by mobile devices, that allows access to email, calendar, contacts, and tasks. ActiveSync is enabled by default on Office 365 Exchange Online mailboxes. In some scenarios, you might wish to disable ActiveSync.

To disable ActiveSync on a specific mailbox, perform the following steps:

1. In the Recipients area of the Exchange Admin Center, select the user for which you wish to disable ActiveSync, and click the Edit (Pencil) icon on the toolbar.

2. In the Mailbox Features section, shown in Figure 4-48, click Disable Exchange Active-Sync.

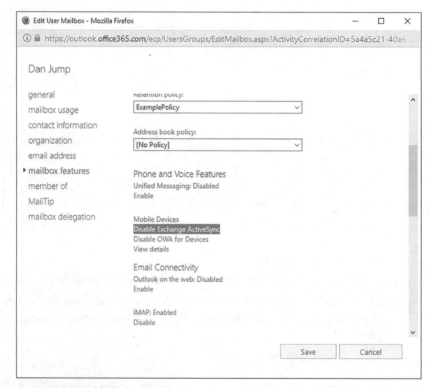

FIGURE 4-48 Disable ActiveSync

3. On the Warning dialog box, click Yes.

4. Click Save to close the User Mailbox properties page.

You can use the Set-CASMailbox Windows PowerShell cmdlet to enable or disable Active-Sync. For example, to disable ActiveSync for the don.funk@contoso2017er.com mailbox, issue the command:

```
Set-CASMailbox -Identity don.funk@contoso2017er.com -ActiveSyncEnabled $False
```

You can use the Get-Mailbox cmdlet in conjunction with the Set-CasMailbox cmdlet to disable ActiveSync for all users in an organization. To do this, issue the command:

```
Get-Mailbox -ResultSize Unlimited -Filter {RecipientTypeDetails -eq "UserMailbox"} |
Set-CasMailbox -ActiveSyncEnabled
$False
```

To enable ActiveSync for the don.funk@contoso2017er.com mailbox, issue the command:

```
Set-CASMailbox -Identity don.funk@contoso2017er.com -ActiveSyncEnabled $False
```

> **MORE INFO** **OFFICE 365 AND ACTIVESYNC**
>
> You can learn more about managing ActiveSync for Office 365 at *https://support.office.com/en-us/article/Set-up-and-manage-mobile-access-for-your-users-01fff219-4492-40f2-82d3-fd2ffc0ad802.*

Mobile Device Management

Mobile Device Management (MDM) for Office 365 allows you to manage certain devices that interact with Office 365. You can control how Office 365 email and documents are accessed and Office 365 MDM allows you to remotely wipe devices to eradicate sensitive organizational information.

Office 365 MDM supports the following devices:

- iOS 7.1 and later
- Android 4 and later
- Windows 8.1 (limited)
- Windows 10 (requires that the device be joined to the Office 365 Azure AD instance)
- Windows 10 Mobile (requires that the device be joined to the Office 365 Azure AD instance)

You can use Office 365 MDM policies to configure the following policies shown in Figure 4-49:

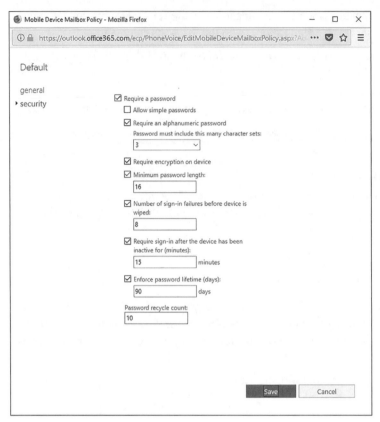

FIGURE 4-49 Mobile Device Mailbox Policy

- Require a password
- Allow simple password
- Require an alphanumeric password (specify number of character sets required)
- Require encryption on device
- Minimum password length
- Number of sign-in failures before device is wiped
- Require sign-in after the device has been inactive for (minutes)
- Enforce password lifetime (days)
- Password recycle count

> **MORE INFO   OFFICE 365 AND MOBILE DEVICE MANAGEMENT**
>
> You can learn more about managing mobile devices using Office 365 at *https://support. office.com/en-us/article/Capabilities-of-built-in-Mobile-Device-Management-for-Office-365-a1da44e5-7475-4992-be91-9ccec25905b0.*

Data Loss Prevention

Data Loss Prevention (DLP) policies allow you to accomplish the following goals:

- **Identify information that is sensitive across a variety of locations including Exchange Online, SharePoint Online, or OneDrive for Business** Sensitive information can include credit card numbers, passport numbers, or any readily identifiable combination of characters.

- **Prevent accidental sharing of information** Block access to documents that contain sensitive information from being accessed by unauthorized people, including those outside the organization. Block email messages that include sensitive information from being sent.

- **Monitor and protect sensitive information in desktop versions of Excel 2016, PowerPoint 2016, and Word 2016** Identify sensitive information as it is generated and apply DLP policies.

- **View DLP reports showing content that matches your organization's DLP policies** Allows you to determine how well your organization is complying with specific DLP policies. Also allows you to view false positive reports.

DLP policies can be configured to protect some or all SharePoint sites or OneDrive accounts. At present it isn't possible to select specific mailboxes, so if you choose to apply DLP policies to Exchange Online, it will apply to Exchange Online in its entirety.

DLP policies

DLP policies contain one or more rules. A rule includes conditions, actions, user notifications, user overrides, and incident reports.

Conditions determine the type of information being searched for and whether to take an action. Conditions can include:

- A type of sensitive information, as shown in Figure 4-50. This can include common types of sensitive information, such as credit card numbers, national ID numbers, and passport numbers. Detection goes beyond looking for a specific string of numbers, but also includes contextual content examination and regular expressions.

- A specific label is applied to the content. A label may be applied manually or through another mechanism such as a transport rule.

- Content is shared with people outside the organization. A determination is made as to the identity of the person trying to access the information.

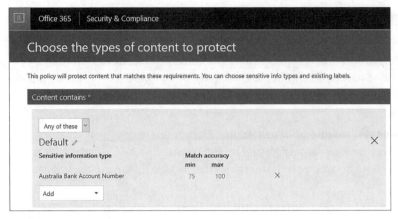

FIGURE 4-50 DLP conditions

Actions determine what occurs automatically when specific sensitive information is detected. Figure 4-51 shows access to the content being restricted. Depending on the action options selected, this would block access to the document to everyone except the primary site collection administrator, document owner, and the person who last modified the document or would just apply to blocking people from outside the organization. This action would also block a message that contained the sensitive information, either in the message body, or as an attachment, from being sent.

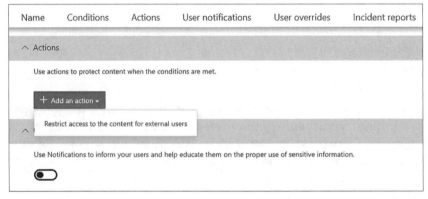

FIGURE 4-51 DLP actions

User notifications, shown in Figure 4-52, determine what happens when a rule is triggered. You can choose to have no notification occur, to send a notification to the user who sent, shared, or modified the content, or to send a notification to a specific person, such as a compliance officer. You can customize the notification. If the rule applies to content generated in Word, Excel, PowerPoint, Outlook, OWA, SharePoint Online or OneDrive for Business, a policy tip text may be configured that will inform the person interacting with the content that the content includes sensitive information.

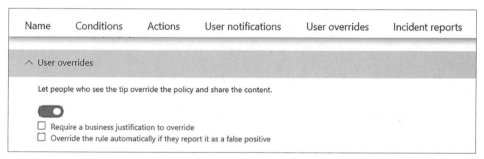

FIGURE 4-52 DLP notification

You can also configure the rule to allow users to override the restriction. You can allow them to provide a business justification to override the rule, or to submit a false positive report as a method of overriding the restriction. User override options are shown in Figure 4-53.

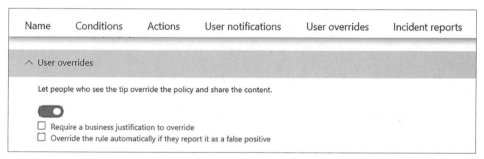

FIGURE 4-53 User override

Incident reports allow you to have a report generated and to be sent when the rule is triggered. For email message, the report includes the original message that triggered the rule. You can configure the following items for the report, as shown in Figure 4-54.

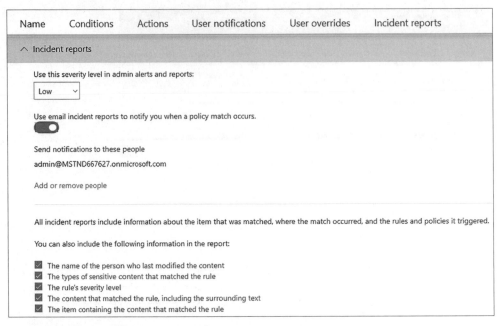

FIGURE 4-54 User override

- The Name Of The Person Who Last Modified The Content
- The Types Of Sensitive Content That Matched The Rule
- The Rule's Severity Level
- The Content That Matched The Rule, Including The Surrounding Text
- The Item Containing The Content That Matched The Rule

Rules are assigned a priority based on the order in which the rule is created. You can't change the priority of a rule, other than by deleting and re-creating the rule. If content matches multiple rules, the rules are processed in priority order, and the most restrictive action is applied.

> **MORE INFO   DATA LOSS PREVENTION**
>
> You can learn more about managing Data Loss Prevention Office 365 at *https://support. office.com/en-us/article/Overview-of-data-loss-prevention-policies-1966b2a7-d1e2-4d92- ab61-42efbb137f5e.*

EXAM TIP

Remember the Windows PowerShell cmdlets used to configure and manage litigation hold.

Skill 4.4: Manage Skype for Business global external communications settings

This skill deals with managing tenancy level settings for Skype for Business. These settings allow you to manage, at the tenancy level, which external users Skype for Business clients are able to communicate with, including whether communication is allowed with the consumer version of Skype.

> **This skill covers the following topics:**
> - Manage external communication and domains
> - Manage Skype consumer connectivity
> - Customize meeting invitations
> - Disable push notifications
> - Cloud PBX
> - PSTN Conferencing
> - Skype Meeting Broadcast

Manage external communication and domains

In the previous chapter, you read about how to manage external communication for Skype for Business Online users using the browser and the Skype for Business Admin Center, as shown in Figure 4-55.

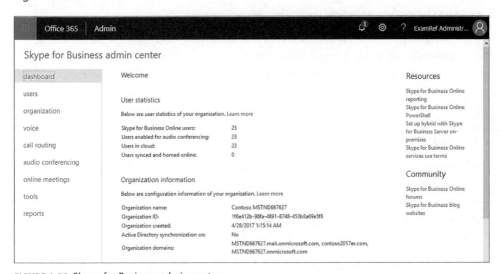

FIGURE 4-55 Skype for Business admin center

You can also use a set of Skype for Business Online specific Windows PowerShell cmdlets to manage external communication settings. These cmdlets are as follows:

- **New-CsEdgeAllowAllKnownDomains**   This cmdlet allows Skype for Business Online users to communicate with any domain, except those on the block list.

- **New-CsEdgeAllowList**   Use this cmdlet to configure the domains with which Skype for Business Online users can communicate. This cmdlet must be used in conjunction with the New-CsEdgeDomainPattern and Set-CsTenantFederationConfiguration cmdlets.

- **New-CsEdgeDomainPattern**   You use this cmdlet to modify the list of allowed or blocked domains because string values cannot be passed directly to the cmdlets used to manage the list.

- **Get-CsTenantFederationConfiguration**   You can use this cmdlet to view information about the allowed domains and the blocked domains.

Managed allowed domain list

The following Windows PowerShell code allows users to only communicate with users in the tailspintoys.com and wingtiptoys.com domains.

```
$x = New-CsEdgeDomainPattern -Domain "tailspintoys.com"
$y = New-CsEdgeDomainPattern -Domain "wingtiptoys.com"
$newAllowList = New-CsEdgeAllowList -AllowedDomain $x,$y
Set-CsTenantFederationConfiguration -AllowedDomains $newAllowList
```

To remove a domain from the allowed list, you need to use a set of commands. First you need to place the current list of allowed domains in a variable:

```
$x = (Get-CsTenantFederationConfiguration).AllowedDomains
```

You then need to determine the number of the domain that you want to remove. You do this by issuing the variable as a command and then counting the number of lines until the domain that you want to remove, with the first line as zero. For example, if you had the following list output when you issued the variable as a command:

```
adatum.com
contoso.com
fabrikam.com
```

The domain contoso.com would be number 1, and adatum.com would be 0. Once you've determined which domain you want to remove, you issue the command $x.AllowedDomain. RemoveAt(Y), where Y is the number of the domain you want to remove. So if you wanted to remove fabrikam.com from the list, you would issue the command:

```
$x.AllowedDomain.RemoveAt(2)
```

You can repeat the process to remove other domains from the list. Once you've pruned all of the domains that you want to remove, you can then assign the list using the following command:

```
Set-CsTenantFederationConfiguration -AllowedDomains $x
```

The following command removes all domains from the current allow list:

```
$newAllowList = New-CsEdgeAllowList -AllowedDomain $Null
Set-CsTenantFederationConfiguration -Tenant -AllowedDomains $newAllowList
```

You can use the Get-CsTenantFederationConfiguration cmdlet to view the list of allowed domains by issuing the following command:

```
Get-CsTenantFederationConfiguration | Select-Object -ExpandProperty AllowedDomains
 | Select-Object AllowedDomain
```

Manage blocked domain list

To add a domain to the blocked list, use the `BlockedDomains` parameter. For example, to add margiestravel.com to the list of blocked domains, issue the following command:

```
$x = New-CsEdgeDomainPattern ''margiestravel.com''
Set-CsTenantFederationConfiguration -BlockedDomains @{Add=$x}
```

You can use the Get-CsTenantFederationConfiguration cmdlet to view the list of blocked domains by issuing the following command:

```
Get-CsTenantFederationConfiguration | Select-Object -ExpandProperty BlockedDomains
```

To remove the domain margiestravel.com from the domain blocked list, perform the following steps:

```
$x = New-CsEdgeDomainPattern ''margiestravel.com''
Set-CsTenantFederationConfiguration -BlockedDomains @{Remove=$x}
```

You can remove all domains from the blocked domain list by issuing the following command:

```
Set-CsTenantFederationConfiguration -BlockedDomains $Null
```

> *MORE INFO* **MANAGE EXTERNAL COMMUNICATION**
>
> You can learn more about managing external communication using Windows PowerShell for Skye for Business Online at: *https://technet.microsoft.com/en-us/library/dn362813(v=ocs.15).aspx.*

Manage Skype consumer connectivity

As you read about in the last chapter, you can use the Turn On Communication With Skype Users And Users Of Other Public IM Service Providers option, found in the External Communications area of the Skype for Business Admin Center, as shown in Figure 4-56, to allow or block Skype for Business users from communicating with Skype users.

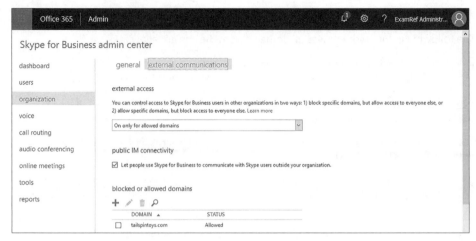

FIGURE 4-56 Allow Skype communication

You can use the Set-CsTenantFederationConfiguration cmdlet to also disable and enable public IM connectivity. The following command enables public IM connectivity:

```
Set-CsTenantFederationConfiguration –AllowPublicUsers $True
```

Once you've enabled public IM connectivity, you can allow or block specific providers. You do this with the Set-CsTenantPublicProvider cmdlet. When using this cmdlet, you must specify the tenant identifier. You can determine the tenant ID using the following command:

```
Get-CsTenant | Select-Object TenantID
```

Once you have the tenant ID, you can enable connectivity to Skype using the following command:

```
Set-CsTenantPublicProvider -Tenant "TenantID" -Provider "Skype"
```

The following command disables public IM connectivity:

```
Set-CsTenantFederationConfiguration –AllowPublicUsers $False
```

> **MORE INFO PUBLIC IM PROVIDER CONNECTIVITY**
>
> You can learn more about allowing access to public IM providers at: *https://technet.micro-soft.com/en-us/library/dn362809(v=ocs.15).aspx*.

Customize meeting invitations

You can customize meeting invitations, including a logo, help URL, legal URL, and meeting footer text. The logo can be up to 188 pixels by 30 pixels in size and can be in .jpg or .gif format. By default, meeting invitations are not customized.

To configure custom meeting invitations, perform the following steps:

1. Select the Meeting Invitation section in the Skype for Business Admin Center.

2. Provide information in the following areas, as shown in Figure 4-57:

   - **Logo URL**   The URL of a JPG or GIF file no larger than 188 pixels by 30 pixels.
   - **Help URL**   The URL of documentation providing assistance to meeting attendees.
   - **Legal URL**   The URL of any legal information necessary for meeting attendees to be aware of.
   - **Footer text**   Text that is included in the footer of any meeting invitation.

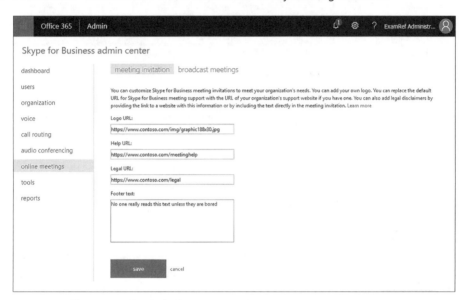

FIGURE 4-57 Custom meeting invitation

***MORE INFO*   CUSTOMIZE MEETING INVITATIONS**

You can learn more about customizing Skype for Business Online meeting notifications at: *https://support.office.com/en-us/article/Customize-meeting-invitations-9af52080-dd56-4b66-b056-41ed1a7aaae3.*

Disable push notifications

Push notification allows alerts about incoming and missed instant messages to be displayed whenever the user is not actively using Skype for Business on their phone or tablet. Push notifications are enabled by default in Skype for Business. Users are able to disable them through the options in the Skype for Business client on their own device. If you want to disable push notifications, users will receive alerts about incoming and missed instant messages the next time they use the Skype for Business client on their mobile device.

To disable push notifications, perform the following steps:

1. Select the Organization section in the Skype for Business Admin Center.

2. Ensure the General section is selected.

3. Under Mobile Phone Notifications, shown in Figure 4-58, and remove the check next to each of the notification types that you would like to remove.

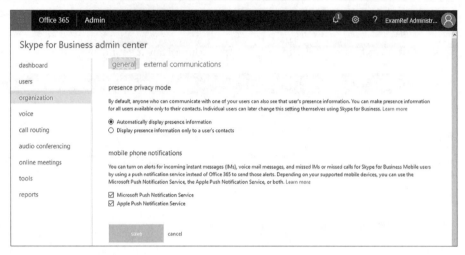

FIGURE 4-58 Push notifications

4. Click Save to apply the changes.

You use the Set-CsPushNotificationConfiguration cmdlet to enable or disable the Push Notification Service. To disable the Apple and Microsoft Push Notification Services, issue the following command:

```
Set-CsPushNotificationConfiguration -EnableApplePushNotificationService $False
-EnableMicrosoftPushNotificationService $False
```

You can disable the push notification for one service while keeping the push notification for the other service running. For example, to disable the Microsoft Push Notification Service, but enable the Apple Push Notification Service, issue the following command:

```
Set-CsPushNotificationConfiguration -EnableApplePushNotificationService $True
-EnableMicrosoftPushNotificationService $False
```

> **MORE INFO PUSH NOTIFICATIONS**
>
> You can learn more about configuring push notifications at: *https://support.office.com/en-us/article/Turn-off-mobile-phone-notifications-2de47013-4f09-493c-abc5-372f56ad69e3.*

Cloud PBX

Cloud PBX, also known as Phone System in Office 365, allows organizations to replace their existing PBX deployment with Office 365. Phone System for Office 365 performs the following basic call tasks:

- Placing calls to the PSTN network
- Receiving calls from the PSTN network
- Transferring calls
- Muting and unmuting calls

Users are able to place and receive calls using their mobile devices, a headset with a laptop or desktop PC, or IP phones that support Skype for Business. You can connect Phone System in Office 365 to the PSTN network in one of the following ways:

- Purchasing a calling plan add-on for Office 365. In this scenario Microsoft is the provider of both core calling and PSTN services. Microsoft is also able to provide or port your user's existing phone numbers.
- Using on-premises PSTN connectivity, where on-premises software connects to an existing telephony interface. Cloud Connector is a set of packaged virtual machines that provide on-premises PSTN connectivity with Phone System for Office 365. This solution is appropriate for organizations that want to allow Skype for Business Online users to use existing PSTN connections with call control managed by Office 365 in the cloud.

> **MORE INFO   CLOUD PBX**
>
> You can learn more about Cloud PBX at: *https://technet.microsoft.com/en-us/library/mt612869.aspx.*

PSTN Conferencing

Office 365 PSTN Conferencing is an Office 365 E5 feature that provides the ability for meeting attendees to connect to the audio portion of a Skype for Business meeting using a dial-in phone number as an additional option to using the Skype for Business client.

To enable PSTN conferencing, perform the following steps:

1. In the Office 365 Admin Center, navigate to Skype for Business under Admin Centers.
2. In the Skype for Business Admin Center click Audio Conferencing.
3. On the Users tab, shown in Figure 4-59, select the user you wish to assign a dial-in conferencing number to, and click the edit (pencil) icon.

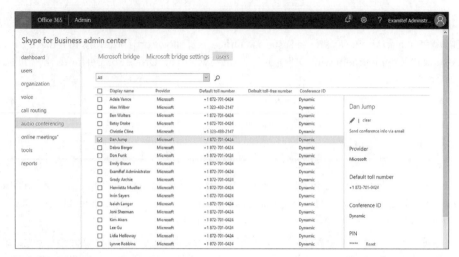

FIGURE 4-59 Audio conferencing users

4. On the Properties page, shown in Figure 4-60, select a default number. This will be the default number used for all meeting invites sent by this user.

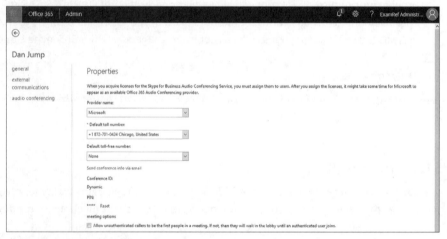

FIGURE 4-60 User toll number properties

5. Once you click Save, the user is sent an email message informing them that they have been configured for Skype for Business Dial-In conferencing, the telephone number to access conference, their personal conference ID, and their organizer PIN.

6. On the Microsoft bridge settings page, shown in Figure 4-61, you can configure the following options.

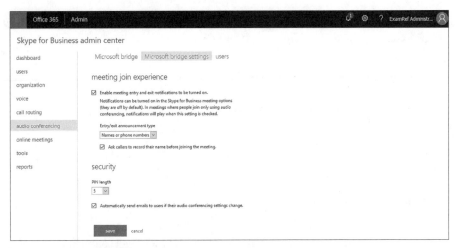

FIGURE 4-61 Microsoft bridge settings

- Entry and exit notification settings. Allows you to determine whether or not entry and exit notifications are made and the nature of those notifications.
- Whether callers are asked to record their name prior to entering the meeting.
- Length of the PIN.
- Sending an email when changes are made to a user's dial-in conference settings.

> **MORE INFO   PSTN CONFERENCING**
>
> You can learn more about PSTN conferencing at: *https://blogs.technet.microsoft.com/skype-hybridguy/2016/01/30/cloud-pbx-modern-voice-pstn-calling-in-office365-2/.*

Skype Meeting Broadcast

Skype Meeting Broadcast allows you to schedule, produce, and broadcast meetings online for audiences of up to 10,000 attendees. To enable Skype meeting broadcast, perform the following steps:

1. In the Office 365 Admin Center, navigate to Skype for Business under Admin Centers.
2. In the Skype for Business admin center, navigate to Broadcast meetings under Online meetings, and then select Enable Skype Meeting Broadcast, as shown in Figure 4-62.

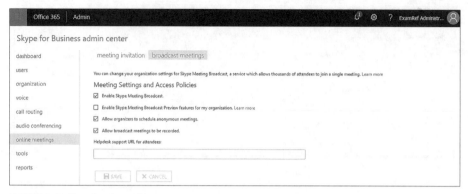

FIGURE 4-62 Broadcast meetings

You can enable broadcast meetings using the following PowerShell command:

```
Set-CsBroadcastMeetingConfiguration -EnableBroadcastMeeting $True
```

> **MORE INFO   SKYPE MEETING BROADCAST**
>
> You can learn more about Skype Meeting Broadcast at: *https://support.office.com/en-us/ar-*
> *ticle/What-is-a-Skype-Meeting-Broadcast-c472c76b-21f1-4e4b-ab58-329a6c33757d.*

EXAM TIP

Remember the different Windows PowerShell cmdlets you would use to manage allowed and blocked domains.

Thought experiment

In this thought experiment, demonstrate your skills and knowledge of the topics covered in this chapter. You can find answers to this thought experiment in the next section.

You are in the process of planning the alteration of the default spam filter used for your organization's Office 365 tenancy. Currently, messages that have an SCL of 7 are being placed in a user's junk email folders. Many of these messages are turning out to be legitimate, so for the next six months you want to have them moved to quarantine instead, where they can be examined by members of your team to check if they are being classified appropriately.

Recently, for reasons that aren't entirely clear, several email accounts at your organization are being sent email from addresses in New Zealand. The contents of these emails are entirely in the Esperanto language. A variety of different IP addresses are used to send the emails, so filtering based on IP addresses hasn't been entirely successful. You have been asked to ensure that all messages of this nature are classified as spam.

You are also in the process of planning an IMAP migration from a third-party on-premises messaging system that hosts 200 mailboxes to Office 365. You are reviewing the migration process.

You are looking at replacing the current practice of using litigation hold at Tailspin Toys when users are subject to discovery requests with instead switching to in-place hold. Management is especially interested in using the query functionality of in-place hold to locate items subject to discovery requests that are stored across multiple mailboxes. Management is also interested in what changes occur in terms of archive mailbox functionality when in-place hold is applied.

You are in the process of configuring Skype for Business Online using Windows PowerShell. You are interested in configuring public IM connectivity, disabling the Apple push notification service, and removing all of the currently blocked domains from the blocked domain list. To do this, you need to research the appropriate Windows PowerShell commands to accomplish these tasks.

With all of this in mind, answer the following questions:

1. What steps do you need to take to modify the default spam filter policy to ensure that messages with an SCL of 7 are placed in quarantine?

2. What steps do you need to take to modify the default spam filter policy to ensure that all messages in the Esperanto language that originate from New Zealand are marked as spam?

3. Which Windows PowerShell cmdlet and parameter should be used to release a message to all recipients if that message is currently in quarantine?

4. What is the first step in an IMAP migration?

5. What step should an administrator take after all IMAP mailboxes that will be migrated are successfully synchronized to corresponding Office 365 mailboxes and are successfully performing periodic synchronization every 24 hours?

6. When should the tenant administrator delete the IMAP migration batches?

7. Which Exchange Administrator role must a user be a member of to configure a query-based in-place hold?

8. When an in-place hold is applied on a mailbox, what is the new quota value assigned to the archive mailbox?

9. Which Windows PowerShell command, including parameters and values, would you use to disable public IM connectivity?

10. Which Windows PowerShell command, including parameters and values, would you use to disable the Apple Push Notification Service?

11. Which Windows PowerShell command, including parameters and values, would you use to remove all domains from the blocked domains list?

Thought experiment answers

This section contains the solutions to the thought experiment.

1. Edit the default spam filter policy and alter the Spam action to Quarantine message.

2. Edit the international spam settings of the default spam filter policy and specify the Esperanto language and the New Zealand country or region.

3. Use the Release-QuarantineMessage cmdlet with the `ReleaseToAll` parameter to release a message currently in quarantine to all recipients.

4. The first step in an IMAP migration is to create user accounts in Office 365 that correspond to the on-premises IMAP accounts that must be migrated.

5. Once synchronization is successful and periodic synchronization is proceeding without problem, the administrator should update MX records to point to Exchange Online.

6. The tenant administrator should delete the IMAP migration batches after mail flow is occurring successfully to Exchange Online and not the on-premises IMAP messaging system.

7. A user must be a member of the Discovery Management Exchange Administrator role to be able to configure a query-based in-place hold.

8. When an in-place hold or litigation hold is applied on a mailbox, the archive mailbox quota is increased from 30 GB to 100 GB.

9. You would use the Set-CsTenantFederationConfiguration –AllowPublicUsers $False command to disable public IM connectivity.

10. You would use the Set-CsPushNotificationConfiguration –EnableApplePushNotificationService $False command to disable the Apple Push Notification Service.

11. You use the Set-CsTenantFederationConfiguration -BlockedDomains $Null command to remove all domains from the blocked domains list.

Chapter summary

- The malware detection response settings are Delete Entire Message, Delete All Attachments And Use Default Alert Text, and Delete All Attachments And Use Custom Alert Text.

- You can configure the following notification options when malware is detected: Notify Internal Senders, Notify External Senders, Notify Administrators About Undelivered Messages From Internal Senders, and Notify Administrators About Undelivered Messages From External Senders.

- You can create different anti-malware policies and then apply them to different groups of mail users.

- When creating a new custom anti-malware policy, you need to configure the Applied To setting. This setting takes the form of an If statement with a condition and exceptions.

- Spam filter blocks lists and allows lists, allowing you to filter on the basis of email address and sender domain.

- Spam filter international settings allow you to filter based on language and country, or region of origin.

- Outbound spam policy allows you to configure how spam originating from within your organization is managed.

- Use the cmdlets with the MalwareFilterPolicy noun to view, modify, create, and remove malware filter policies.

- Use the cmdlets with the MalwareFilterRule noun to view, modify, create, and disable malware filter rules.

- Use the cmdlets with the HostedConnectionFilterPolicy noun to manage connection filter policies.

- Use the cmdlets with the HostedContentFilterPolicy noun to view and edit spam filter settings.

- Use the Get and Release-QuarantineMessage cmdlets to search for and release messages from quarantine.

- Cutover migration is suitable if your on-premises environment has Exchange Server 2007 or later, less than 200 mailboxes, and you will perform cloud-based account management.

- Staged migration is suitable if you have an on-premises deployment of Exchange 2007 deployment with any number of user accounts. Staged migration can be used with on-premises or cloud-based user account management.

- Remove move migrations are appropriate if you have more than 2,000 user accounts, have Exchange 2007 or later, and intend to manage migrated users using cloud tools.

- IMAP migration is appropriate if you have non-Exchange on-premises messaging solutions.

- Use the New-CsEdgeAllowAllKnownDomains cmdlet to allow Skype for Business Online users to communicate with any domain, except those on the blocked list.

- Use the New-CsEdgeAllowList cmdlet to configure the domains with which Skype for Business Online users can communicate. This cmdlet must be used in conjunction with the New-CsEdgeDomainPattern and Set-CsTenantFederationConfiguration cmdlets.

- Use the New-CsEdgeDomainPattern to modify the list of allowed or blocked domains.

- Use the Get-CsTenantFederationConfiguration to view information about the allowed domains and the blocked domains.

- You can use the Set-CsTenantFederationConfiguration cmdlet to also disable and enable public IM connectivity.

- You can customize meeting invitations, including a logo, help URL, legal URL, and meeting footer text.

- Skype for Business push notification allow alerts about incoming and missed instant messages to be displayed whenever the user is not actively using Skype for Business on their phone or tablet.

- You can disable push notifications for the Microsoft and Apple Push Notification Service through the Skype for Business Admin Center, or by using the Set-CsPushNotification-Configuration.

- Archived mailboxes can be accessed by clients running Outlook 2007 and later, as well as people running Outlook Web App on computers.

- Archive mailboxes cannot be accessed from mobile versions of Outlook and cannot be accessed from Outlook Web App when used from a mobile device web browser.

- Litigation hold is applied to an entire mailbox and preserves the contents of that mailbox until the duration of the litigation hold expires, including modified and deleted items.

- It can take up to 60 minutes for a litigation hold to be enforced by Exchange Online after an administrator enables the hold.

- You can enable litigation hold on a mailbox using the Set-Mailbox Windows PowerShell cmdlet.

- When litigation hold or in-place hold are enabled, the quota on the archive mailbox is increased to 100 GB from 30 GB.

- In-place hold differs from litigation hold in that only the items that meet the query condition will be protected, rather than all items in the mailbox.

- Only users who have been assigned membership of the Discovery Management role group can configure query-based in-place holds.

- In-Place hold is managed from Windows PowerShell using cmdlets with the Mailbox-Search noun and the InPlaceHold parameter.

- You can disable and enable Outlook Web App (OWA), also termed Outlook on the Web, through Exchange Admin Center, or by using the Set-CasMailbox cmdlet with the OwaEnabled parameter.

- You can disable and enable ActiveSync through the Exchange Admin Center or by using the Set-CasMailbox cmdlet with the ActiveSyncEnabled parameter.

CHAPTER 5

Configure and secure Office 365 Services

Office 365 has a variety of services beyond SharePoint and Exchange Online that can be very useful to the organizations you support. In this chapter, you'll learn about implementing Microsoft Teams, configuring and managing OneDrive for Business, automating with Microsoft Flow, creating Apps with PowerApps, configuring and managing StaffHub, as well as the steps to take to configure security and governance for your Office 365 tenancy.

Skills in this chapter:

- Skill 5.1: Implement Microsoft Teams
- Skill 5.2: Configure and manage OneDrive for Business
- Skill 5.3: Implement Microsoft Flow and PowerApps
- Skill 5.4: Configure and manage Microsoft StaffHub
- Skill 5.5: Configure security and governance for Office 365 services

Skill 5.1: Implement Microsoft Teams

This skill deals with implementing Microsoft Teams, which is a chat-based collaboration tool. In this section, you'll learn how to configure Microsoft Teams, and how to manage licenses and teams, and how to configure Office 365 connectors for Microsoft Teams.

> **This section covers the following topics:**
> - Configure Microsoft Teams
> - Manage licenses
> - Manage teams
> - Configure Office 365 Connectors

Teams and channels

To effectively configure Microsoft Teams, it is important to understand the difference between the concepts of Teams and Channels.

- **Team**   This is a collection of users, content, and apps associated with separate projects and tasks within an organization. Teams can be created to be private with membership only open to invited users. Teams can also be created as public. Public teams are open to anyone within the organization. By default, an Office 365 tenancy can have a maximum of 500,000 Teams, and each team can have a maximum of 2500 members. A global admin can create an unlimited number of teams. A normal Office 365 user can create up to 250 teams. By default, all users have the ability to create a team within Microsoft Teams.

- **Channels**   They are sections within a team that allow conversations to be segmented by specific topic. Team channels are for open conversations between team members. Private chats are only visible to private chat participants. It is possible to extend a channel with Apps. These Apps can include Tabs, Connectors, and Bots. The General channel is created automatically when a new team is created. The General channel cannot be removed or unfavorited. Microsoft recommends pinning information about the purpose of the team to this channel. Any member of a team can create a channel.

> **MORE INFO   TEAMS AND CHANNELS**
>
> You can learn more about Teams and Channels at *https://docs.microsoft.com/en-us/microsoftteams/teams-channels-overview.*

Setting up Teams in Office 365

Teams is enabled by default for all Office 365 organizations. To enable or disable Teams for an organization, perform the following steps:

1.   In the Office 365 Admin Center, click on Services & Add-ins under Settings.

2.   On the Services & add-ins page, shown in Figure 5-1, click Microsoft Teams.

FIGURE 5-1 Services & add-ins

3. In the Settings By User/License type section of the Microsoft Teams page, shown in Figure 5-2, use the drop down to select each license type used in your organization, and use the slider to turn Microsoft Teams on or off.

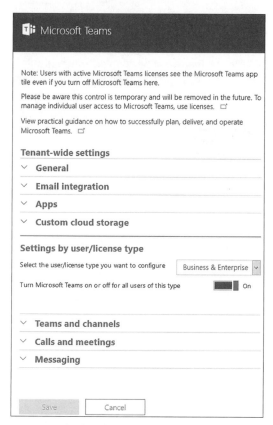

FIGURE 5-2 Settings by user/license type

MORE INFO **ENABLE OR DISABLE TEAMS**

You can learn more about enabling and disabling Teams at *https://docs.microsoft.com/en-us/microsoftteams/office-365-set-up.*

Manage Teams licensing

Teams is available for the following Office 365 subscription types:

- Office 365 Business Essentials
- Office 365 Business Premium
- Office 365 Enterprise F1
- Office 365 Enterprise E1

- Office 365 Enterprise E3
- Office 365 Enterprise E5
- Office 365 Education
- Office 365 Education Plus
- Office 365 Education E5

If a user has the appropriate Office 365 license, Teams will be enabled automatically. You can disable Teams on a per-user basis on the user's Product Licenses page as shown in Figure 5-3.

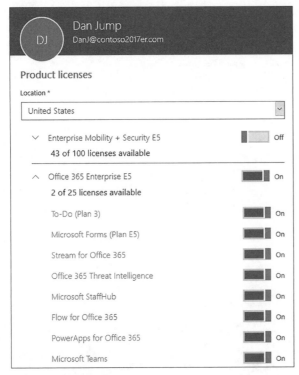

FIGURE 5-3 Microsoft Teams license

You can enable or disable Teams for specific license types through the Microsoft Teams section of the Services and add-ins area of the Office 365 Admin console as shown in Figure 5-4. If you only want to enable Teams for specific users, disable Teams at the license type level and then enable Teams for the specific users.

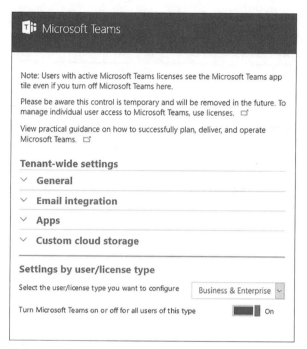

FIGURE 5-4 Microsoft Teams settings

> **MORE INFO**   **MANAGING TEAMS LICENSING**
>
> You can learn more about managing Teams licensing at *https://docs.microsoft.com/en-us/ microsoftteams/office-365-licensing*.

Manage Teams functionality

Teams functionality, including functionality for channels, is enabled on a tenant wide basis, rather than on a per Team or per-channel basis. You can configure the following general tenant wide settings as shown in Figure 5-5.

- **Show organizational chart in personal profile**   When enabled, it displays an organizational chart icon in the user's contact card. When this icon is clicked, it displays the user's place in the organizational chart.

- **Use Skype for Business for recipients who don't have Microsoft Teams**   It allows users of Microsoft Teams to contact other people in the organization who aren't configured for Microsoft Teams using Skype for Business.

- **Allow T-bot proactive help messages**   T-bot, the Microsoft Teams bot, will automatically start a chat session with users to assist them with Microsoft Teams.

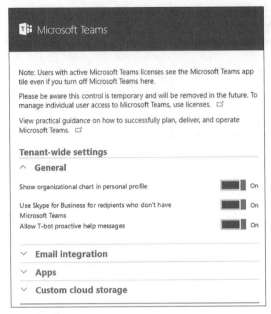

FIGURE 5-5 General Teams settings

You can allow users to send email to Microsoft Teams channels at the tenancy level as shown in Figure 5-6. You can restrict which email domains are allowed to send email to channels on the allowed senders list. To determine a channel's email address, click More Options next to the channel name and then click Get email address.

FIGURE 5-6 Teams email integration

You can configure the following Apps settings at the tenancy level as shown in Figure 5-7.

- **Disable default apps** Allows you to disable or enable default apps. By default, default apps are disabled. The default apps are Planner, PowerApps, and Website.

- **Allow external apps in Microsoft Teams** Allows or disallows users from adding tabs and bots that are available to the Office 365 tenant.

- **Allow sideloading of external apps** Allows or disallows users from installing and enabling custom bots and tabs.

- **Allow new external apps by default** Allows or disallows external apps that are added to the Office 365 tenant by default.

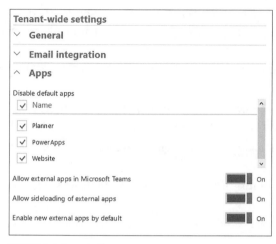

FIGURE 5-7 Apps in Teams

By default, Microsoft Teams users can upload and share files in Teams channels and chats from OneDrive and OneDrive For Business. Custom cloud storage tenancy level settings, shown in Figure 5-8, allow you to configure additional cloud storage services users that can use as a location for uploading and sharing files in Microsoft Teams channels and chats. Options include Box, Dropbox, Google Drive and ShareFile.

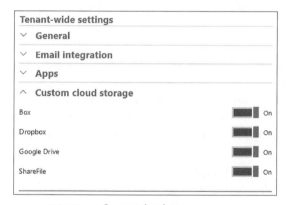

FIGURE 5-8 Custom cloud storage

The Teams and Channels settings provide links to the Groups dashboard in the Office 365 Admin Center for team management. It also provides a link to configure permissions on who on a team can add and manage channels. By default, any user in the organization can create a Team. The same creation settings configured for Office 365 Groups apply to Microsoft Teams. You will learn more about assigning roles and permissions for teams later in this chapter.

Meetings allow between two and eighty people to have an audio or video conference through Teams. The Calls and meetings settings, shown in Figure 5-9, allow you to configure the following:

- **Allow scheduling for private meetings**   If enabled, users are able to schedule private meetings. These meetings will not be listed in any channel. The maximum number of people in a private chat is 20.

- **Allow ad-hoc channel meetup**   If enabled, users can initiate ad-hoc channel meetups.

- **Allow scheduling for channel meetings**   If enabled, users are able to schedule channel meetings. All channel members can join channel meetings.

- **Allow videos in meetings**   If enabled, allows users to have video communication in a meeting.

- **Allow screen sharing in meetings**   If enabled, allows users to share desktop screen sessions within meetings.

- **Allow private calling**   If enabled, users are able to make private calls using Teams.

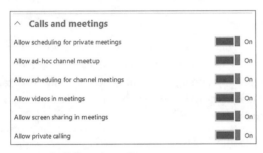

FIGURE 5-9 Calls and meetings

The messaging settings determine the types of content and control that you allow in Teams. For example, you may wish to allow the use of gifs, stickers and memes from the internet. If you do enable these settings, you may wish to pin a post describing what constitutes acceptable content for your organization, because allowing the posting of some internet memes is likely to trigger a visit from the denizens of the human resources department. You can configure the following settings, as shown in Figure 5-10.

- **Enable Giphy so users can add gifs to conversations**   Allows users to add animated images to conversations. You can set a content rating to determine how risqué the animated images allowed can be. The content rating can be set to No Restriction, Moderate, and Strict. It is enabled by default at the Moderate content rating.

- **Enable memes that users can edit and add to conversations**   Allows users to create and add memes to conversations, and is enabled by default.

- **Allow owners to delete all messages**   Allows channel owners to delete all messages in the channel, and is disabled by default.

- **Allow users to edit their own messages**   Allow users to modify their messages to channels in Teams, and is enabled by default.

- **Allow users to delete their own messages**   Users are able to delete their own messages, which is enabled by default.

- **Allow users to chat privately**   Allow users to initiate private chats, which is enabled by default.

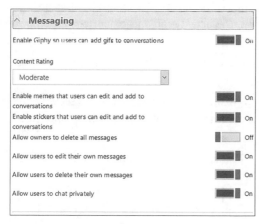

FIGURE 5-10 Messaging settings

MORE INFO   **ENABLE TEAMS FUNCTIONALITY**

You can learn more about enabling Teams functionality at *https://docs.microsoft.com/en-us/ MicrosoftTeams/enable-features-office-365.*

Roles and permissions

Microsoft Teams have two administrative roles: Owner and Member. Any user that creates a new team is assigned the Owner role. Owners are able to delegate the Owner role to other members of the same Team. Table 5-1 lists the permissions that are available to holders of the Owner and Member roles.

TABLE 5-1 Teams permissions

	Owner	Member
Create team	Yes	No
Leave team	Yes	Yes
Edit team name/description	Yes	No
Delete team	Yes	No
Add channel	Yes	Yes
Edit channel name/description	Yes	Yes
Delete channel	Yes	Yes
Add members	Yes	No
Add tabs	Yes	Yes
Add connectors	Yes	Yes
Add bots	Yes	Yes

You can restrict the permission to create new Teams from all users to members of a specific security group. Doing so involves also changing the permissions of which users can create Office 365 Groups, because the permission to create Office 365 Groups is the same permission that allows the creation of Microsoft Teams. This activity can only be performed in PowerShell and involves the following steps:

1. Create the security group to which you want to delegate the permission to create Office 365 Groups and Microsoft Teams.

2. Configure Office 365 Group settings to only allow the newly created security group to create Office 365 Groups using the following PowerShell script when connected to an Azure AD session:

```
$Template = Get-AzureADDirectorySettingTemplate -Id 62375ab9-6b52-47ed-826b-
58e47e0e304b
$Setting = $template.CreateDirectorySetting()
$setting["EnableGroupCreation"] = "false"
$setting["GroupCreationAllowedGroupId"] = "<ObjectId of Group Allowed to
  Create Groups>"
New-AzureADDirectorySetting -DirectorySetting $settings
```

> **MORE INFO   TEAMS ROLES AND PERMISSIONS**
>
> You can learn more about assigning Teams roles and permissions at *https://docs.microsoft.com/en-us/microsoftteams/assign-roles-permissions*.

Configure Office 365 Connectors

Connectors allow organizations to siphon content from services outside Microsoft Teams directly into Teams channels. For example, connectors allow Teams users to receive information directly into the chat stream from services including Twitter, Trello, GitHub, and Visual Studio Team Services.

Any member of a specific Team can connect that team to a cloud service using a connector. This allows all members of that Team to be notified of activities from that service. Removing a user from the Team removes any connectors added to the Team by that user.

Users can add a connector to a Team using either the Microsoft Teams Desktop or web client. To add a connector, perform the following steps:

1. Enter the Teams channel to which you wish to add the Connector.

2. Next to the channel name, click the ellipses (...) icon, and then click Connectors.

3. From the list of Connectors, shown in Figure 5-11, select the Connector that you wish to add and then click Configure.

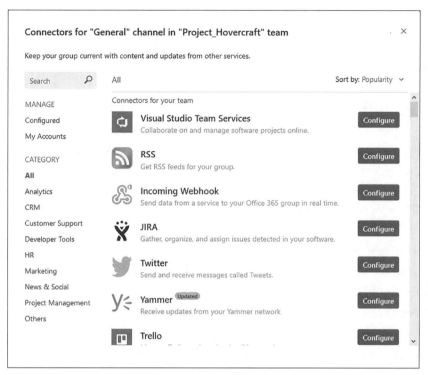

FIGURE 5-11 Available connectors

4. Depending on the Connector, you'll need to provide information that allows information to be streamed from the connecting service into Teams. Figure 5-12 shows the details of the Twitter Connector, which requires a sign in to an existing Twitter account.

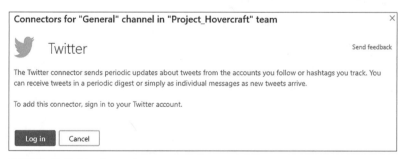

FIGURE 5-12 Twitter Connector

5. Once the Connector is configured, data will automatically be streamed into the channel for which the Connector is configured.

Organizations can develop custom Connectors to integrate with Line of Business applications using the included Incoming Webhook connector. This Connector creates an endpoint for a channel, and is able to extract data from applications using HTTP post methods.

Teams Cmdlets

You can use the following PowerShell cmdlets to manage Microsoft Teams:

- **Add-TeamUser**   Add a user or owner to a team.
- **Connect-MicrosoftTeams**   Connect an authenticated account so that it can use the Microsoft Teams cmdlets.
- **Disconnect-MicrosoftTeams**   Disconnect an account from a session where it can use Microsoft Teams cmdlets.
- **Get-Team**   View all of the Teams that a specific account belongs to.
- **Get-TeamChannel**   View all of the channels associated with a team.
- **Get-TeamFunSettings**   View the settings for posting GIFs and memes to a Team.
- **Get-TeamGuestSettings**   Views a Team's guest settings.
- **Get-TeamHelp**   View all Teams related cmdlets.
- **Get-TeamMemberSettings**   View member settings for a Team.
- **Get-TeamMessagingSettings**   View messaging settings for a Team.
- **Get-TeamUser**   View the users of a Team.
- **New-Team**   Create a new Team.
- **New-TeamChannel**   Create a new channel within a Team
- **Remove-Team**   Remove an existing Team.
- **Remove-TeamChannel**   Remove a channel from a Team.
- **Remove-TeamUser**   Remove a user from a Team.
- **Set-Team**   Configure the properties of a Team.
- **Set-TeamChannel**   Configure the properties of a Team channel.
- **Set-TeamFunSettings**   Configure the settings for posting GIFs and memes to a Team.
- **Set-TeamGuestSettings**   Configure Team guest settings.
- **Set-TeamMemberSettings**   Configure Team member settings.
- **Set-TeamMessagingSettings**   Configure messaging settings for a Team.
- **Set-TeamPicture**   Configure the picture associated with the Team.

EXAM TIP

Remember how to configure Teams licensing so that only a subset of the users in your organization have access. Remember the general steps required to allow only members of a specific group to create Teams.

Skill 5.2: Configure and manage OneDrive for Business

This skill deals with OneDrive for Business. OneDrive for Business is a tool that allows the synchronization of files across multiple devices and Office 365. In this section, you'll learn how to manage OneDrive for Business, including how to migrate files to OneDrive for Business, configure alerts to tell you useful information, configure permissions to the service, and how to manage document deletion policies. You'll also learn how to configure file activity reports, manage OneDrive for Business bandwidth utilization, configure storage for OneDrive for Business in Office 365, manage device access to the service, and deploy the OneDrive for Business client.

This skill covers the following topics:

- Migrate files to OneDrive for Business
- Configure Alerts
- Configure permissions
- Configure document deletion policies
- Configure file activity reports
- Control network bandwidth
- Manage OneDrive for Business by using OneDrive admin center
- Configure storage
- Configure device access
- Deploy OneDrive for Business clients

Manage OneDrive for Business by using OneDrive admin center

The OneDrive admin center enables you to manage your organization's OneDrive for Business settings. You can use the OneDrive admin center, shown in Figure 5-13, to perform the following tasks:

- Manage external sharing
- Enable sharing notification
- Prevent users from installing the OneDrive sync client
- Allow syncing only from computers joined to a specific AD DS domain
- Block syncing of specific file types
- Set the default storage space
- Preserve OneDrive files after a user leaves the organization
- Control access based on network location or app
- Control access to features in the OneDrive and SharePoint mobile apps

FIGURE 5-13 OneDrive admin center

MORE INFO **ONEDRIVE ADMIN CENTER**

You can learn more about the OneDrive admin center at: *https://support.office.com/en-us/article/OneDrive-admin-center-b5665060-530f-40a3-b34a-9e935169b2e0?ui=en-US&rs=en-US&ad=US.*

OneDrive for Business Limitations

When migrating files to OneDrive for Business, you need to consider that files that may be stored on a local PC or on a file share may not be able to be stored in OneDrive for Business because of limitations that the OneDrive for Business client or service has. You will need to ensure that files that you are attempting to migrate don't conflict with these limitations. Limitations are listed in Table 5-2.

TABLE 5-2 OneDrive for Business limitations

Invalid characters	<,>,:,",|,?,*,/,\
Unsupported file names	Icon, .lock, CON, PRN, AUX, NUL, COM1, COM2, COM3, COM4, COM5, COM6, COM7, COM8, COM9, LPT1, LPT2, LPT3, LPT4, LPT5, LPT6, LPT7, LPT8, LPT9, _vti_
Unsupported folder names	_t, _w, _vti_
Unsupported root folder name in a library	Forms
Number of items to be synced	Sync performance declines when more than 100,000 files are stored in a single OneDrive for Business site or team site library. If there are more than 100,000 files, store them in multiple folders/libraries.
File size limit	Files cannot exceed 15GB
Synced folder location	You cannot configure a network or mapped drive as the OneDrive sync location
Symbolic Links or soft links	OneDrive for Business doesn't support symbolic links where the Link and Target are stored in the same library location.
OneNote notebooks	Have their own sync mechanism and shouldn't be stored in a folder synchronized using OneDrive for Business
Open files	Open files can't be synced by OneDrive for Business
Roaming, Mandatory, and Temporary Windows Profiles	Cannot be synced to OneDrive for Business
Terminal Services / Remote Desktop Services	Not supported on Windows Server 2008, Windows Server 2008 R2 and Windows Server 2012 Terminal Services, also known as Remote Desktop Services

> *MORE INFO* **SYNCHRONIZATION LIMITATIONS**
>
> **You can learn more about OneDrive for Business limitations at: *https://support.microsoft.com/en-au/help/3125202/restrictions-and-limitations-when-you-sync-files-and-folders*.**

Migrating known local folders

Many organizations have known folders such as the Documents folders directed to an on-premises file share. As part of a migration strategy to move these files to Office 365, you can redirect these folders from an on-premises file share to OneDrive for business. This can be done through group policy for organizations where computers are members of Active Directory domains. In organizations where computers aren't members of a domain, you will have to instead use more manual and intensive methods of moving files into folders used by OneDrive for Business. This process is manual because in non-domain environments where users have more freedom to configure computers as they see fit, rather than being subject to domain policy, users are more likely to store their files in idiosyncratic locations.

When redirection of known folders to OneDrive for Business is implemented, users continue to use folders such as the Documents folder in the normal manner. In the background, the contents of these known folders will automatically be synced with OneDrive for Business. When using this method, Group Policy will determine if the OneDrive for Business folder has been configured on the target computer. If the folder doesn't exist, known folders, such as the Documents folder, will not be redirected. Once the OneDrive for Business folder is present, because the sync client has been deployed, known folders will automatically be redirected.

When you have redirected known folders, shortcuts to those folders will point to the new location linked with OneDrive for Business. The existing folder structure will still be in place and the contents of those folders will remain in the original location. Similarly, if known folders are currently redirected to network shares, you will need to migrate data from that location to OneDrive for Business after you redirect the known folders to OneDrive for Business. Microsoft recommends scripts that use XCopy or Robocopy to perform this task.

You can only use this strategy if OneDrive files are being stored in the default location, which is %userprofile%\OneDrive - <TenantName>. If OneDrive for Business files are being stored in another location, you can't use the known folder redirection strategy.

As mentioned earlier, the known folder redirection strategy requires that computers be members of an Active Directory Domain Services Domain. The other step to take is to download and install the OneDrive for Business Group Policy objects onto a Domain Controller. The ADML and ADMX files are located in the OneDrive installation directory, %localappdata%\Microsoft\OneDrive\BuildNumber\adm\, of a computer with the OneDrive client installed. Redirecting known folders to OneDrive involves the following steps:

1. Open the Group Policy Management Editor and edit the policy that will apply to users whose folders you will redirect to OneDrive for Business.

2. Edit the User Configuration\Policies\Administrative Templates\OneDrive\Prevent users from changing the location of their OneDrive policy, and set it to enabled. This will block users from moving their OneDrive for Business folder.

3. Create a new environment variable using the User Configuration\Preferences\Windows Settings edit the Environment item and create a new Environment Variable named OneDriveSync that has the value %userprofile%\<SyncFolder>, where <SyncFolder> is the name of your default folder. An example is OneDrive – Adatum, as shown in Figure 5-14.

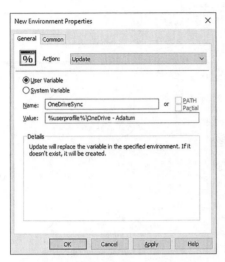

FIGURE 5-14 New environment setting

4. On the Common tab of the New Environment Properties dialog box, select Item-level targeting, click Targeting, click New Item, and then click File Match. Choose the Folder exists from the Match type drop down and in the Path box, type **%userprofile%\<SyncFolder>**, where <SyncFolder> is the name of your OneDrive folder, as shown in Figure 5-15.

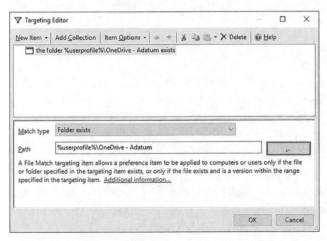

FIGURE 5-15 Folder targeting

5. Click OK twice to close the Targeting Editor dialog box and the New Environment Properties dialog box.

6. Edit the properties of the User Configuration\Policies\Windows Settings\Folder Redirection\Documents node, and choose Basic – Redirect Everyone's Folder To The Same Location. Under Target Folder Location, choose Redirect To The Following Location. In the Root Path box, type the **%OneDriveSync%\Documents** option, as shown in Figure 5-16.

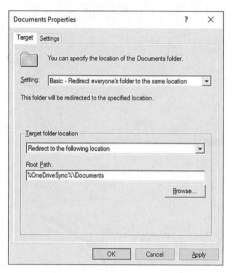

FIGURE 5-16 Document redirection policy

7. In the Settings tab, clear the Move the contents of Documents to the new location check box. The reason you do this is that if there are files in both locations with the same name, you may lose data. If there are no files in the new location, you can leave this setting enabled and files will be migrated without the need for scripts.

8. Use this same process to redirect other known folders such as Pictures, Music, Videos, Downloads, and others.

> **MORE INFO** **REDIRECTING FOLDERS**
>
> You can learn more about Redirecting known folders to OneDrive for Business at *https:// support.office.com/en-us/article/Redirect-known-folders-to-OneDrive-for-Business-e1b3963c-7c6c-4694-9f2f-fb8005d9ef12.*

Configure Alerts

You can configure notifications to alert owners of OneDrive for Business folders when certain activities, such as users being granted external access, occur. You can configure the following notifications, shown in Figure 5-17, for OneDrive for Business:

- **Other users invite additional external users to shared files** The owner of the One-Drive for Business folder is sent an email if other users who have permission to the folder add additional external users.

- **External users accept invitations to access files** The owner of the OneDrive for Business folder is sent an email if external users accept invitations to access files.

- **An anonymous access link is created or changed** The owner of the OneDrive for Business folder is sent an email if an anonymous access link is created or changed.

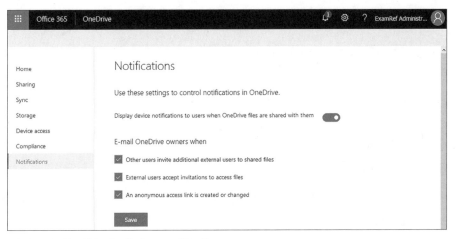

FIGURE 5-17 OneDrive for Business notifications

> **MORE INFO**   **ONEDRIVE FOR BUSINESS NOTIFICATIONS**
>
> You can learn more about OneDrive for Business notifications at *https://support.office. com/en-us/article/Turn-on-external-sharing-notifications-for-OneDrive-for-Business-b640c693-f170-4227-b8c1-b0a7e0fa876b?ui=en-US&rs=en-US&ad=US.*

Configure permissions

Permissions allow you to restrict the actions that can be taken in OneDrive for Business. In the Sharing section of the OneDrive for Business console, shown in Figure 5-18, you can select the default type of link offered when users share items. This setting allows you to determine whether links will be:

- **Sharable: Anyone with the link**   Users don't need to authenticate with an account that is present within the Office 365 Azure Active Directory Instance.
- **Internal: Only people within your organization**   Users need to authenticate with an account that is present within the Office 365 Azure Active Directory instance. This is the default setting.
- **Direct: Specific people**   A specific set of people that need to authenticate to access the OneDrive for Business content.

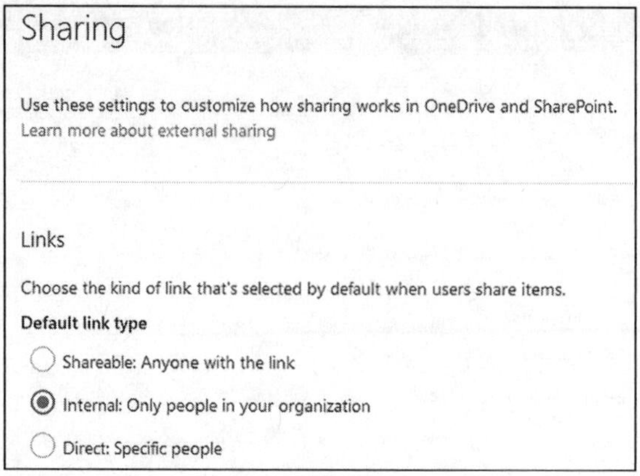

Sharing

Use these settings to customize how sharing works in OneDrive and SharePoint.
Learn more about external sharing

Links

Choose the kind of link that's selected by default when users share items.
Default link type

- ◯ Shareable: Anyone with the link
- ⦿ Internal: Only people in your organization
- ◯ Direct: Specific people

FIGURE 5-18 Sharing settings

Using the advanced settings for sharable links options section of the OneDrive for Business admin center, shown in Figure 5-19, you can configure the following:

- **Links must expire within this number of days**   This setting allows you to specify how long a link remains valid before it cannot be used to access OneDrive for Business content. The default is 14 days.

- **Files**   This setting allows you to configure permissions for files in OneDrive for Business in the scope of the shared link. By default this is set to View, Edit, and Upload. It can also be configured as View only.

- **Folders**   This setting allows you to configure permissions for folders in OneDrive for Business in the scope of the shared link. By default this is set to View, Edit, and Upload. It can also be configured as View only.

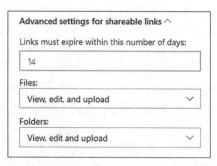

Advanced settings for shareable links ∧

Links must expire within this number of days:

14

Files:

View, edit, and upload ∨

Folders:

View, edit and upload ∨

FIGURE 5-19 Advanced Settings For Sharable Links

Using the external sharing settings, shown in Figure 5-20, you can configure permissions for sharing for both SharePoint and OneDrive for Business. You can use the slider to set different permissions for each service. The permissions that you can set include:

- **Anyone**   When you set this permission, users are able to create sharable links that don't require the person using the link to sign-in.

- **New and existing external users**   When you set this permission, external users must authenticate to access content.

- **Existing external users**   When you set this permission, external users are only able to access content if they have an external user account registered as a guest user in Azure Active Directory.

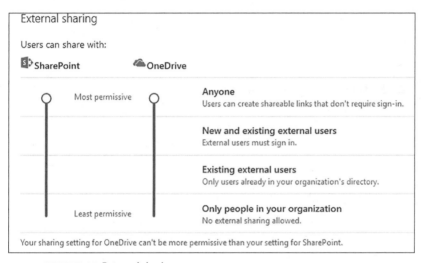

FIGURE 5-20 External sharing

Through the Advanced Settings For External Sharing section of the OneDrive for Business admin center, you can configure settings around restricting how external users can interact with content stored in your tenancy's OneDrive for Business instance. These settings are shown in Figure 5-21 and can be configured as follows:

- **Allow or block sharing with people on specific domains**   Allows you to configure specific domains as allowed or blocked. Users with accounts from these email domains aren't able to authenticate to access OneDrive for Business content.

- **External users must accept sharing invitations using the same account that the invitations were sent to**   This option allows you to block accounts other than the one an invitation is sent to from accessing OneDrive for Business content.

- **Let external users share items they don't own**   Allows external users to share content stored in your organization's OneDrive for Business instance.

- **Display to owners the names of people who viewed their files**   Allows file owners to view which authenticated accounts have been used to access those files.

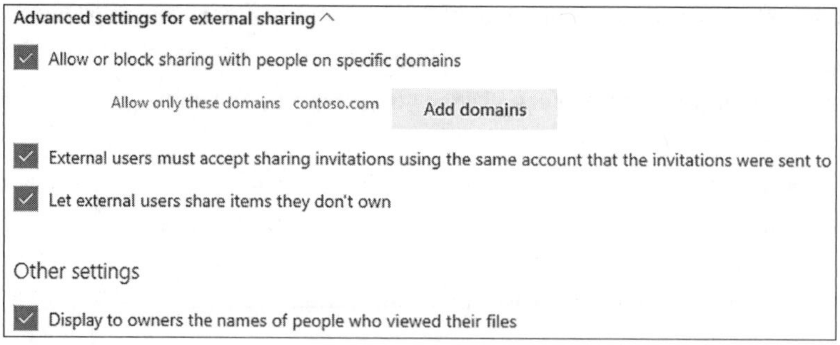

FIGURE 5-21 Advanced settings for external sharing

> *MORE INFO*   **ONEDRIVE FOR BUSINESS SHARING PERMISSIONS**
>
> You can learn more about sharing permissions for OneDrive for Business at: *https://sup-port.office.com/en-us/article/Manage-sharing-in-OneDrive-and-SharePoint-ee8b91c5-05ec-44c2-9796-78fa27ec8425.*

Configure document deletion policies

When you delete a user account, OneDrive for Business removes the contents of the user's OneDrive for Business site. The amount of time between the deletion of the account and the removal of the content is configured in the Storage section of the OneDrive for Business Admin Center as shown in Figure 5-22. The default amount of time that a user's data is retained in OneDrive for Business is 30 days.

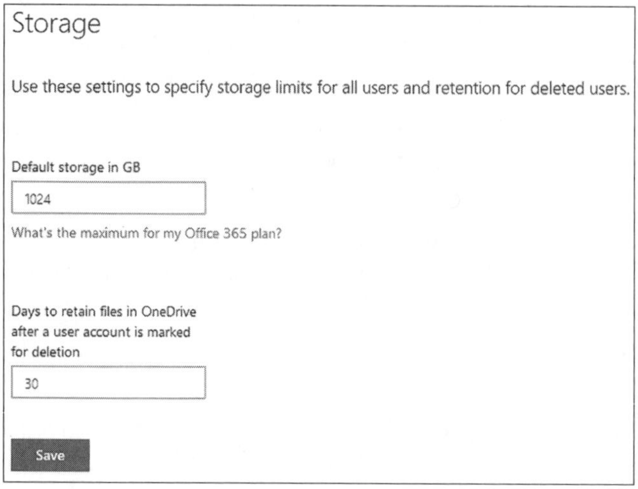

FIGURE 5-22 Keep for 30 days

Retention policies allow you to configure automatic deletion of documents in OneDrive for Business after a certain amount of time has passed. For example, you might choose to configure a document deletion policy that automatically deletes documents seven years after creation. You configure document deletion policies using Retention under Data Governance in the Office 365 Security & Compliance Center. To create a document deletion policy for OneDrive for Business, perform the following steps:

1. In the Retention section, click Create to create a new retention policy.

2. In the Name your policy section, shown in Figure 5-23, provide a name and description for the retention policy.

FIGURE 5-23 Retention policy name

3. On the Settings page, specify whether you want to retain content, delete content, or both. You can specify the amount of time and whether the age of the content is determined based on creation date or when the content was last modified. Figure 5-24 shows content that will be deleted seven years after it was created.

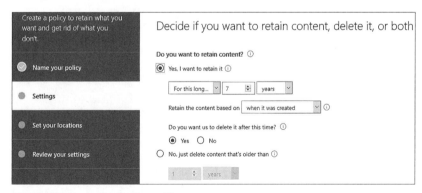

FIGURE 5-24 Content retention settings

4. On the Set your locations page, ensure that OneDrive accounts is selected. You can also choose to apply the retention policy to other locations within your Office 365 subscription.

5. When creating the policy, you can also choose to enable Preservation Lock. Doing this means that the policy can't be deleted, but that you can make modifications to the policy itself.

> ***MORE INFO*** **RETENTION POLICIES**
>
> **You can learn more about document retention policies at:** *https://support.office.com/en-us/article/Overview-of-retention-policies-5e377752-700d-4870-9b6d-12bfc12d2423*.

Configure file activity reports

You can view the OneDrive for Business activity report by performing the following steps:

1. In the Office 365 Admin center, click Usage under Reports.

2. In the Select a report drop down, click OneDrive Activity.

3. The OneDrive file activity report, shown in Figure 5-25, provides the following information:

- Files viewed or edited
- Files synced
- Files shared internally
- Files shared externally

FIGURE 5-25 OneDrive activity

You can also use the activity report to view information on a per-user basis, including the user's:

- Last OneDrive for Business activity date
- Number of files viewed or edited
- Number of files synced
- Number of files shared internally
- Number of files shared externally

> **MORE INFO**   **ACTIVITY REPORTS**
>
> You can learn more about OneDrive for Business activity reports at: *https://support.office. com/en-us/article/Office-365-Reports-in-the-Admin-Center-OneDrive-for-Business-activi- ty-8bbe4bf8-221b-46d6-99a5-2fb3c8ef9353?ui=en-US&rs=en-US&ad=US.*

Control network bandwidth

You can configure how much bandwidth the OneDrive for Business client uses by configuring the following Group Policy policies when the OneDrive group policy templates are installed:

- User Configuration\Policies\Administrative Templates\OneDrive\Set the maximum upload throughput that OneDrive.exe uses.
- User Configuration\Policies\Administrative Templates\OneDrive\Set the maximum download throughput that OneDrive.exe uses.
- Computer Configuration\Policies\Administrative Templates\OneDrive\Set the maximum percentage of upload bandwidth that OneDrive.exe uses.

Set the maximum upload throughput that OneDrive.exe uses

The Set the maximum upload throughput that OneDrive.exe uses policy, shown in Figure 5-26, allows you to specify maximum upload bandwidth in kilobytes per second. Note that this is different from usual measures of bandwidth that use bits rather than bytes. This policy is primarily useful when a large amount of data has been placed into the OneDrive for Business folder on a client, and you don't want the upload of that data consuming a disproportionate amount of bandwidth.

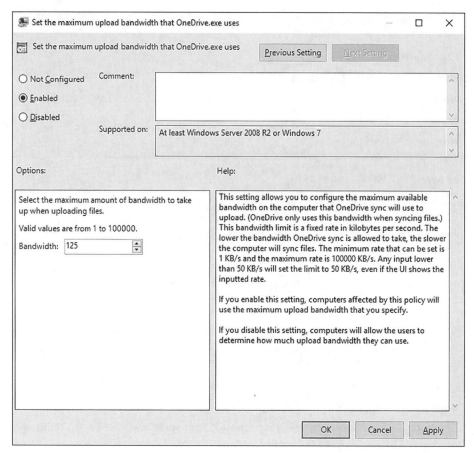

FIGURE 5-26 Maximum upload bandwidth

Set the maximum download throughput that OneDrive.exe uses

The Set the maximum download throughput that OneDrive.exe uses policy, shown in Figure 5-27, allows you to set the maximum download bandwidth in kilobytes per second that OneDrive for Business uses to retrieve files and folders from your organization's Office 365 subscription.

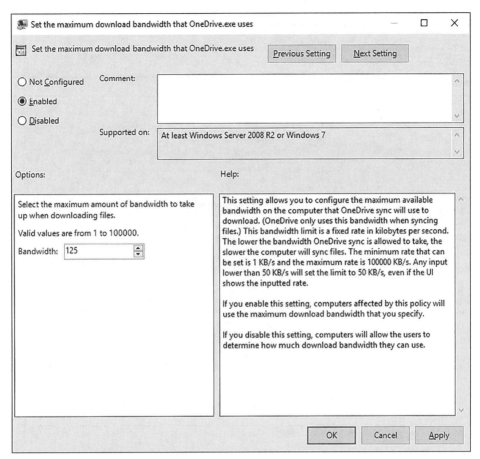

FIGURE 5-27 Maximum download bandwidth

Set the maximum percentage of upload bandwidth that OneDrive.exe uses

Unlike the other policies, which are configured in the User Configuration section of group policy, the Set the maximum percentage of upload bandwidth that OneDrive.exe uses policy, shown in Figure 5-28, is configured in the Computer Configuration section. Rather than specifying an amount in kilobytes, this policy uses a technique where measurements of actual bandwidth are taken by the client and upload throttling occurs based on the result of that measurement. The bandwidth measurements occur over a sixty second period and are revised every 10 minutes.

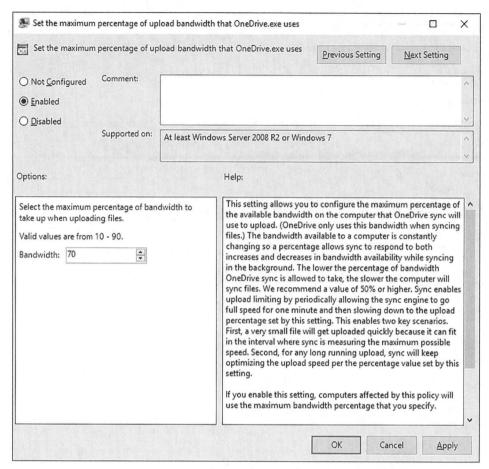

FIGURE 5-28 Maximum percentage upload bandwidth policy

> **MORE INFO** **CONTROLLING ONEDRIVE CLIENT**
>
> You can learn more about controlling OneDrive client through group policy at: *https://sup-port.office.com/en-us/article/Use-Group-Policy-to-control-OneDrive-sync-client-settings-0ecb2cf5-8882-42b3-a6e9-be6bda30899c*.

Configure storage

By default, each user is allocated 1 TB of storage space in OneDrive for Business. Organizations that have the following Office 365 plans are able to increase each user's default storage space up to 5 TB:

- Office 365 Enterprise E3 and E5
- Office 365 Government E3 and E5
- Office 365 Education and Office 365 Education E5
- OneDrive for Business Plan 2 and SharePoint Online Plan 2

Your Office 365 subscription must have a license allocated to at least one user before it is possible to increase the default amount of storage allocated to OneDrive for Business. Organizations that have more than five users can set a higher allocation than 5 TB, but can only do so after consulting with Microsoft support. You set the default allocation for all users in the Storage section of the OneDrive for Business admin center as shown in Figure 5-29.

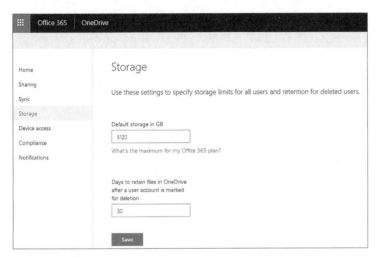

FIGURE 5-29 Storage settings

> **MORE INFO   ONEDRIVE FOR BUSINESS STORAGE**
>
> You can learn more about configuring OneDrive for Business storage at *https://support. office.com/en-us/article/Set-the-default-OneDrive-for-Business-storage-space-cec51d07-d7e0-42a3-b794-9c00ad0f0083*.

Configure device access

You can block the synchronization of specific file types and block synchronization from computers that are not joined to specific domains in the Sync section of the OneDrive for Business Admin center as shown in Figure 5-30. Domains can only be added as GUIDs, rather than fully qualified domain names. This feature is useful where OneDrive for Business is deployed in multiple domain environments.

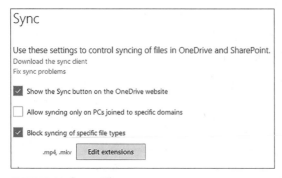

FIGURE 5-30 Sync settings

You can use the Device Access section of the OneDrive for Business Admin center, shown in Figure 5-31, to allow access to OneDrive for Business only from specific IP address ranges and to allow or block access from applications that don't use modern authentication.

Device access

Control access based on network location

☑ Allow access only from specific IP address locations

192.168.42.0/24, 192.168.50.0/24 **Edit**

Control access from apps that can't enforce device-based restrictions

☑ Allow access from apps that don't use modern authentication

FIGURE 5-31 Device Access

> **MORE INFO   ONEDRIVE FOR BUSINESS DEVICE ACCESS**
>
> You can learn more about sharing permissions for OneDrive for Business at *https://support.office.com/en-us/article/Manage-sharing-in-OneDrive-and-SharePoint-ee8b91c5-05ec-44c2-9796-78fa27ec8425*.

Deploy OneDrive for Business clients

The OneDrive for Business client can be deployed using enterprise deployment tools including System Center Configuration Manager. The command to setup the OneDrive for Business client when configuring deployment in Configuration Manager is:

```
<pathToExecutable>\OneDriveSetup.exe /silent
```

Computers that are running Windows 10 or have Office 2016 installed may already have an updated sync client installed. While this may be the case, it is important to note that OneDrive needs to be installed for each user and Office is usually installed on a per-computer basis.

The next important step when deploying OneDrive for Business in an enterprise environment is ensuring that the OneDrive.admx and OneDrive.adml file are added to the group policy store so that the group policy settings they host can be included in GPOs deployed in your organization. The group policy store is located in the SYSVOL\domain.name\Policies\PolicyDefinitions folder on a domain controller.

> **MORE INFO   DEPLOY ONEDRIVE FOR BUSINESS CLIENT**
>
> You can learn more about deploying the OneDrive for Business client at *https://support.office.com/en-us/article/Deploy-the-new-OneDrive-sync-client-in-an-enterprise-environment-3f3a511c-30c6-404a-98bf-76f95c519668.*

EXAM TIP

Remember what sort of policy you would configure if you wanted content to be automatically deleted from OneDrive for Business seven years after it is created.

Skill 5.3: Implement Microsoft Flow and PowerApps

This skill deals with Microsoft Flow and PowerApps. Flows allow you to create automation where specific actions are taken, such as sending an email, in response to triggers, such as the sending of a tweet with specific keywords. PowerApps allows users with minimal coding experience to generate an app that uses an existing data source such as SharePoint, Excel, or SQL Server.

> **This section covers the following topics:**
> - Create flows
> - Create flow actions
> - Create PowerApps

Create flows

A flow allows you to create automated workflows between applications and services. You can use flows to synchronize files, collect data, and collect notifications. To use Microsoft Flow, it is necessary to have an account with Microsoft Flow. You can sign up for an account at *https://flow.microsoft.com*. Users with Office 365 accounts automatically have Microsoft Flow accounts and simply have to activate those accounts at the Microsoft Flow website. An account can have up to 50 flows associated with it.

You can create a flow from a template or from scratch. To create an account from scratch, perform the following tasks:

1. Sign into the website at *https://flow.microsoft.com* and then click My Flows on the navigation bar. The navigation bar is shown in Figure 5-32.

FIGURE 5-32 Flow navigation bar

2. On the My Flows bar, shown in Figure 5-33, click Create from blank. You also have the option to create a flow from a pre-generated template or to import an existing flow.

FIGURE 5-33 My flows

3. The next step is to choose a trigger that will start the flow. A number of popular triggers are provided as shown in Figure 5-34, or it is possible to search for existing Connectors. This example will involve creating a flow that provides an email notification when a tweet is sent using a specified keyword. It requires access to an existing Twitter account.

FIGURE 5-34 Popular triggers

4. Click on the When A New Tweet Is Posted trigger. You will be prompted to sign in to your Twitter account to create a connection. You will need to authorize Microsoft PowerApps and Microsoft Flow for this Twitter account to continue.

5. In the search text box, shown in Figure 5-35, provide the text of the information that you want to be emailed about.

FIGURE 5-35 New tweet posted trigger

6. Click New Step and then click Add An Action as shown in Figure 5-36 to specify what action to take when the trigger triggers.

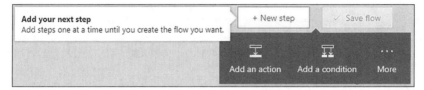

FIGURE 5-36 Add an action

7. In the Choose an action section, shown in Figure 5-37, select Office 365 Outlook – Send An Email.

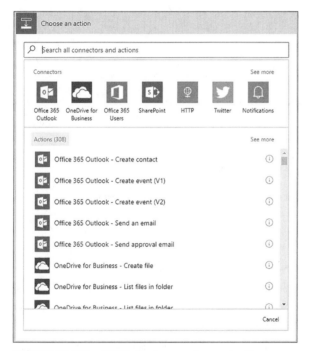

FIGURE 5-37 Office 365 Outlook connectors and actions

8. In the Send An Email action form, shown in Figure 5-38, provide an address in which to send the email, the subject that will be used, and the Body of the text. You can use the Add Dynamic Content option to select dynamic content, such as Name of the person who wrote the tweet and the text of that tweet.

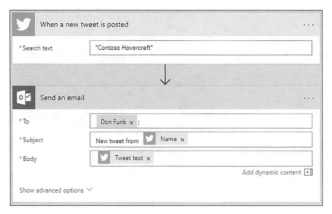

FIGURE 5-38 Send an email action

9. Click Create Flow to create the flow.

> **MORE INFO   CREATE FLOWS**
>
> You can learn more about creating flows at: *https://docs.microsoft.com/en-us/flow/get-started-logic-flow.*

Create flow actions

You can add multiple actions and advanced actions for the same trigger on a Flow. For example, you might not only have a flow that sends an email when someone tweets about "Contoso Hovercraft," but which also creates a file in OneDrive for Business that contains information about the tweet that was sent in the email.

To add actions to an existing flow, perform the following steps:

1. When signed in to *https://flow.microsoft.com*, select My Flows in the navigation bar. In the list of flows that you've created, shown in Figure 5-39, click the edit (pencil) icon next to the flow to which you wish to add an action.

FIGURE 5-39 List of flows

2. Click New Step and then click Add An Action.

3. Click OneDrive for Business as shown in Figure 5-40, and then click OneDrive for Business - Create File.

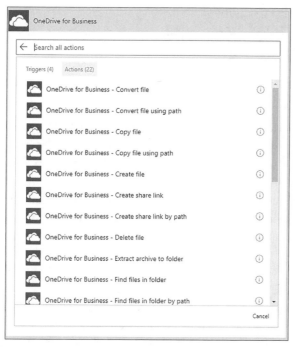

FIGURE 5-40 OneDrive for Business actions

4. On the Create File dialog box, shown in Figure 5-41, provide the path of the OneDrive for Business folder. Also, be sure to use Dynamic Content to add information such as User Name and Tweet Text.

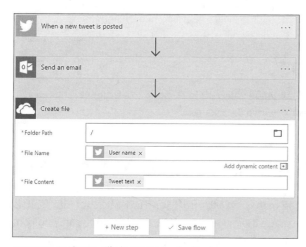

FIGURE 5-41 Create File in OneDrive for Business

5. Click Save Flow to save the additional action to the flow and then click Done.

Create PowerApps

PowerApps is an Office 365 service that allows users to create business apps that will run in a browser or on a mobile device such as a phone or tablet. PowerApps is designed to allow users with minimal coding experience to generate an app that uses a data source such as SharePoint, Excel, SQL Server, SalesForce, Dynamics 365, or other common data services.

Apps can be generated automatically simply by specifying the data source that the app will use. Microsoft provides a large number of templates that can be used as the basis of Power-Apps. You can create PowerApps using PowerApps Studio for Windows on a computer that has the Windows 8, Windows 8.1, or Windows 10 operating system. There is also a version of PowerAlls Studio for Web that runs in a standards compliant browser that can be used to author PowerApps.

Candidates for the 70-347 exam aren't expected to create a PowerApp in the exam, but should be aware of when PowerApps would be a useful solution to solve a particular problem. In this case, you need an app that will run in a browser or on a mobile device that uses a specific data source such as SharePoint, Excel, SQL Server, SalesForce, Dynamics 365 or other common data sources.

EXAM TIP

Remember that you choose a Flow when you want to respond to a trigger event and a PowerApp when you want to work with a data source.

Skill 5.4: Configure and manage Microsoft StaffHub

This skill deals with configuring and managing Microsoft StaffHub. Microsoft StaffHub is a tool that can be used by workers to manage their work schedule, share information, and connect to other work-related apps and resources. In this section, you'll learn how to manage StaffHub teams, StaffHub members, and StaffHub account provisioning.

StaffHub Setup

Enable StaffHub on the Office 365 tenant by performing the following steps:

1. In the Services and Add-Ins section, which is under Settings in the Office 365 Admin Center, click on StaffHub as shown in Figure 5-42.

FIGURE 5-42 StaffHub in Services & Add-ins

2. On the StaffHub flyout, shown in Figure 5-43, click Update StaffHub Settings For Your Organization.

FIGURE 5-43 Update StaffHub settings

3. Ensure that Enable Microsoft StaffHub is set to On, as shown in Figure 5-44.

FIGURE 5-44 Enable StaffHub

MORE INFO   **STAFFHUB SETUP AND CONFIGURATION**

You can learn more about StaffHub setup and configuration at: *https://blogs.technet.micro-soft.com/skypehybridguy/2017/08/07/staffhub-overview-initial-setup-configuration/*.

Manage StaffHub Teams

To create the first StaffHub team, perform the following steps:

1. Navigate to *https://staffhub.office.com* and sign in. If you don't have a team configured, you'll automatically be redirected to *https://staffhub.office.com/setup*. This will start the StaffHub Team setup wizard shown in Figure 5-45.

FIGURE 5-45 Welcome to StaffHub

2. On the Name your team page, shown in Figure 5-46, specify a name for your team.

FIGURE 5-46 Name Your Team

3. On the Confirm Your Team's time Zone page, shown in Figure 5-47, specify the team's time zone.

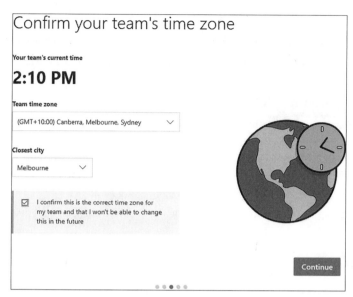

FIGURE 5-47 Time zone setup

4. On the Get The Mobile App page you can send an SMS message with a link to the Staff-Hub app in each mobile App vendor's App store. You can also skip this page.

5. On the Who's On Your Team page, shown in Figure 5-48, you can populate your team with members. You'll need the team member's email address or phone number to add them to the team.

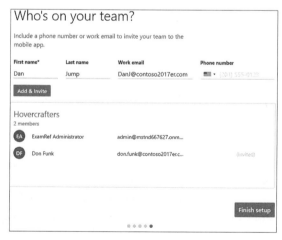

FIGURE 5-48 Team members

6. If you want to create additional teams, navigate to: *https://staffhub.office.com/app/setup*.

To give a Team Member administrator privileges for the team, perform the following steps:

7. Navigate to *https://staffhub.office.com*, sign in, and then click Team in the navigation menu, as shown in Figure 5-49.

FIGURE 5-49 Team in navigation menu

8. In the list of team members, click the team member that you want to make a team administrator.

9. Under Admin, set the slider to Allow Team Member To Create Or Modify Schedules as shown in Figure 5-50.

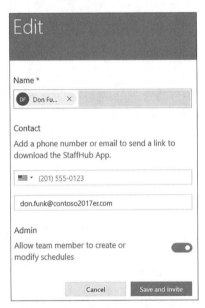

FIGURE 5-50 Edit StaffHub user

> **MORE INFO   STAFFHUB TEAMS**
>
> You can learn more about StaffHub Teams at: *https://support.office.com/en-us/article/Getting-started-with-Microsoft-StaffHub-92e9480f-0a37-47d2-ac96-2d11ee5f0656?ui=en-US&rs=en-US&ad=US*.

Manage StaffHub members

To add a team member to a schedule, perform the following steps:

1. In the Team, select Schedule in the navigation menu as shown in Figure 5-51.

FIGURE 5-51 Schedule in navigation menu

2. In the Schedule, shown in Figure 5-52, click Add Member.

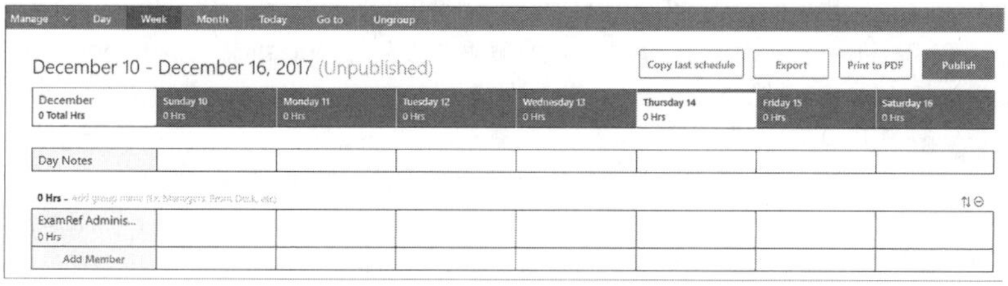

| Manage ∨ Day   Week   Month   Today   Go to   Ungroup | | | | | | | |

December 10 - December 16, 2017 (Unpublished)					Copy last schedule	Export	Print to PDF	Publish
December 0 Total Hrs	Sunday 10 0 Hrs	Monday 11 0 Hrs	Tuesday 12 0 Hrs	Wednesday 13 0 Hrs	Thursday 14 0 Hrs	Friday 15 0 Hrs	Saturday 16 0 Hrs
Day Notes							
0 Hrs - Add group name (Ex, Manager's Team Desk, etc)							⇅⊖
ExamRef Adminis... 0 Hrs							
Add Member							

FIGURE 5-52 Add member to Schedule

To add a group to the schedule, perform the following steps:

3. In the Schedule, click Add Group.

4. Provide the name of the group and then begin to add team members. Figure 5-53 shows a team named Alpha Team with Don Funk and Dan Jump as members.

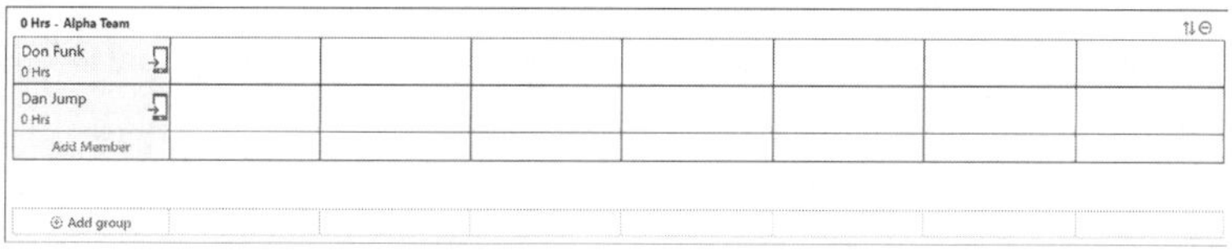

0 Hrs - Alpha Team							⇅⊖
Don Funk 0 Hrs							
Dan Jump 0 Hrs							
Add Member							
⊕ Add group							

FIGURE 5-53 Add team members

MORE INFO   STAFFHUB TEAM MEMBERS

You can learn more about StaffHub team members at: *https://support.office.com/en-us/article/Add-employees-or-groups-in-Microsoft-StaffHub-f56ba0bb-8ca2-4583-8c0e-e10be3fc8985.*

Manage StaffHub account provisioning

StaffHub is only available to users with Office 365 Enterprise licenses (F1, E1, E3, E5 or Edu). Staff-Hub can automatically create new Office 365 accounts for workers who don't already have an identity in Azure Active Directory. When StaffHub provisions an account, it does the following:

- Creates an ID in the form firstname.lastname@domain.com. If the name already exists in the directory, then a number is appended to the end of the alias. For example, don.funk1@contoso.com. Creates an associated account in Azure AD.

- Adds the newly provisioned account to the StaffHubProvisionedUsers security group. This provides you with a simple method of keeping track of all accounts that are provisioned through StaffHub rather than through other methods such as Azure AD Connect.

- Does not assign a license. StaffHub does not automatically assign a license and StaffHub does not enforce licensing. You can configure StaffHub to enforce licencing.

To provide StaffHub with the ability to provision accounts, perform the following steps:

1. Access the StaffHub Admin Center at *https://staffhub.office.com/admin*.

2. Under Self Provision Accounts, shown in Figure 5-54, set the slider to On and specify the name of the Azure AD domain they will be provisioned in, the security group, and the company name.

FIGURE 5-54 Self Provision Accounts

To have StaffHub require licenses when provisioning accounts, select the Apply License Check checkbox, as shown in Figure 5-55.

FIGURE 5-55 Apply license check

MORE INFO **STAFFHUB ACCOUNT PROVISIONING**

You can learn more about StaffHub account provisioning at: *https://support.office. com/en-us/article/Let-Microsoft-StaffHub-provision-accounts-for-firstline-workers-22ef209e-603c-4b32-98a0-4a9a9b50eec9*.

EXAM TIP

Remember which group the accounts that StaffHub automatically provisions are added to by default.

Skill 5.5: Configure security and governance for Office 365 services

This skill deals with configuring security and governance for Office 365 services. Security and governance is increasingly important for organizations that not only have to effectively respond to legal and regulatory imperatives, but who also need to ensure that their intellectual property is not accidentally leaked or stolen. In this section, you'll learn how to configure eDiscovery, advanced eDiscovery settings, data governance, Office 365 encryption, and how to use the Office 365 Compliance and Security center.

> **This skill covers the following topics:**
> - Configure eDiscovery
> - Configure advanced eDiscovery settings
> - Implement advanced data governance
> - Enable and configure Secure Store
> - Protect data and enforce data compliance by using the Office 365 Compliance and Security Center

Configure eDiscovery

eDiscovery allows organizations to put certain types of content on legal hold or to run content searches so that they can respond to legal or regulatory requests. You perform eDiscovery in Office 365 using the Security & Compliance Center. eDiscovery is performed through the creation and management of eDiscovery cases. eDiscovery cases allow you to control who can perform eDiscovery actions, place a hold on content relevant to a discovery request, and to associate content searches with a specific case.

eDiscovery roles and permissions

eDiscovery permissions allow you to control what actions users of the Security & Compliance center can perform. An administrator must be a member of the Organization Management role group or be assigned the Role Management role to be able to assign eDiscovery related permissions. The built in eDiscovery roles are shown in Figure 5-56 and included in the following list.

FIGURE 5-56 Permissions and roles

- **Compliance Administrator** Users assigned this role can manage settings for device management, data loss prevention, reports, and preservation.

- **eDiscovery Manager** Users assigned this role can create and manage eDiscovery cases. Users assigned this role are able to add or remove users from a case, place content locations on hold, create and configure content searches associated with a case, export content search results, and configure search results for analysis in Advanced eDiscovery. This role is segmented into two separate sub-roles: eDiscovery Manager and eDiscovery Administrator.

    - **eDiscovery Manager** Is able to view and manage any eDiscovery cases they create or are a member of. Is also able to access the cases they are associated with in Advanced eDiscovery.

    - **eDiscovery Administrator** The same permissions as eDiscovery Manager, but is also able to view all cases listed on the eDiscovery page, not just those they are associated with. Are able to add themselves to cases so that they can manage those cases. Perform administrative tasks in Advanced eDiscovery.

- **Organization Management** When assigned this role, a user is able to control permissions for accessing features in the Security & Compliance Center. They are also able to manage settings for data loss prevention, device management, preservation, and reports.

- **Reviewer** When assigned this role, a user is only able to view and open the list of cases on the eDiscovery page. Users assigned this role are unable to create cases, add members to a case, create holds, create searches or export search results. While users that are assigned this role are unable to prepare results for Advanced eDiscovery, they can access cases in Advanced eDiscovery to perform analysis tasks.

- **Supervisory Review** Users assigned this role are able to create and configure policies that determine which communications are subject to review in an organization.

- **Security Administrator** Members of this role are often cross-service administrators, external partner groups, and can include Microsoft Support. Members of this group have administrative permissions to Azure Information Protection, Identity Protection Center, Privileged Identity Management, Monitor Office 365 Service Health, and Security & Compliance Center.

- **Security Reader** Similar to the Security Administrator role, members of this role can include cross-service administrators, external partner groups, and Microsoft Support. It has view only permissions. Members of this group have read only access permissions to Azure Information Protection, Identity Protection Center, Privileged Identity Management, Monitor Office 365 Service Health, and Security & Compliance Center.

- **Service Assurance User** Members of this role are able to view reports and documents that describe Microsoft's security practices when it comes to customer data stored in Office 365. Members of this role are also able to access independent third-party audit reports on Office 365.

To assign users to a role, perform the following steps:

1. In the Security & Compliance Center, select the Permissions node.

2. Select the role to which you wish to add the user and then click Edit.

3. On the role page, click Edit role group. Figure 5-57 shows the eDiscovery Manager role.

FIGURE 5-57 eDiscovery Manager

4. On the Choose Members page, click Choose Members, click Add and then specify the user that you wish to add to the role. Figure 5-58 shows the Choose Members page. When you have added members to the role, click Done and then click Save to save the modifications to the role group.

FIGURE 5-58 Choose members

Creating eDiscovery cases

To create a new eDiscovery case, perform the following steps:

1. In the Security & Compliance Center, click eDiscovery under Search & Investigation.

2. On the eDiscovery page, shown in Figure 5-59, click Create a case.

FIGURE 5-59 eDiscovery

3. On the New case page, shown in Figure 5-60, provide a name and a description and then click Save.

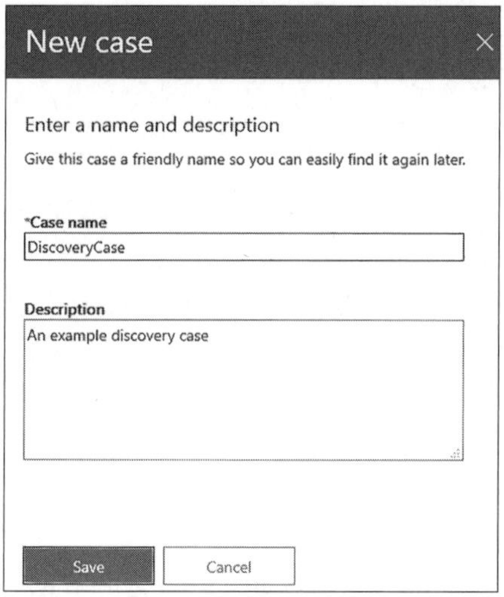

FIGURE 5-60 New Case

Add members to a case

To add members to a case, perform the following steps:

1. In the eDiscovery section of the Security & Compliance console, click the case to which you wish to add a user.

2. On the Manage this case page, shown in Figure 5-61, click Add to add a user and then add the user. You can also click Remote to remove a user from the case. When you have finished modifying the case membership, click Save.

FIGURE 5-61 Manage This Case

Place content on hold

Placing content on hold stops that content from being modified or deleted. When creating a hold, you can choose to:

- **Create an indefinite hold**   When you do this, all content is placed on hold.
- **Create a query-based hold**   When you do this, only data stored in Office 365 that matches the parameters of the query is placed on hold.
- **Create a date-range based hold**   When you do this, content that was created, sent, or received between specific dates is placed on hold.

To create a hold, perform the following steps:

1. In the eDiscovery section of the Security & Compliance admin center, click Open next to the case for which you want to create the hold.

2. On the Hold page, click the New (+) icon.

3. On the Create A New Hold page, shown in Figure 5-62, provide a name for the hold, specify which mailboxes and sites are subject to the hold, and select whether to hold all public folders.

FIGURE 5-62 Create A New Hold

4. On the Create a new hold page, shown in Figure 5-63 you can add keywords to search for. You can also create conditions including:

- Common
  - Date
  - Size
  - Sender/Author
  - Subject/Title
  - Compliance Tag
- Mail
  - Participants
  - Sender
  - To
  - Recipients
  - Subject
  - Received Date
  - Sent date
  - Message type
  - Message class
- Documents
  - Author
  - Title
  - Created data
  - Last modified date
  - File type

FIGURE 5-63 New hold conditions

5. If you don't add keywords or conditions, all content based on your mailbox, sites, and public folder selections will be held. If you do select keywords or conditions, content that matches those keywords and conditions will be held.

Performing content searches

To create a content search associated with a case, perform the following steps:

1. In the eDiscovery section of the Security & Compliance admin center, click Open next to the case for which you want to create the content search.

2. On the Search page, shown in Figure 5-64, click the New (+) icon.

FIGURE 5-64 Start new search

3. On the New Search page, shown in Figure 5-65, specify whether you want to search existing content that has been placed on hold, search across the entire Office 365 tenancy, or search specific locations. If you specify all case content, this will search all data that is being held, not just the data from one specific hold. If you choose to search specific locations, you can select specific mailboxes, specific sites, and none or all public folders.

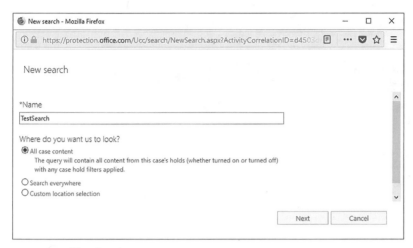

FIGURE 5-65 New Search

4. As is the case when configuring a hold, you can then choose to search for specific keywords or specific conditions. The conditions available are the same as those listed in the procedure on creating a hold.

> **MORE INFO   CONFIGURING EDISCOVERY**
>
> You can learn more about Topic at: *https://support.office.com/en-us/article/Manage-eDiscovery-cases-in-the-Office-365-Security-Compliance-Center-9a00b9ea-33fd-4772-8ea6-9d3c65e829e6*.

Configure Advanced eDiscovery settings

Advanced eDiscovery allows for the analysis of unstructured data within Office 365 provides a more efficient process for document review and allows you to reduce the amount of irrelevant data returned when you perform eDiscovery. Once you have configured a search in the eDiscovery section of the Security & Compliance center, you can use Advanced eDiscovery to perform further analysis of the returned data. Advanced eDiscovery requires an Office 365 E3 with the Advanced Compliance add-on or Office 365 E5.

Advanced eDiscovery has the following functionality:

- Allows for the extraction of text from images.
- Identifies redundant information including near-duplicates

- Identifies e-mail threads
- Applies predictive deep learning technology to identify relevant documents

To access a case in Advanced eDiscovery, perform the following steps:

1. In the eDiscovery section of the Security & Compliance admin center, click Open next to the case for which you want to perform Advanced eDiscovery.

2. On the home page for the case, shown in Figure 5-66, click Switch to Advanced eDiscovery.

FIGURE 5-66 Switch to Advanced eDiscovery.

Once you have accessed Advanced eDiscovery, you can perform the following tasks:

- **Analyze case data**   This allows you to identify and organize files returned by a search by various parameters.
- **Relevance Setup and Relevance**   Allows you to enable assessment and relevance training based on a random sample of files. This allows the deep learning process to create a model of your data to assist with analysis.
- **Export**   Allows you to export the data found by the Advanced eDiscovery process.
- **Report**   Allows you to generate reports related to the Advanced eDiscovery process. These reports are output in .csv format.

MORE INFO   **ADVANCED EDISCOVERY**

You can learn more about advanced eDiscovery at: *https://support.office.com/en-us/article/ Office-365-Advanced-eDiscovery-fd53438a-a760-45f6-9df4-861b50161ae4.*

Enable and configure Secure Store

Secure Store is an authorization service that runs with SharePoint and stores credentials in a manner similar to Azure Key Vault. Secure Store is able to support storing multiple sets of credentials that are used to access multiple systems through Business Connectivity Services (BCS). You can access Secure Store from the SharePoint admin center as shown in Figure 5-67.

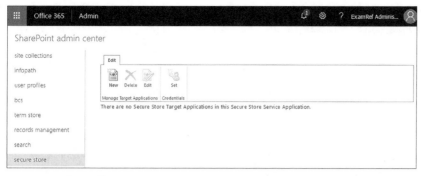

FIGURE 5-67 Secure Store

When Secure Store is correctly configured, the following process can occur:

- A user wishing to access specific data connects to SharePoint Online using their Office 365 credentials.

- Inside SharePoint Online, the Secure Store Service leverages stored credentials known to the external business application to connect to and retrieve external data that will be displayed on the SharePoint Online site to the user that is attempting to access that data.

- This data from the external source is displayed to the user without requiring the user to enter additional credentials. The Secure Store service performs a check of user rights to determine whether they can leverage those mapped credentials to access the external data.

To create a target application that will connect to the external data source using credentials stored in Secure Store, perform the following steps:

1. Open the SharePoint Online Admin Center

2. Click Secure Store and then click New in the Manage Target Applications group

3. In the Target Applications Settings dialog box, shown in Figure 5-68, provide the following information:

- **Target Application ID** This is the name of the target application.

- **Display Name** A friendly name for the target application. Can be the same or different to the Target Application ID.

- **Contact e-mail** An address that can be used by people having difficulty with the application.

- **Target Application type** Set by default in SharePoint Online to Group Restricted.

- **Credentials Fields** In this section, enter the credentials that will be used to access the remote target application.

- **Target Application Administrators** The administrators of the target application. These users are able to make modifications to the target application settings.

- **Members** This is the list of Azure Active Directory users who are able to leverage the target application to access the remote data.

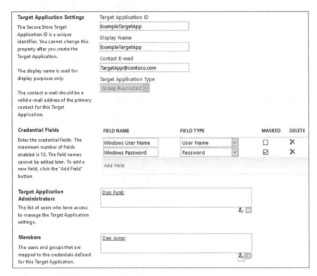

FIGURE 5-68 Target Application Information

To set the credentials of a target application:

1. Select the application in the Secure Store section of SharePoint Admin Center, and then click Set in the Credentials group on the ribbon.

2. On the Set Credentials for Secure Store Target Application dialog box, shown in Figure 5-69, provide the additional credentials you want associated with the target application in Secure Store.

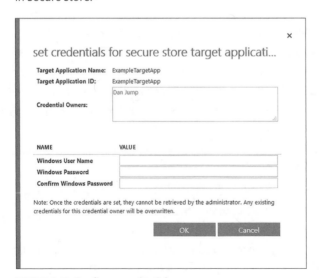

FIGURE 5-69 Configure credentials

Protect data and enforce data compliance

Many organizations work with sensitive data such as credit card numbers or medical records. This sensitive data is often subject to regulation on how it is handled, with harsh punishments for organizations that are found to have mishandled this information. Data loss prevention policies allow you to perform the following tasks:

- **Identify sensitive information across the Office 365 tenancy** For example, you can locate documents that contain Australian Tax File Numbers in specific people's OneDrive for Business folders or Exchange mailboxes.

- **Prevent the sharing of sensitive information** For example, you can block documents that contain sensitive information from being accessed by people outside the organization. You can also block users from sending email messages containing sensitive information.

- **Monitor and protect sensitive information as it is generated in Office desktop applications** DLP policies allow for the automatic identification of sensitive information as it is generated. For example, if someone types an Australian Medical Account Number into an Excel spreadsheet, they can be provided with a visible warning about the sensitive nature of that data as well as having rights management policies automatically applied to the file.

- **Allow users to override DLP policies if there is a business justification** You can configure DLP policies so that users are able to apply overrides if they provide a business justification. Appropriate users are notified when such an override is applied and they can follow up with the user to determine if the override was legitimate or if the user has violated organizational rules.

- **View DLP reports showing content that has matched DLP policies** The Security & Compliance Center offers extensive reporting on matches of content against configured DLP policies.

DLP policies contain the following:

- **Locations** Where the content is located. This can include Exchange Online, SharePoint Online and OneDrive for Business.

- **How to protect the content:**
  - **Conditions** The rules used to identify content. For example, locating credit card numbers.
  - **Actions** The action to take when content meets the conditions. For example, block access to a document containing sensitive information.

- **User notifications**   Determines the information provided to the user when the content they are interacting with meets the conditions of a DLP policy.
- **User overrides**   Provides the user with an ability to override a DLP policy, but requires the user to provide a justification.
- **Incident reports**   When a DLP rule generates a match, you can configure an incident report to be sent to one or more people. For email messages, the report will also include an attachment containing the original message.

> **MORE INFO**   **DATA LOSS PREVENTION POLICIES**
>
> You can learn more about data loss prevention policies at: *https://support.office.com/en-us/article/Overview-of-data-loss-prevention-policies-1966b2a7-d1e2-4d92-ab61-42efbb137f5e.*

Implement Advanced Data Governance

Office 365 Advanced Data Governance uses machine learning to allow organizations to locate and keep critical data while removing trivial, redundant, and obsolete data. Rather than having a completely manual process when it comes to the identification and management of sensitive data, machine learning algorithms can more quickly and effectively examine data in an Office 365 subscription and then make and implement recommendations on how to manage that data. Office 365 Advanced Data Governance provides the following functionality:

- **Proactive policy recommendation and automatic data classification**   Requires analysis of the data stored in your organization's Office 365 tenancy.
- **System default alerts that identify governance risks**   This includes noting events such as unusual file deletion volumes.
- **Apply compliance controls to on-premises data**   This includes filtering and migrating data from on-premises locations to Office 365.

> **MORE INFO**   **ADVANCED DATA GOVERNANCE**
>
> You can learn more about advanced data governance at *https://blogs.office.com/en-us/2017/04/04/announcing-the-release-of-threat-intelligence-and-advanced-data-governance-plus-significant-updates-to-advanced-threat-protection/.*

EXAM TIP

Remember the functionality of each of the roles in the Security & Compliance admin center.

Thought experiment

In this thought experiment, demonstrate your skills and knowledge of the topics covered in this chapter. You can find answers to this thought experiment in the next section.

You are in the process of configuring and securing Office 365 services. Your manager is currently very interested in ensuring that content from the company's twitter account is visible to everyone in the organization, without requiring them to sign on to twitter. With this in mind, you'd like the content from the twitter account streamed into a channel in Microsoft Teams as well as archived in OneDrive for Business.

Your manager is also increasingly interested in ensuring that your organization is meeting its compliance obligations. You want to ensure that content is deleted automatically from OneDrive for Business after a certain amount of time. You also want to know which roles have the ability to view all currently open eDiscovery cases.

With all of this in mind, answer the following questions:

1. Which eDiscovery role in Office 365 has the ability to view the content of all open eDiscovery cases?

2. What should you configure to ensure that content from the corporate twitter account is always sent to a channel in Teams?

3. What should you configure to ensure that content from the corporate twitter account is always stored in OneDrive for Business?

4. What would you configure to ensure that files in OneDrive for Business were automatically deleted seven years after they were created?

Thought experiment answers

This section contains the solutions to the thought experiment.

1. The eDiscovery Administrator role has the ability to view the content of all open eDiscovery cases.

2. You would configure an Office 365 Connector to ensure that content from the corporate twitter account was automatically posted in a channel in Teams.

3. You would configure a Microsoft Flow to ensure that content from the corporate twitter account was automatically stored in OneDrive for Business.

4. You would configure a retention policy to ensure that documents stored in OneDrive for Business were automatically deleted seven years after they were created.

Chapter summary

- A Microsoft Team is a collection of users, content, and apps associated with separate projects and tasks within an organization.
- Teams can be created to be private with membership only open to invited users.
- Public teams are open to anyone within the organization.
- By default, an Office 365 tenancy can have a maximum of 500,000 Teams.
- Teams have a maximum of 2500 members.
- Channels are sections within a team that allow conversations to be segmented by specific topic.
- Teams is enabled by default for all Office 365 organizations.
- You can allow users to send email to Microsoft Teams channels.
- Microsoft Teams users can upload and share files in Teams channels and chats from OneDrive and OneDrive For Business.
- Microsoft Teams uses two administrative roles, Owner and Member. Any user that create a new team is assigned the Owner role.
- Connectors allow organizations to siphon content from services outside Microsoft Teams directly into Teams channels.
- You can configure notifications to alert owners of OneDrive for Business folders when certain activities, such as users being granted external access, occur.
- Through the advanced settings for external sharing section of the OneDrive for Business admin center, you can configure settings around restricting how external users can interact with content stored in your tenancy's OneDrive for Business instance.
- The amount of time between the deletion of an Office 365 account and the removal of the content is configured in the Storage section of the OneDrive for Business Admin Center.
- The default amount of time that a user's data is retained in OneDrive for Business is 30 days.
- Retention policies allow you to configure automatic deletion of documents in OneDrive for Business after a certain amount of time has passed.
- You can configure how much bandwidth the OneDrive for Business client uses by configuring Group Policy.
- By default, each user is allocated 1 TB of storage space in OneDrive for Business. Organizations that have the following Office 365 plans are able to increase each user's default storage space up to 5 TB.
- You can block the synchronization of specific file types and block synchronization from computers that are not joined to specific domains in the Sync section of the OneDrive for Business Admin center.

- Flows allow you to create automation where specific actions are taken, such as sending an email, in response to triggers, such as the sending of a tweet with specific keywords.

- PowerApps allows users with minimal coding experience to generate an app that uses an existing data source such as SharePoint, Excel, or SQL Server.

- You can add multiple actions and advanced actions for the same trigger on a Flow.

- Microsoft StaffHub is a tool that can be used by workers to manage their work schedule, share information, and connect to other work-related apps and resources.

- StaffHub can automatically create new Office 365 accounts for workers who don't already have an identity in Azure Active Directory.

- eDiscovery allows organizations to put certain types of content on legal hold or to run content searches so that they can respond to legal or regulatory requests.

- eDiscovery is performed through the creation and management of eDiscovery cases. eDiscovery cases allow you to control who can perform eDiscovery actions, place a hold on content relevant to a discovery request and to associate content searches with a specific case.

- Advanced eDiscovery allows for the analysis of unstructured data within Office 365, provides a more efficient process for document review and allows you to reduce the amount of irrelevant data returned when you perform eDiscovery.

- Secure Store is an authorization service that runs with SharePoint and stores credentials in a manner similar to Azure Key Vault.

Index

E

F

G

H

I

K

L

M

O

About the author

ORIN THOMAS is an MVP, a Microsoft Regional Director, an MCT, and has a string of Microsoft MCSE and MCITP certifications. He has written more than 3 dozen books for Microsoft Press on topics including Windows Server, Windows Client, Azure, Office 365, System Center, Exchange Server, Security, and SQL Server. He is an author at PluralSight and is completing a Doctorate of Information Technology at Charles Sturt University. You can follow him on Twitter at *http://twitter.com/orinthomas*.